Unions, Unemployment and Innovation

Unions, Unemployment and Innovation

Eric Batstone
and
Stephen Gourlay

With Hugo Levie and Roy Moore

Basil Blackwell

© E. V. Batstone and S. N. Gourlay 1986

First published 1986

Basil Blackwell Ltd
108 Cowley Road, Oxford OX4 1JF, UK

Basil Blackwell Inc.
432 Park Avenue South, Suite 1503,
New York, NY 10016, USA

British Library Cataloguing in Publication Data

Batstone, Eric
    Unions, unemployment and innovation.
    1. Trade-unions—Great Britain
    I. Title II. Gourlay, Stephen
    331.88′0941   HD6664

    ISBN 0–631–14961–9

Library of Congress Cataloging in Publication Data

Batstone, Eric
    Unions, unemployment, and innovation.
    Bibliography: p.
    Includes index.
    1. Trade-unions—Great Britain. 2. Unemployment—
Great Britain. 3. Technological innovations—Great
Britain. I. Gourlay, Stephen, 1949–   . II. Title.
HD6664.B335 1986   331.88′0941   85–30679
ISBN 0–631–14961–9

Typeset by Photo·Graphics, Honiton, Devon
Printed in Great Britain by T J Press, Padstow

To the memory of Mick Mellish – that others engaged in the study and practice of industrial relations may emulate his qualities, standards and commitment.

Contents

Preface

The study on which this volume is based was financed by the Economic and Social Research Council over a two-year period from January 1983. It consisted of two types of research: the first was a survey of over 1,000 shop stewards drawn from a variety of unions and industries. The second was four case studies. These were linked to a wider project, undertaken in five countries, focusing upon the disclosure of information to workers and their representatives in the context of new technology.

As in all empirical research we owe many debts: we would like to thank the stewards who took considerable time and care to complete our somewhat lengthy questionnaire and the union officials who commented upon various drafts of the questionnaire and who helped us draw the samples. Similarly, we owe great debts to the stewards, workers and managers who co-operated in our case studies. We hope that our findings will be of some use to these people.

We were also helped by many people within the university. Toni Batstone, our research secretary, did a great deal of the initial analysis of the case studies as well as bearing a sizeable workload in helping to administer the survey. Nick Martin, Keith Grint and Bernie Harris helped with the coding of the questionnaires. Ken MacDonald, Clive Payne and Martin Range gave invaluable advice on statistical, computer and word processing. The secretaries at Nuffield, and in particular Trude Hickey, gave invaluable and cheerful help in typing, printing and collating the questionnaires. Finally, the industrial sociology group at Nuffield once more provided a stimulating context in which to work. To all of these, our thanks.

Glossary of Abbreviations

ASTMS   Association of Scientific, Technical and Managerial Staffs
AUEW   Amalgamated Union of Engineering Workers
BIFU   Banking, Insurance and Finance Union
CPSA   Civil and Public Services Association
EETPU   Electrical, Electronic, Telecommunication and Plumbing Union
NGA   National Graphical Association
POEU   Post Office Engineering Union, now called the National Communications Union
SCPS   Society of Civil and Public Servants
TGWU   Transport and General Workers Union
USDAW   Union of Shop, Distributive, and Allied Workers

1 Introduction

This book investigates the way in which workplace trade unionism in both the public and private sectors has been affected by the last five years of recession and of political hostility. It is based upon a survey of over 1,000 shop stewards from a wide range of industries and unions. In addition, we undertook four detailed case studies: these are used for illustrative purposes in this volume, but are reported at length elsewhere (Batstone *et al.*, 1986). We investigate this issue in two related ways. The first is through looking at the general pattern of union organization and labour relations; the second is by taking a critical case – that of new technology – in order to permit a more detailed investigation. The increasingly unfavourable environment has seriously weakened trade unionism, according to some commentators. The balance of power has been shifted in favour of the employer, who has not been slow to exploit the opportunities thereby presented. In the view of others, the impact of unemployment and the state has been far less dramatic, either because unions within the workplace have been able to isolate themselves from broader forces, or because employers have found it inadvisable fully to exploit the state of the labour market, or both. Given the centrality of this question to our research, it is useful to consider these differing views more fully, before going on to look at the nature of trade union organization.

Recession and Trade Unionism

Views differ on the question of the extent to which trade union power and strategy are affected by recession and, in particular, unemployment. It is not our intention here to discuss the wider debates concerning the causes of unemployment, but simply to focus upon the relationship between unions and unemployment. (For a useful review of the more general debate, see Deaton, 1983.) According to many commentators, particularly within industrial relations, high levels of unemployment seriously weaken trade unions. On the other hand, many economists, particularly macro-economists, stress the limited extent to which market forces impinge upon the power and influence of unions. This difference in large part reflects their different starting points. Those within the industrial relations tradition typically stress the way in which institutional factors constrain the operation of the market, whereas, of course, economists start with the importance of market-related factors. If one starts from the former view, then it is likely – ironically – that in any real situation one might be particularly impressed by the importance of the market. Conversely, if one expects market forces generally to be 'effective', then stress may often be placed upon factors that constrain their full operation. It follows, however, that neither side in this debate claims either that the market is totally ineffective or all-powerful. Nevertheless, it is convenient to distinguish between a market and a monopoly model in order to highlight the different arguments.

Both approaches accept that trade unions introduce a degree of monopoly into the labour market. By organizing collectively, workers achieve greater influence. An aggrieved worker who decides to withdraw his or her labour is unlikely to have much effect upon the employer, who can easily find a replacement. The situation is very different if workers collectively engage in such action. This, then, is the key characteristic of a trade union: it combines the power of individual workers and the sum is more powerful than its parts. However, the difference between the monopoly and market models of trade unionism rests upon the degree and stability of that monopoly.

The market model stresses the way in which recession (or other factors leading to unemployment, such as labour-saving new technology) affects the bargaining power of trade unions. This is seen to occur in three related ways. First, it is claimed that employers have less need for output, since demand is slack. Consequently, a stoppage of work imposes fewer costs upon them in a period of recession (and indeed may even be profitable) than when demand is more buoyant; thus they will be less ready to concede to union demands backed up with sanctions. Secondly, the bargaining power of the union is weakened by the availability of alternative labour, when unemployment is high. That is, if unions try to impose demands, employers can more easily sack union members and replace them with alternative labour, when unemployment is high. Third, reduced bargaining power means that union membership becomes less attractive to workers. According to this view, workers join a union when the gains thereby achieved are thought to exceed the costs. If unions are less able to win wage increases, and if employers are able to adopt a more hostile approach towards union members, then the gains of membership fall relative to the costs. Accordingly, union density declines. It is therefore possible to imagine a vicious circle of declining union strength: unions lose their bargaining power, with the result that membership declines. This further reduces the monopoly of the unions, and so still more workers quit their unions (see, e.g., Bain and Elsheikh, 1976; Burkitt, 1980).

These factors, then, are seen to lead to a reduction in union bargaining power. If, however, a union is aware of the vicious circle just outlined, then it may be prepared to make concessions to the employer. For example, given the possibility that the employer will employ alternative labour at a lower price, the union may be prepared to accept reductions in wages for its members; or it may accept changes in working practices which serve to reduce unit labour costs. In other words, the union adjusts its actions to recognize the increased competition associated with high unemployment.

The monopoly model places less emphasis upon these market forces than upon the continuing significance of union monopoly power. From this perspective, unemployment may have to reach extremely high levels before union power is weakened to any significant degree. The precise form that such approaches take varies (and indeed economists frequently merely assume stability of money or real wages – suggesting the importance of union monopoly – without explaining precisely why this should be so; see Thurow, 1983).

Here, we will consider one approach that currently appears to enjoy considerable popularity in certain quarters in Britain. It is claimed that two factors explain the current high level of unemployment in Britain: the nature of the benefit system and the monopoly power of trade unions. Through the use of their monopoly power, trade unions are able to raise wages and impose constraints upon efficient working within the union sector; those unable to find employment in this high-pay sector are therefore forced to accept employment in the non-union sector or else be unemployed. The demands of the unions in the union sector lead to reductions in employment and the labour that is shed moves into the non-union sector or else into unemployment. The decline of union membership does not, according to this argument, affect union behaviour or power directly. However, a market model might indicate that as the supply of labour increases in the non-union sector, wages would fall and this would impose constraints upon wages in the union sector. This does not happen, according to the monopoly model, because of the nature of the benefits system. For this imposes constraints upon how far wages in the non-union sector can fall. At some point workers will choose not to work in the non-union sector, preferring to be 'voluntarily' unemployed: that is, they do not offer themselves on the labour market, since they can make as much money by drawing benefit. The benefit system, therefore, is a central factor and this permits trade unions to maintain their monopoly power. For the nature of the benefit system means that the pressures that would otherwise serve to challenge union power are diverted into voluntary unemployment (see, e.g., Minford, 1983). It is, however, important in this case to note the way in which it is claimed that unemployment should be dealt with. First, unemployment is seen to be voluntary: most of those out of work choose to be. The way to make them seek employment is to reduce the payments they obtain through the benefit system. Then the increase in numbers seeking work in the non-union sector will serve to weaken the monopoly power of the unions. However, it is also argued that union monopoly should be more directly weakened through legislation, so that market forces can operate more effectively at all times.

Given the importance of these different arguments for our subsequent analysis of workplace trade unionism, we need to look at these various arguments more closely.

The State of the Product Market

An important part of the market argument relates to the state of the product market rather than the labour market. In a recession, it is claimed, the employer has less need of output and can therefore endure a strike with greater equanimity. Indeed, if he or she is operating at a loss, it is possible that a stoppage is actually profitable (Tylecote, 1973). Such arguments certainly have some plausibility, but it is not clear how generally applicable they are. In the first place, even when unemployment is high, certain product markets will be thriving. Companies operating in these areas will presumably wish to maximize output and will be enjoying high profits. If this is so, then product market forces will serve to strength the union's bargaining power.

But even when the product market is slack, employers may be keen to avoid a lengthy stoppage. Except in the case of a total monopoly (which, of course, never exists), slack demand for a company's products indicates that competition is strong – all producers of the product will be seeking to grab as much of the market as they can. Under such conditions, a temporary cessation of supply could be catastrophic for an employer, since potential customers can easily switch to alternative sources of supply. Similarly, and depending upon the nature of the product, employers may build up stocks to meet any expected upturn in demand. In both these types of situation, the bargaining power of the union may not be seriously weakened. It is, of course, possible that the employer can 'ride' a stoppage, if stocks have been built up with which he or she can continue to supply customers. In this case, the size of stockpiles – and the ability of the company to achieve access to them – are of crucial importance. But even here there is a limit to the advantages enjoyed by the employer: his or her bargaining advantage can only last as long as supplies last.

Similar points apply to the argument concerning the attractiveness of a stoppage when production is unprofitable. If loss-making is seen as merely temporary, then the employer may be keen to expand markets so as to return to profitability in the longer term; thus he or she will be keen to continue production. If loss-making is seen to be long term, then it would be economically rational to shut down permanently. However, it is possible to envisage other situations where an employer may seek major changes. For example, where a stoppage would effectively destroy the chances of regaining profitability, the employer might adopt a tough approach to the union, since, quite literally, he or she has nothing to lose. Another situation where there might be significant change is where both employer and union recognize their common weakness: the employer cannot hope to survive in the market place if a stoppage occurs, and the unions recognize that their members will therefore become unemployed. In this situation – which probably occurs quite frequently – it is common weakness rather than the relative strength of the employer which is of crucial importance. However, the picture may differ somewhat in a multi-plant company: in this case, the preceding argument may apply as far as plant management are concerned, but the union within an individual plant may be at a severe disadvantage relative to management at company level, who can pick which plants survive and which shut down. In this case, the level at which a union operates (at plant or company level) and the degree and form of co-ordination between different levels of the union may be of crucial importance.

In sum, the extent to which weak product markets shift the balance of power in favour of the employer is likely to vary. Even in a recession, some product markets boom; where demand is slack, employers may be keen to maintain production in order to preserve markets. On the other hand, there are situations, such as those where the employer has nothing to lose no matter what happens, or where a multi-plant company faces a plant-based union organization, where the conventional arguments apply. In still other cases, the situation may best be seen as one of mutual weakness such that there are pressures towards collaboration.

Alternative Labour

The second main factor which is said to weaken trade unions in a recession is the availability of alternative labour. A simple price–auction model, for example, suggests that union power will be weakened when unemployment is high, because an unemployed worker can go along to any employer and offer to do the job of a current worker for less money. The economically rational employer, the model suggests, will accept this offer (or force the current worker to accept a wage cut). The most succinct answer to this model is put forward by Thurow: 'in the real world any employer would think that you were a nut if you really expected him to accept your offer' (1983, pp. 191–2). However, it is necessary to explain why an employer should take this view.

Even in a non-union situation, employers are unlikely to conform to the price–auction model, simply because of the very large transaction costs involved. These would relate to a massive and unpredictable flow of applicants who would have to be assessed; there would be the costs involved in sacking more highly paid workers; there would be continual disruptions to production as replacement labour was introduced and as new workers had to learn their tasks (if only in terms of tacit skills). The administration of steadily declining wage rates would be a major task; team working would be continually disrupted and so on. In short, this pattern of continual, atomistic bargaining would lead to a total shambles even within the sort of firm envisaged in classical economic theory.

More fundamentally, there is reason to suppose that many employers operate on a quite different basis. They have created internal labour markets; they have used security of employment and associated systems to try to achieve a stable workforce, at least as far as key areas of activity are concerned. They have been aware of the importance of factors other than the pay packet, if workers are to co-operate in efficient working. Furthermore, trade unions have not only played an important role in encouraging this isolation of the workplace from the wider labour market, but they would not accept such an atomistic approach towards workers, for this would be contrary to their monopoly position (indeed, stable and strong union organization makes a nonsense of such atomistic approaches).

If an employer were to try to conform to even some modified form of the price–auction model, then it would first be necessary to remove the collective influence of the union. This would be a pre-condition, rather than a consequence, of replacing current workers with alternative labour. This would involve some form of confrontation, which would, in all probability, be costly. The attractions of recruiting replacement labour would have to be extremely high before an employer seriously contemplated such a course of action.

Confrontation may often lead to the use of alternative labour, rather than the reverse. That is, no matter what the level of unemployment, employers do not generally consider replacing union with non-union labour, except when they are faced with a lengthy strike (moreover, although non-union labour has been taken on in a few cases, it generally seems that the threat of such action is either withdrawn or encourages moves towards settlement of the dispute). But even if an employer contemplates such action, the costs of alternative labour may well be very high, since sacked trade unionists may seek to block the movement of 'scab' labour.

Recent discussions have stressed other means by which unionized labour can be replaced by alternative, non-union or less strongly organized labour (see, e.g., Rubery et al., 1984). These arguments have largely focused upon the notion of dual labour markets. Unionized workers are generally seen as part of the primary sector, whereas alternative labour is to be found in the secondary sector. Accordingly, employers can reduce costs and the bargaining power of the unions by shifting work from the primary to the secondary sector. There are two main ways in which this can be achieved: the first is by recruiting secondary workers directly into the firm; the second is subcontracting work to employers who operate with secondary labour.

In some cases, employers may seek to do this directly: that is, by sacking primary-sector workers and replacing them (in the way just discussed), or by increasingly resorting to part-time or casual labour, or by shifting the same workers from primary to secondary status. The most common areas for this type of tactic currently appear to be in the public services through privatization, and possibly more generally in catering and cleaning. In other cases, the same effect appears to come about through more indirect, and possibly non-purposeful, ways. Hence, for example, an employer may reduce primary-sector employment, given what is believed to be a permanent fall in demand. If there is then what is feared might be only a temporary upsurge of demand, then temporary labour may be used to fill it. Or, alternatively, the employer may, in the event of a longer-term resurgence, choose to reduce costs and increase flexibility by using secondary labour. In some cases, unions may accept such tactics, since they are seen to increase the security of unionized workers.

Although the employer may in these ways achieve greater flexibility and thereby partially evade union bargaining power, there are equally constraints upon such strategies. First, the logic of resorting to secondary labour is to have flexibility. If this is so, then there are pressures upon employers to meet falls in demand by shifting work away from the secondary sector into the primary, unionized, sector. The question therefore arises as to whether, at any particular time in a recession, more employers are shedding secondary labour than are recruiting it. Second, it is generally arged that only particular types of work can be subcontracted. It has to be possible to subdivide the production process into clearly defined parts; quality standards must not be too exacting. Hence, the activities which can be most easily sent out are peripheral and require little skill (although information technology may serve to extend the potential for such tactics). In other words, they are likely to be elements of the production process where union power is in any case limited. Indeed, a union whose primary membership is in more central areas may not be too sorry to see such weak groups removed from its bargaining area – the net effect may be to strengthen it.

Two other points are worthy of comment in this context. First, it appears that resort to subcontractors is sometimes a second-best option for employers. This seems to be the case, for example, as far as the maintenance of new technology is concerned in some companies. They are unable to achieve union agreement to the new patterns of training and working required, and hence are forced to subcontract. This may substantially increase costs: for example, it may take several hours, in which production is lost, before the subcontractor arrives. In this instance, subcontracting reflects union power (although evading it at some cost). Second, not all subcontracting is to non-unionized firms or labour. Indeed, some of the largest firms in this country are subcontractors, and their labour forces can generally be seen as primary rather than secondary. In this case, the attractions to the main employer of subcontracting may be simply to buy in expertise and remove the complexities of a marginal activity. For workers, it may have little effect. Moreover, in such cases subcontracting does not necessarily lead to a fall in overall union density.

As yet we lack much systematic data on the trends and scale of resort to secondary labour, and therefore it is difficult to assess its effects upon unionized workers and trade union power. What is important, however, is to recognize that there are reasons to expect that trends vary between companies (and possibly different activities within

companies) and that greater use of so-called secondary labour may have variable implications for unions and their members.

Another option open to employers is to shift production from unionized to non-unionized or less strongly organized plants within the company. Unless the latter already exist and production falls dramatically so that some plants have to be shut down, this is likely to be a long-term and expensive process. To set up totally new plant is a costly exercise and many factors other than the nature of the labour force are likely to be of relevance (see, e.g., Forthergill and Gudgin, 1982). Hence, although strongly unionized plants have lost proportionately more jobs than the more weakly organized, it is not evident that this is primarily attributable to union-evasion strategies on the part of employers (although it may be a factor).

The growth of employment of non-union or less strongly organized labour may also come about through shifts in the pattern of demand for goods and services. For example, if goods made by union labour are more expensive than those produced by non-union labour, then consumers will shift their purchases to the latter. Employment in the non-union firms will grow, as it declines in the unionized sector. The overall impact of trade unions will therefore decline. There are, however, a number of other considerations which need to be taken into account. First, trade union organization tends to be stronger in some sectors than others. It follows that in some areas of activity only unionized firms may be competing, since strong entry barriers exist. Declines in activity rates of unionized sectors may therefore reflect shifts in the general pattern of tastes. Second, union density tends to be greater in larger and inherently more profitable firms (Craig *et al.*, 1982). Here unions achieve economies of scale in recruiting and servicing members and are more able to demonstrate their value to potential members. It follows that as non-unionized firms grow and become more profitable, they are increasingly likely to be unionized. There may of course be a time-lag between the decline of old unionized sectors and the growth of union density in new sectors: however, awareness of the possibility of unionization may induce employers to come to terms with the unions early on or to provide good wages and conditions as part of a union-avoidance strategy.

These considerations are relevant to a widely discussed phenomenon: the presumed distinctive strategies of 'new technology' firms. Our argument would be that, to the extent that their strategies are distinctive, they reflect less their product than the fact that they are new. Since they do not have pre-existing labour forces, they are able to exploit the high level of unemployment in a way in which established

firms cannot. Hence, where they do recognize unions, they can obtain better terms from unions competing to increase their declining membership. Their ability to do this derives from the fact that the new company has no existing labour force which is able to impose sanctions – hence the unions have little power. Once operating, however, the company has a labour force which can use the production process against the employer – as a consequence, the pattern of labour relations may change as workers develop in-plant organization and exert their bargaining power (cf. Dubois, 1976). Second, the perspective of the larger union is likely to be different to that of the in-plant union. The former suffers from high levels of unemployment, since, even if membership declines less fast than employment, it loses economies of scale in its operation and may also lose influence in such bodies as the TUC. In-plant unions are likely to be less concerned about such matters, since their focus is upon the membership within the plant.

Games, Strategies and Constraints

We have argued above that as long as the employer wants production, then workers have some degree of power. The exact sources of power vary according to the position of workers in the production process and the more general nature of that process: this is discussed more fully below. This is true whether we are considering unionized or non-unionized plants. The importance of trade unionism is that through combination workers increase this power: the sum is greater than the parts. The nature of this power is such that an employer cannot operate solely through coercion, but needs to win the compliance of the workforce. Given the importance of worker discretion and tacit skills even in the most routine of jobs, the employer has no alternative.

In part as a recognition of this fact, many large employers have developed internal labour markets, isolating their employees from the forces of the wider market. We have argued above that, in part because of union power, but also due to other factors relating to skills, the nature of the production process and costs of administration, there are limits as to how far employers can, or would wish to, break down this isolation (as is recognized, for example, in some forms of implicit contract theory, see Okun, 1981). If this is correct, then it follows that the extent to which union bargaining power within the workplace is reduced depends primarily upon events within the company. Hence, it is changes in the labour requirements of the company itself that are the key factor (although, of course, changes in relative factor prices are important here).

In the attempt to maintain or improve competitiveness, employers

may adopt a variety of strategies. Some of these may have no effects, or only indirect effects, upon the labour force. These include creating new products, introducing new technology (a central theme in this volume), or simply improving design and the organization of production – for example, by ensuring that the right components are at the right place at the right time. Labour, then, is not the only means of adjustment. It is, however, clearly an important one. But in seeking to reduce employment or increase efficiency, it is also generally important for the employer to maintain some minimal degree of compliance (the exception was noted above, where, literally, the employer has nothing to lose: see Batstone, 1984a). With this exception, and assuming some degree of flexibility on the part of the union, the employer is likely to seek to adjust manning levels through co-operation with the union and workforce, rather than through head-on confrontation. That this is generally the case has been indicated by a number of recent studies (e.g. Batstone, 1984a; Edwards, 1985) and it is also found to be the case in this study – at least as far as the private sector is concerned. However, some writers have suggested that the increased consultation with both unions and workers may be a moderate form of 'union-bypassing' (e.g. Sisson, 1984).

Such bypassing may be an accurate description in some cases, but it is by no means inevitably so. First, it is necessary to distinguish between intent and effect: that is, employers may seek to bypass the unions, but may fail to do so. In the case of employee involvement techniques, for example, there is reason to doubt their efficacy, particularly when they fit ill with other forms of labour control (see, e.g., Batstone, 1984a; Elden, 1977; Fox, 1974; Gustavsen and Hunnius, 1981; Turner and Lawrence, 1967). As a consequence, such techniques may have the effect of increasing the centrality of the union in workers' eyes and may even be used as a means to impose even greater pressure upon the employer. Similarly, the growth of union-based consultation can be seen as union bypassing only if it is at the expense of negotiation; that is, issues that were formerly negotiated are now simply matters for consultation. But it seems that frequently the issues for consultation serve to expand the range of union–management deliberations, rather than intruding upon previously jointly-negotiated matters: certainly for much of the post-war period this was the case.

Nevertheless, it is generally claimed that changes in working practices have been widely introduced in companies facing competitive pressures, and this can be seen as indicative of a decline in union influence. The pattern is reminiscent of debates on productivity bargaining in the 1960s and 1970s: there may, for a period, be an increase in the range of joint regulation, as changes in working practices are

negotiated, but thereafter union power declines because it has bar-gained its powers away. However, there is a risk of forgetting that past experience: productivity bargaining frequently failed to reduce union power or increase productivity (Batstone, 1984a). It may be that, without changes in working practices, productivity would have declined. If output has fallen dramatically, then – particularly where the same equipment is being employed – it is clearly necessary to change working arrangements; manning requirements do not change in proportion to output, so that no jobs may be lost when output falls by 20 per cent; but 40 per cent of jobs may be lost when output falls a further 20 per cent. In addition, allowance has to be made for cyclical patterns and time-lags, and there are also serious measurement problems (Muellbauer, forthcoming). Our assessment of the growth of productivity depends upon the point from which we measure it. If, for the present, we take growth of productivity as the inverse of union power, we would have to say that in the first move union power increased, whereas in the second it was reduced to its previous level.

The current situation may also differ from previous experience because, in the face of few alternative job opportunities, unions might be expected to demonstrate greater concern over job loss than they did in the past. However, the nature of union priorities as between wages and jobs is likely to vary according to a number of factors. One of these is the precise pattern of union organization. The importance of this factor can best be seen by contrasting the approach likely to be adopted by a highly centralized, powerful union confederation with that of a workplace union organization that enjoys a high degree of autonomy. The former is likely to act as a class-based organization: that is, it defines its scope of interest as embracing all workers, rather than a particular sectional group of union members. Moreover, its strength and structure permit it to make meaningful deals with the state concerning a trade-off between jobs and pay levels, and this will be facilitated by the fact that union leaders are likely to have more autonomy. Accordingly, they are ready and able to moderate wages in the interests of employment. On the other hand, the workplace organization in a decentralized union movement cannot be sure that, even if it moderates wages, others will follow suit. It may therefore find itself lagging behind on pay, without having made any substantial contribution to employment levels. This will be all the more galling since the key unit of organization – those working in the workplace – is not of a kind to encourage such wider interests: it is responsible primarily for its members rather than the working class as such. It is therefore likely to place a greater priority upon its own wages than upon the general level of unemployment. Hence, we see that where

centralized confederations exist, real wages have typically not grown in recent years, whereas they have in countries approximating our second type, even when unemployment has been much higher (this point is developed more fully in chapter 8).

It might be argued, however, that workplace organizations would trade off wages in favour of employment when the jobs to be lost are those of their own members. However, this will be so only under certain conditions. The explanation in large part depends upon the fact that at workplace level – as distinct from confederal level – the views of individual members can be more easily expressed. One can identify at least two situations in which a workplace organization will not trade money for jobs. First, if an employer wishes to reduce employment by 10 per cent and 10 per cent of workers volunteer for redundancy – for example, because they have major short-term financial problems, which can be resolved by taking redundancy pay – then the union is not confronted with a trade-off. Indeed, in some situations it appears that unions wish to oppose job loss, but that this option is effectively destroyed by members volunteering for redundancy (this suggests the interesting hypothesis that individualism applies to leaving, and in part entering, the workplace, but not to action within it). The second is a situation where a majority of workers wish to retain their jobs, when the company is seeking job reductions of less than 50 per cent. As long as the majority of workers can be sure that it is not their jobs that will be lost, then it is economically rational for them to support the proposed redundancies. This will be all the more true if lower manning levels provide them with greater security and/or with increases in pay (for example, from performance-related bonuses or promotion). Such action by the membership may also have an added advantage for the union: it avoids a major confrontation, which it may well lose. Accordingly, its power might be reduced less than would otherwise be the case.

It is important to keep arguments of this kind in perspective. Few unions will happily forgo employment of even a small minority of their members. The readiness of members to volunteer for redundancy may often reflect a sense of impotence and desperation. The moves discussed in the preceding paragraph have therefore to be seen as 'suboptimal', from a union viewpoint. The reason for discussing them at some length, however, is to stress that there are likely to be situations in which substantial job loss is not as catastrophic for trade unions as a good deal of recent discussion would suggest.

There are, of course, other factors that will affect union and member thinking, not least elements of solidarity. In addition, faced with insecurity, workers may increasingly turn to the union for support and

protection. Nevertheless, there does appear to be a degree of validity in the preceding arguments. There are, however, other situations where the union will seek to preserve jobs and will be forced or prepared to make concessions to this end. This is particularly likely where workers cannot be certain whether they will be made redundant, and where some concessions are necessary in order to prevent the whole plant being shut down. (The latter may provide particular scope for employer games when it operates a number of plants and where the key focus of union organization is the workplace rather than the company.) It is in these situations that the union's bargaining position is most seriously weakened, and it may be forced to concede changes in working practices or wage moderation in exchange for continued employment; in the course of doing so, it may also be required to accept some job loss.

Even in this case, however, if the employer wishes to maintain the compliance of workers and the co-operation of the union, it may be necessary to make concessions. That is, changes in working practices may be less than the technically optimal from the employer's point of view. Moreover, as in new union situations, the balance of advantage for the employer may be only temporary. Once the risk of job loss has receded, then the power of the union is likely to return: for the ultimate basis of union power within the workplace is not its absolute size, but its ability to stop production when the employer wants it. This, then, is another important factor shaping management thinking and encouraging it to seek change through co-operation rather than confrontation.

In this section, we have argued that the way in which the company itself fares is central to the impact of the recession upon many union-ized workplaces. We have indicated that when the company faces market problems, unless these are of a particularly severe nature, it has good reason to adopt a co-operative approach to the unions, if they appear to be at all flexible. Second, we have pointed to a number of situations in which proposed job loss may have less effect upon union power and influence than might be expected. This is not to deny that unions may be seriously weakened in certain situations; all that has been argued is that serious weakening of trade unions is likely to be a good deal less common than often seems to be supposed.

The State and Removing Obstacles to the Operation of Market Forces

Operating on what we have termed the monopoly model, some com-mentators have argued that it is necessary to use non-market means to reduce the power of trade unions, and more generally to introduce

downward flexibility of wages. More specifically, they have argued for changes in the benefits system and legislation that reduces the monopoly power of the unions.

It is not our intention to discuss at length the question of the benefits system. Three points can, however, be noted. The first is a moral one. Unemployment is largely a reflection less of choice on the part of the unemployed, than of the operation of market forces and the priorities of the state, which can adopt policies to reduce the size of the dole queue. There is also a strong case for arguing that, in a civilized society, the state should ensure that all its citizens enjoy some minimal standard of living.

Second, it should be remembered that the introduction of welfare benefits is in large part a reflection of pressures deriving from the labour movement, in both its political and union forms. To the extent that these remain strong, and to the extent that governments are guided by the criterion of political legitimacy, then there are limits to how far reductions in benefit are likely to be made. In other words, the very existence of benefits is in part attributable to union monopoly; it therefore follows that there are limits to how far such benefits can be reduced, without first removing that monopoly. This is not, of course, to suggest that no changes can be made; indeed, in the past there has been a risk of exaggerating the constraints upon such moves (e.g. Goldthorpe, 1978). Nevertheless, we would maintain that there are limits to how far policies of this kind can be pursued.

Third, one might question the efficacy of reduced benefits. This depends upon the proportion of people who would both seek and find work, if benefits were lower. If worker choice were the primary factor explaining unemployment, then one would expect that unemployment would increase when benefits were increased. But such patterns appear to account for only a small proportion of changes in levels of unemployment (Atkinson *et al.*, 1984; Micklewright, 1985; Narendranathan *et al.*, 1985). In other words, there is reason to doubt the efficacy of such a strategy.

Our primary concern, however, is with the question of legislation as a means of reducing union power. Over the last few years we have seen a number of measures to this end. It is too early to assess their overall efficacy. Certainly, at first sight, it seems reasonable to argue that the existence of the closed shop and of the deduction of union dues at source serve to provide institutional checks upon the ability of union members to vote with their feet. In other words, these institutional devices may constitute an important means by which union density – and hence bargaining power – is maintained. However, if the union maintains its bargaining power, then one would expect that

union members would not wish to leave the union, since the gains of membership exceed the costs. Hence, as one would expect, ballots over the continuation of the closed shop – despite the very high levels of support legally required (roughly double the support obtained by the Conservative government in the 1983 election) – have generally supported its continuation. A total ban on the closed shop might lead to a decline in union membership. But, internationally, there is no relationship between the coverage of the closed shop and union density. Even if Britain were to prove an exception to this pattern, the explanation may reflect less any disillusion with the union, but rather an ability to free-ride: that is, within a workplace the main gains of union action may go to all workers, although only union members pay their dues. But in such situations, the social pressures for continued membership may be considerable.

This is particularly likely if the employer sees advantages in dealing with the workforce collectively. Surveys indicate that many employers see advantages in the closed shop and in dealing with trade unions (Brown, 1981). Hence, they may encourage union membership, even when there is no formal closed shop (e.g., Seglow *et al.*, 1982, on the Federal Republic of Germany). Moreover, we have argued that in the recession there are strong pressures upon many employers to maintain co-operative relations with the union: to the extent that this is the case, then they will neither encourage workers to quit the union, nor will they use other legal means to endanger the position of the union.

Another factor discouraging legal resort on the part of employers is the very nature of the law. It is clear that the pattern of labour relations varies considerably between employers: the pattern consists of a complex web of formal agreements, informal understandings, and custom and practice. It has been found that even formal agreements made within the workplace often sit uneasily with pre-existing practices and may therefore be largely ignored (Batstone, 1984a; Terry, 1977). If this is true of agreements made within the workplace, then it is likely to be even more true of legislation that is imposed or offered by an external body. Such opportunities, for example, over secondary action, are likely to be used only *in extremis* by employers who are acting rationally.

Other legislation is based upon the assumption that union leaders are unrepresentative of their members and therefore adopt policies that are in their own, rather than members', interests. In any set of large organizations, such possibilities clearly exist: the question of their importance therefore arises. In this area, we come to conventional arguments concerning the personal and institutional interests of union leaders. However, the rationale of the legislation is directly con-

tradictory to the assumptions underlying much of the academic debate. For oligarchy is generally seen to lead to incorporation – that is, moderation on the part of the leaders, where members would prefer to apply stronger challenges to the employer. In any event, there is a risk of exaggerating the divergence between member and institutional interests: the union's survival as an organization depends upon member support. Conversely, if formal organizational structures did not exist, then the collective expression of worker interests would become that much more difficult, since, on every occasion, organization would have to be created afresh.

To the extent that the interests of members and leaders diverge, it seems probable that union leaders may be more ready to make concessions in order to maintain the level of employment than would members. This seems likely for a number of reasons. First, in many unions benefits are paid to the unemployed, who do not pay dues: hence, instead of being a source of income, the unemployed are a drain upon resources. Second, we have noted that trade unions achieve economies of scale where there are large numbers of members; hence the costs for a national union of a declining membership are significant. Third, union income depends upon numbers of members rather than their incomes – that is, the union has an interest in maximizing membership rather than maximizing members' earnings. The importance of these considerations is indicated both by the decline in absolute membership of many unions – the membership of TUC affiliated unions, for example, fell from over 12 million at the end of 1979 to just under 10 million in 1985 – and by the severe financial problems which many unions have faced. These pressures do not impinge upon workplace organizations to anywhere near the same degree: typically, they enjoy high levels of density in concentrated areas, and, at the same time, they are far less dependent upon finances for their activity (or, to put it differently, they depend upon the voluntary activity of members and financial support from the employer, who, for example, often pays the wages of stewards while they are carrying out union business).

In short, there is reason to doubt the efficacy of recent legislation, at least as far as the private sector is concerned. The situation may, however, be rather different in the public sector, where the government is the employer. In this instance, the arguments we have outlined above concerning the pressures in favour of co-operation may still apply to 'managers', who see their primary function to be carrying out particular sets of activities. Such pressures may also operate upon the government itself to some degree, even when it is committed to breaking union monopoly. This can arise in two ways, although both

are based upon the priority of the government – the maintenance of political legitimacy (the equivalent of profits in the private sector). The first of these is where attacks upon trade unions are electorally unpopular. This, to date, does not appear generally to have been the case. The second is where challenges to the union adversely affect the provision of goods and services on the part of the state, and these are an important basis of political legitimacy. It seems that this may be a more serious constraint upon the state.

Nevertheless, it might be expected that the state can adopt a tougher approach to the unions than can many employers in the private sector. Precisely because it does not operate on a profit criterion and has access to such massive resources, it is able to confront trade unions in situations where a private employer would not. And where a government can claim to have come to power in part upon a commitment to challenge union power, the pursuit of political legitimacy may encourage it to adopt such a course of action. There is, however, a balance between such action and endangering the provision of services upon which political legitimacy rests. Hence it is worthy of note that the main challenges to the unions have been in areas where such problems have been limited – for example, in public corporations where demand is slack and stocks are high. Morever, in these cases, the public corporation has been making losses, so that the government is able to impose its demands as a pre-condition of continued financial support. The same sorts of influence may also occur during the process of privatization. In short, given the nature of the political market in legitimacy, one might expect that under certain circumstances the state will be more likely to challenge unions in the public sector than will employers in the private sector. The latter may be hesitant to use even the legislation with which the government supplies them.

Trade Unions

The preceding discussion has focused primarily upon the extent to which changes in product and labour markets affect the power and influence of trade unions, both directly and through management strategy. However, the nature of trade unions themselves is also likely to shape their experiences in a recession. Three sets of factors shaping union power and strategy are of especial relevance for our present purposes: factors relating to the power of individual workers and work groups within the production process; factors shaping member attitudes and perceived interests; and the nature of union organization itself.

Worker Power in the Production Process

Three features of work are generally seen as providing workers with a significant degree of power within the production process (Hickson *et al.*, 1973). The first of these concerns the ease with which they can be replaced, that is, their substitutability. Clearly the state of the labour market is of relevance here, but generally speaking the greater the skill level, the less easily can workers be replaced (Clegg, 1970, p. 31). This is most obviously true of such groups as craftsmen, but it may also apply to other workers who have firm-specific and 'tacit' skills.

Second, workers who are more central to the production process are generally seen to have greater power, for action by such central groups will have a widespread effect upon other workers, bringing production to a halt (e.g. Sayles, 1958, p. 4). A related factor is the immediacy with which a group can disrupt production. For example, a small group directly working on part of an integrated production system may be able to stop the whole system immediately. In contrast, stoppages by maintenance workers may have little effect for some time – that is, until machines break down.

Third, work groups that cope with uncertainty for larger groups within the organization generally have greater power than those in more routinized situations, for their work permits others to operate upon more certain grounds. It follows that the withdrawal of their coping activities will introduce disarray into the traditionally routine activities of other groups.

These various sources of power can, to a large extent, be related to the nature of the production process and the exact relationship of workers to it. Hence, for example, production workers within integrated production systems – such as continuous-flow and, in particular, assembly-line operations – are likely to have considerable centrality. On the other hand, skilled workers in unit and small-batch production and maintenance workers more generally are likely to derive power from their coping with uncertainty, even though the latter may lack immediacy. Similarly, clerical workers involved in non-routine administration may be seen as deriving power from their coping with uncertainty, and are also likely to have limited substitutability.

However, although worker power in part derives from their position within the work process, action by both employers and unions can also affect it. For example, a union may reduce the substitutability of

workers by ensuring that other workers refuse to work with any replacement labour. The use of picket lines and the extension of the range of workers engaged in strike action can effectively change the centrality of the aggrieved group; the immediacy with which workers affect production can be affected by purposely running down stocks of components. The manipulation of rules – that is, rule-breaking, or in some cases rule conformity as with working to rule, or the withdrawal of acts of 'utilitarian sabotage' – can affect the extent to which a group copes with or creates uncertainty within the work process. In short, collective organization on the part of workers can change the bases of worker power within the production process (for a fuller discussion of these themes, see Batstone *et al.*, 1978, pp. 27–32).

Member Orientations

The extent to which workers make use of their power resources and the extent to which they are prepared to create further resources through combination depend upon their orientations and the extent to which these are consistent with their employment situation. Non-work factors, such as domestic responsibilities and social ties, serve to shape workers' work-related goals and their views on the legitimacy of collective action (see, e.g., Goldthorpe *et al.*, 1968; Rubery *et al.*, 1984). But, in addition, factors within the work situation shape worker expectations. For example, social interaction with workmates and the operation of work-group norms influence worker views and behaviour (Batstone *et al.*, 1975). In addition, as has been increasingly recognized in discussions of labour control strategies, employers also seek to shape the attitudes of workers through a variety of involvement techniques as well as by career structures and payment systems (Edwards, 1979). Day-to-day work experience may also foster certain attitudes. For example, as Fox (1974) has argued, detailed control over workers implies that they are not to be trusted; they may therefore reciprocate by demonstrating low trust in management. Unions themselves may also affect worker attitudes: indeed, an important aspect of strong union organization is the education of members into certain principles and perspectives (see, e.g., Batstone *et al.*, 1977 and 1978).

However, worker readiness to employ collective means of interest pursuit is not only dependent upon the particular pattern of expectations, or perceived interests, which they hold, but also the extent to which they are met. Hence, for example, although manual workers may, in general terms, be more ready than non-manual workers to resort to collective action, it is quite possible that the latter actually

demonstrate a higher level of strike action. This may arise simply because the expectations which they have developed are not being met by employers, whereas those of manual workers are. Moreover, the experience of collective action may serve to shape expectations and orientations.

One indicator of member orientations of relevance in this context is union density. The higher the proportion of workers who are union members, the greater is the likelihood that workers will act collectively. However, it should be remembered that collective sanctions are not confined to unionized workers; nor are all union members equally ready to engage in such action (see, for example, Blackburn, 1967). As noted above, traditionally it has been argued that manual workers are more collectively oriented than non-manual workers. The same has in the past been thought to be true of men as compared with women, and full-timers as compared with part-timers. However, these patterns may have become less marked with changes in absolute and relative pay levels, job security and broader changes in the organization of work and patterns of labour control.

Union Structure and Strategy

It has been observed at a number of points in the preceding discussion that trade unions can affect the power of workers and their expectations and perspectives. However, it is equally the case that the nature of the membership affects the nature of trade unions. This is most clearly the case in terms of union structure: the early patterns of trade union organization reflected the goals of their founders. For example, those committed to a class-based definition of worker interests sought to develop broad-based, open forms of union organization. In contrast, those who defined their interests in craft terms set up exclusive organizations, confining membership to the relevant craft. Although a great deal of change has occurred in union organizations subsequently, the nature of that change has in part been affected by previous union structure. As Turner has argued, 'the character of organizations is very much a product of their ancestry and the circumstances of their early growth' (1962, p. 14). Unions, then, are products of their past and agents of their future: it follows that their futures are to a degree shaped by their past.

Our concern, however, is less with the historical development of trade unions than with how they are confronting the current situation. To a significant extent, therefore, we can take union structure as given: we can then look at how structure affects union power and strategy.

Two key dimensions of union structure can be distinguished for our purposes: union scope and organizational sophistication. We will discuss these two dimensions in general terms and then go on to apply them to different aspects of union organization. It should be stressed, however, that we do not claim that these are the only factors which explain union behaviour; many other factors are relevant. Moreover, in multi-union situations, the actions of one union may have 'knock-on' effects, some of which are unforeseen. There are therefore limitations to the utility of rational models of the kind we are outlining. But recognition of this point does not deny their utility.

Union scope. By union scope, we wish to refer to the nature of a union's membership, or aspired membership. Union scope, we will argue, affects the way in which a union defines members' interests. The scope of a trade union can be further divided into two aspects: first, the proportion of a workforce which the union has in membership or aspires to have as members – its relative size – and, second, the particular nature of that membership.

The importance of the relative size of a union can be best explained in Olsonian terms, although similar arguments are common in industrial relations (for example, in the context of debates on multi-unionism). A union that represents all workers within an employment unit is likely to adopt a rather different perspective to one representing only a small, specific group. The reason for this is as follows: any union demand, if successful, provides gains to its members, but may also impose costs upon the workforce more generally. A union representing a small, sectional group will alone obtain the gains from its actions, but may incur only a small proportion of the costs of its action. On the other hand, an all-encompassing union – that is, one that represents all workers – will not only achieve all of the gains of its actions, but also all of its costs. It therefore follows that it will tend to take a broader perspective than a more sectional organization. Or, as Olson puts it: 'the more inclusive the special-interest group, the greater will be the share of any inefficient policies to be borne by its own membership. This internalization of external effects rises monotonically with the share of the population and other resources that a special-interest group includes' (1983, p.23).

If this argument is correct, then it follows that all-encompassing organizations are more likely to concern themselves with a wider range of issues and, in particular, with the general nature of employer strategy – that is, the broader factors which shape more immediate aspects of the wage–effort bargain. Less inclusive organizations are

not only less concerned with such issues, but also – to the extent that they are concerned – see them very much through their own sectional perspective. The precise nature of that perspective depends upon the sorts of groups covered by the union.

To argue that more inclusive organizations adopt a wider perspective is not, however, to suggest that they necessarily adopt a more co-operative approach. There is a no *a priori* reason to believe that a wider definition of member interests should lead to incorporation. In some cases it may do so, but in others it is possible that an all-encompassing organization will pose a greater challenge to employers than more sectional organizations. The precise approach adopted by any union is likely to reflect both the nature of the membership and the strategies adopted by employers.

The second aspect of union scope relevant to an understanding of union behaviour concerns the precise nature of the membership it represents. In addition to the personal characteristics of members, such as sex, ethnicity and age, the sorts of occupations it covers and their relationship to the production process are likely to be of particular relevance. Given the nature of our survey, we can usefully focus here upon the following groups: semi-skilled workers, craftsmen both in production and maintenance areas, and white-collar workers. Cross-cutting these variations is whether or not members work in the public or private sector. Compared with unions covering semi-skilled workers, craft unions have traditionally placed particular emphasis upon the protection of the craft: this has meant seeking to control the supply of labour into a particular job territory and maintaining skill levels in other ways, such as ensuring adequate training. Non-manual unions have traditionally exercised less widespread control over issues relating to work organization and even pay: this is because, traditionally, individualistic means of pursuing interests have been more open to their members. To a large extent, therefore, the role of the union has been concerned with preserving the relative status of members and protecting the career structure.

The importance of the distinction between the private and public sectors has been mentioned in the preceding discussion. Particularly if we compare unions in classic areas of the public sector, such as the civil service, with those in parts of the private sector which are rela-tively independent of the state as a controller or buyer of goods and services, then their logics of action are significantly different. Ultimately, union power depends upon the ability to damage the employer's interests. This means, in the private sector, that union power rests ultimately upon the ability to damage profits; in the public sector, it means the ability to damage the political legitimacy of the government (for a fuller discussion of this point, see Batstone *et al.*, 1984).

In brief, we have argued that two aspects of union scope are important for an understanding of union strategy: relative size or inclusiveness, and the precise nature of the membership represented. In practice, there is often a relationship between these two variables. All-inclusive unions, for example, will by definition include all types of worker within any employment unit. Those representing craftsmen, particularly maintenance craftsmen, will generally be smaller and less inclusive than those representing less skilled workers. However, there can clearly be exceptions to this general pattern, due to the particular mix of occupations within an employment unit.

Union sophistication. The strategy and influence of a trade union is not merely shaped by its scope, but also by its sophistication. By this we mean its internal organizational arrangements and resources. In order effectively to pursue members' interests, a union has to be able to undertake three things: first, it has to be able to identify and permit the expression of different interests; second, it has to have mechanisms that permit the collation and reconciliation of different interests; and, third, it requires resources not only to define members' interests, but also, given these, to formulate and implement coherent and effective strategies which take into account the context within which the union finds itself.

Unless differing interests can be expressed and thereby taken into account, it is unlikely that union strategy will optimally reflect members' interests. It is likely, for example, that some groups will systematically suffer relative to those who can more easily express their views. This may not only mean that costs are imposed upon the former, but also that the union becomes weakened. Those whose interests remain unrepresented may be forced to resort to 'unconstitutional' means to pursue their special interests within the union: or they may quit, possibly joining another union or seeking to form a breakaway organization (see Hemingway, 1978; Hirschman, 1970; Lerner, 1961). At the least, the disadvantaged groups may become increasingly apathetic and disillusioned, with the result that the union cannot rely upon their support at crucial times.

The precise ways in which different interests may be expressed can vary widely. In some unions, for example, differences of interest may largely reflect geographical location, in which case conventional structures may suffice. In other cases, however, there may be distinctive occupational interests, which cut across regions and areas:

unions sometimes create special decision-making structures for these different interests or else ensure that all the interests have some minimal representation upon key committees or councils. At workplace level, the representation of different interests is of equal importance: if they are to be effective, workplace organizations need to ensure that the structure of shop-steward constituencies reflects the different interests which exist and that none of these positions remains vacant.

Not only does organizational structure need to reflect different interests, it is also necessary that those interests be reconciled in some way, if an overall strategy is to be formulated and pursued. Unless this is done, there is a risk that sectionalism dominates: this will mean that certain common interests will not be pursued and, at the same time, the various sectional groups will impose costs upon each other as they seek to pursue their own particular interests. Equally, it is important not only that different views be known at some central, co-ordinating level, but also that they be represented there. Where this is not the case, we may speak of an oligarchical structure: under such conditions, the reconciliation of interests may be arbitrary and member interests may be subordinated to institutional concerns and the personal interests of the oligarchs. In other words, there needs to be some structure at the highest level of the organization through which representatives of different interests achieve some form of accommodation. In the case of workplace organizations, this may take the form of a shop stewards' committee; at national level, annual conferences or executive councils may play a similar role.

Third, we have argued, a union requires resources not only to permit the expression and reconciliation of interests, but also to investigate and understand the second dimension crucial to effective policy formation – the context in which the union operates. The nature of these resources may vary widely between unions. In some cases, they may take the form of specialist officers working full-time for the union; in other cases, the union may rely more heavily upon lay officials – but even these require resources, if only in the form of time off to fulfil their union responsibilities. Moreover, if central-level strategies are to be important, and if complex issues in the union's environment are to be tackled seriously, it is likely that specialist skills and personnel who spend the bulk of their time on such matters will be needed. Hence, an effective workplace union organization may require a hierarchy of stewards and possibly one or two full-time stewards; it may also require specialist advice, an obvious source being the union nationally. In the same way, unions nationally require full-time officials and specialist staff in a range of areas. (It is possible to extend the list of organizational resources: for example, to include large strike funds.)

Where these three elements – representation of sectional interests, means by which different interests may be reconciled, and organizational resources – exist, along with 100 per cent union density, then we may talk of a union being sophisticated. The degree of union sophistication, and the way in which it is achieved, are likely to be related to union scope. For example, a national union with a homogeneous membership in terms of occupation and industry may have fewer problems of reconciling different interests; at the same time, it can achieve economies of scale in the use of its resources, in so far as it needs to develop expertise only in relation to one industry and occupation. Similarly, we have argued that an all-encompassing organization is likely to demonstrate a broader range of interests and, accordingly, it may require greater specialist resources.

There is also an important size effect upon the degree of union sophistication. This can best be demonstrated by considering workplace union organization. Where a union has few members, it is likely to have only one steward. At first sight, problems of co-ordination would therefore appear to be few. However, in such situations members may often act individualistically, the steward may have little time to pursue union matters, and he or she may find it difficult, with few resources and little experience, to develop any coherent policy. Discussions of union policy are likely to be informal and *ad hoc*; union organization may therefore be extremely fragile. On the other hand, where the membership is larger, there are clearly greater pressures for some type of formal organization: at the same time, the greater workload of the union will mean that these formal structures are used and that stewards build up expertise both individually and collectively (see, e.g., Batstone *et al.*, 1977). In short, the larger the membership, the more sophisticated union organization is likely to be.

Levels and Units of Union Organization

The preceding discussion has been in very general terms. We need, therefore, to move on to a more detailed consideration of the realities of trade union organization. For our purposes, two cross-cutting aspects of union organization are relevant: the distinction between workplace and national levels of union organization, and secondly, the distinction between individual trade unions and trade unions collectively at either of these levels. That is, the preceding arguments can be applied to individual trade unions within the workplace, to the unions collectively within that workplace, to individual unions nationally or to the union movement nationally. However, the precise implications or the relative importance of the various arguments presented vary according to which of these units of union organization we are talking about. Moreover, further questions arise concerning the relationship between these different units of union organization. The focus of our research was upon the workplace, and hence we will consider the question of union organization at this level first.

Workplace union organization. In order to distinguish between individual unions and the totality of unions representing manual workers/white-collar workers within the workplace, we will refer to intra- and inter-union organization. Inter-union organization, to the extent that it exists, is by definition all-encompassing, and hence our focus will be upon the degree of sophistication of organization between unions. Intra-union organizations may, on the other hand, vary widely in terms of the degree of inclusiveness, as well as in terms of type of membership and sophistication. But the relationships between the two types of organization are also important: intra-union organization may be sophisticated in the case of a particular union, whereas inter-union organization may be unsophisticated; both may be high or low in their levels of sophistication. The interesting situation, however, is that in which intra-union sophistication for a particular union is low, but inter-union sophistication is high. In such cases (and also possibly where both types of organization are sophisticated), it is likely that individual unions have forsaken a good deal of their individual identity. Less sophisticated unions, we have argued, are often small, and therefore they may constitute only a low proportion of the total union membership within a plant. They would normally, therefore, adopt a somewhat parochial approach and have a rather limited bargaining range. However, particularly where there are larger unions within the workplace which are more sophisticated, the small, less sophisticated union may find it attractive or necessary to co-operate with the larger unions. It may be that this is the only way in which it can ensure that its members do not suffer as the larger groups pursue their interests; co-operation may also mean that the smaller union can 'ride on the back' of the larger unions, thereby achieving greater influence; and it may find that unilateral actions that run against the wishes of larger unions meet with little success. But the condition of such co-operation is likely to be that it adopts a less self-interested approach. In brief, under these conditions, the unions collectively within the workplace become the dominant form of union organization. (This is not to suggest that smaller unions will totally merge their interests with those of the larger body of union members; indeed, inter-union co-operation may be fraught with tensions and, on occasion, to such a degree that it collapses.)

National-level organization. In the same way as we have distinguished between intra- and inter-union organization within the workplace, so it is possible to employ a similar distinction at national level: indeed, inter-union sophistication has assumed considerable importance in recent discussions of social and economic policy and performance (e.g. Goldthorpe, 1984). However, for our present purposes we will concentrate upon intra-union organization: that is, individual unions at national level; in the concluding chapter, we look at inter-union organization at national level.

At workplace level, the primary distinctions concerning types of union member relate to occupation. In the case of unions nationally, however, a further distinction is also important: the degree to which a union's membership is confined to a single employer or industry, or cuts across a wide range of industries. For convenience, we can distinguish between four types of national union as follows:

Range of occupations covered:

	Single	*Multi*
Range of employers/industries:		
Single	1	2
Multi	3	4

Generally speaking, the most all-encompassing form of union organization at industry level is the single-industry/employer, multi-occupation union (type 2). In this instance, the welfare of the union is intimately tied to that of the industry/employer. This, along with its multi-occupational membership, means that it is likely to seek a wide range of influence and demonstrate a concern with broad, strategic issues. Moreover, the fact that the union deals with only one employer/industry means that it can focus its resources and thereby, for any level of resources, achieve greater expertise than could a union that was forced to spread its resources more widely.

The single-employer/industry, single-occupation union (type 1) is likely to demonstrate many of the characteristics of its multi-occupational equivalent. Its fate is similarly tied to that of a single employer or industry. However, it is likely to differ according to two factors: first, the precise nature of the occupation covered (e.g. craft, non-manual) and, second, the relative importance of the occupation/union within the industry/company. The higher the proportion of workers that the union represents, the more similar it is likely to be to a multi-occupation union in terms of its interests and strategy. Where the union's occupation represents only a small proportion of total union membership, then it is likely to adopt a more sectional approach: that is, it will be more concerned with representing the distinctive interests of its members, with the result that it is somewhat less concerned than an all-encompassing organization with the general strategies of the employer – except in so far as they directly impinge upon the occupation.

The fate of the multi-industry, single-occupation union (type 3) is not tied to a single industry or employer, although the union is able to concentrate its resources upon the welfare of its occupation. Hence it is less likely to show a general interest in employer strategy. On the other hand, single-occupation unions are concerned with the preservation of their occupation and so may bargain more intensively and achieve greater control over factors relating most directly to the work situation. Many craft unions were traditionally of this kind.

The final type of union is the multi-industry, multi-occupation union (type 4). Other things being equal, the fate of such unions is not tied to any individual industry or employer, and at the same time it has to spread its resources across a wide range of different activities. Nationally, therefore, it is less likely to be able to commit time to a detailed consideration of employer strategy. This will be less true the smaller the range of industries/employers covered by the union; it will also be less true if membership is concentrated in a small number of sectors and the union concentrates its resources upon these. On the other hand, a single, centralized union confederation can be seen as approximating to a type 4 union. Such confederations might be expected at national – as distinct from industry – level to act in a manner similar to a type 2 union. This theme is taken up in the final chapter.

These points are not meant to be exhaustive: for example, a wide range of factors affect the resources at the disposal of a union and the efficiency with which they are used, as indicated by the concept of sophistication. The level of resources within a union can be varied and the precise way in which they are used may be affected by both tradition and the political complexion of its leadership. However, it was beyond the scope of our research to investigate these matters in detail, and therefore we have confined our discussion to these general characteristics of trade unions nationally.

External integration. From the perspective of a national union, workplace organization can be seen as one of the basic building blocks of organization – using the notion of sophistication, it constitutes one means of permitting the expression of particular interests as well as being a means through which union policy can be applied. From the perspective of the workplace organization, the larger union may be seen as a source of legitimacy, support and possible constraint. Since the focus of our research was the workplace, we adopt the latter perspective here. Accordingly, we will refer to the links between the workplace and the larger union as 'external integration'.

The relationship between workplace and larger union organizations can vary in both degree and nature. Some workplace organizations have no ongoing relationship with the larger union, whereas others may be in continual contact. In addition, the nature of the relationship may vary. One form of external integration involves persons from the workplace organization being active members of various bodies within the larger union. From the perspective of the workplace organization, such links may not only be a means of influencing the policies of the larger union, but also constitute channels through which it receives a wide range of information, which can be used in the formulation of local policy. However, the larger union may also have a more direct role within the workplace. It may assume important responsibilities for bargaining on behalf of the workplace: these may take the form of multi-employer bargaining or officials playing a direct role in workplace negotiations. The role of the larger union may be of a less direct nature: in some cases, agreements struck locally may have to be ratified by the larger union; the larger union may be a source of advice and information, either of a general kind or tailored specifically to the needs and problems of the workplace.

The degree of external integration is affected by a wide variety of factors: these may include factors relating to the personalities and biographies of key figures within the workplace and national organizations, and particular events and problems within the workplace. However, certain structural features are also likely to be of relevance. Workplace organizations that have large numbers of members, both in absolute terms and relative to the larger union's total membership, are more likely to be integrated. Large concentrations of members are likely to be of greater importance to the larger union and, in addition, they provide economies of scale for it. That is, generally speaking a union official needs no more time to negotiate on behalf of 10,000 members than he or she needs to deal with the problems of only ten members.

Second, the nature of the larger union is likely to affect the degree of external integration. We have argued in the previous section that a union with a more homogeneous membership can develop greater expertise than a more heterogeneous union for any given level of resources; for example, the same basic facts are relevant to all work-place organizations in a single-industry union. Such economies of scale, we would suggest, are likely to be more important for single-industry than for single-occupation unions. It follows that homogeneous, and particularly single-industry, unions are likely to be of greater help and importance to workplace organizations than are more heterogeneous organizations. In addition, there is likely to be a stronger sense of identity between the workplace and the larger organization in such unions. Accordingly, we would expect external integration to be stronger in more homogeneous, and particularly single-industry, unions.

Other factors may also serve to strengthen the ties between the workplace and the larger organization in single-industry unions. First, particularly where they cover a wide range of occupations, single-industry unions are likely to have a strongly concentrated membership; and, we have suggested, this encourages closer ties. In addition, there appears to be a fairly strong tendency for single-employer/industry unions to bargain more centrally: for example, at the level of the employer in the civil service, or at the level of the industry in other cases. Furthermore, where this is the case, there is less likely to be a disjunction between the structures of union government and admin-istration, on the one hand, and of collective bargaining, on the other. These factors are likely to strengthen further the degree of external integration.

Third, the sophistication of the workplace organization itself affects the degree of external integration. In part related to the size effect discussed earlier, sophisticated intra-union workplace organizations are likely to be more externally integrated. Such well-organized bodies are likely to have a strong identification with the larger union and be more aware of its relevance to workplace problems. It may also be the case that intra-union sophistication is a reflection of external integration. However, inter-union sophistication, once we allow for size effects, may serve to reduce external integration. This is par-ticularly so where intra-union organization at the workplace is weak. In such cases, strong ties with other unions within the workplace may act as a substitute for external integration. Inter-union organization may become an important focus of identity rather than the larger union, and it may also provide the resources and supports which in other situations the larger union might supply.

Bargaining Structures and Employer Strategy

Sophistication and union strategy may also be shaped by the employer. As the debate on the reform of workplace industrial relations has shown clearly, the employer can affect the degree of union integration and sophistication by his or her readiness to recognize stewards, by providing facilities for union activities and by being prepared to negotiate at the workplace. But the employer can affect union strategy in a variety of other ways. Most obviously, a powerful employer who refuses to negotiate is likely to limit severely the extent to which a union is able to achieve any widespread influence. On the other hand, a more open management is likely to encourage a union to expand its range of interests.

A long-standing thesis, which has recently been put forward explicitly by Clegg (1976), is that union structure is shaped by the pattern of collective bargaining and that this, in turn, is primarily determined by the employer. This argument confronts a number of problems, among which is the fact that unions may influence the strategies adopted by the employer and the levels at which bargaining occurs. Nevertheless, the pattern of bargaining is likely to be related to union structure and to the strategies pursued by the union: these relationships can be identified without having to accept any single direction of causality. We have already noted that single-industry and single-employer unions are likely to negotiate at a more centralized level, for example. But there are two other important features of bargaining level which can be noted.

Particular types of issue – that is, controlling for employer strategy and union sophistication – can in principle be more easily negotiated at one level than at another. Most obviously, it is extremely difficult to bargain over corporate strategy at shop-floor level. This is so for at least two reasons. First, at this level the sectional interests of particular groups of workers are likely to be dominant, thereby making it more difficult to develop and pursue a broader union policy. Second, the managers with whom a union negotiates at shop-floor level lack the knowledge and authority to shape the general direction of corporate activity. This suggests that more centralized bargaining with an employer – other things being equal – facilitates a broader strategy on the part of the union: the structure of bargaining reduces the strains towards sectionalism, while, at the same time, the union will be negotiating with those who have a greater influence on management policy.

Conversely, it might be suggested that the detailed regulation of work can best be achieved at shop-floor level: but this does not always appear to be the case. Union influence might be greater and more general, if shop-floor bargaining takes place within a framework shaped at a higher level of bargaining. Thereby the weaker have some degree of protection and the patterns of bargaining have greater legitimacy in management's eyes. However, centralized bargaining over work organization issues cannot deal with the detailed formulation and implementation of agreements in a wide diversity of situations. It is for this reason that we would suggest that, on many issues, bargaining at a variety of levels – as long as it is co-ordinated in some way – is likely to give unions greater influence.

If such multi-level bargaining – as we will term it – is important, then we need also to ask what factors affect the number of levels at which a union negotiates. Generally it is easier for unions to negotiate informally below the formal level of bargaining than it is for them to bargain informally at a higher level. In other words, it is easier for a steward to 'bend the ear' of a supervisor than it is for him or her to do the same with the managing director. It follows that the more centralized bargaining is, the greater are the opportunities for multi-level bargaining. In other words, centralized bargaining gives unions two potentially important advantages: first, a greater opportunity to negotiate over a wide range of issues and over matters which might, in other situations, be seen as within the exclusive concern of management. Second, it increases the opportunity for multi-level bargaining, and thereby greater and more secure influence.

It should be stressed, however, that the opportunities presented by more centralized bargaining structures may not be taken up by unions. Employers may seek centralized bargaining in order to reduce the role of the union within the workplace. Similarly, it is possible that unions lack the degree of external integration and workplace sophistication to exploit the possibility of multi-level bargaining. Both of these factors have been important in the past for some unions that bargain centrally. In such cases, sophistication of union organization at national level may be seen as constraining the development of workplace sophistication. However, there has been a trend over the last two decades for a growing sophistication of workplace organization, even where bargaining is centralized. This has occurred in part because of the point noted above: that there are limitations on the extent to which detailed negotiations on matters such as work organization can be conducted meaningfully at the centre. Hence local, supplementary bargaining has developed and, along with this, a growing sophistication of workplace organization.

Finally, one other aspect of employer behaviour is likely to be important: this is the degree of bureaucracy in the administration of labour and industrial relations. Where systems are highly bureaucratic, we would suggest, there are greater opportunities for union influence. This is so for a number of reasons: first, the very bureaucracy can be used as a sanction upon management; second, bureaucratic rules are of a more public nature and are meant to be 'rational' both in themselves and in their application. Hence a union is able to negotiate more easily over inconsistencies in the rules themselves or in their application in more bureaucratic situations. Thereby the pattern of agreements can be made more complex by the development of a 'case law' of interpretations (roughly, in other words, custom and practice). This argument flies in the face of a good deal of traditional industrial relations wisdom, which has stressed the advantages of informal bargaining for shop stewards. We would accept that where shop-steward organization is extremely strong, this may well be true. But, on the other hand, most shop-steward organizations are not, and never have been, extremely strong. Second, this conventional view seriously underestimates the advantages that management gained from informality. Third, our argument suggests that bureaucratic rules and agreements can be a fertile ground for informal bargaining. Fourth, traditional arguments have often been based upon 'workerist' and romantic accounts of atypical situations.

In this section, then, we have looked at union structure and strategy. We have argued that the nature of union strategy is shaped by its scope and sophistication. At workplace level, we have suggested the importance not only of the nature of the membership, but also of a structure of steward constituencies that permits the representation of different interests, structures that permit the representation and reconciliation of those interests centrally, and resources in the form of senior and full-time stewards, as well as 100 per cent union membership. However, we have also pointed to the need to differentiate between intra- and inter-union organization. Nationally we have argued that the nature of union strategy is shaped by the mix of industries and occupations it represents. Third, we have argued that the importance of the larger union for the workplace organization depends upon the scope of the larger union, the nature of workplace organization and various size effects. However, we have also noted the importance of employer strategy and bargaining structures for the role and influence of trade unions in the workplace. These factors are likely to shape both the general pattern of union influence and also its approach to new technology – the theme to which we now turn.

The Question of New Technology

The reasons for relating the question of trade unions in the recession and new technology can be argued from two different starting points:

from that of an interest in the impact of the recession or from that of an interest in new technology.

From the first perspective, the attraction of looking at new technology lies in its being a critical case. Particularly where survey data are used, there is a risk that a general picture of the state of workplace trade unionism and labour relations is excessively crude and, to that extent, misleading. This is particularly true given problems of developing adequate measures of union strength and influence. Not only are these difficult to assess at the best of times, but, in addition, a union may maintain a substantial role, even where its influence has declined. It is therefore useful, in addition to building up a general picture, to focus upon some specific area or issue and analyse it in somewhat greater depth. There still exist, of course, the limitations of the survey method; hence we also undertook a number of case studies. But we can still, using survey methods, develop a more detailed picture in relation to one issue than we are able to obtain generally.

The case for choosing new technology as a 'test case' can be made on a number of grounds. One attraction is that it is in some senses 'new': that is, it is an issue where there may be more scope for change than is the case for many other issues. It is possible, for example, that the pattern of joint regulation remains fairly stable elsewhere, whereas in new technology areas the employer is able to impose new terms and conditions. That is, new technology provides a means by which new sets of principles may be introduced into the workplace. Hence, as the field of application of new technology expands, so would the scope of these new patterns. Accordingly, areas where new technology is applied may be more sensitive to the recession than other areas.

Second, it has often been argued that new technology serves as a form of labour control: for Braverman (1974), for example, new technology constitutes a further and significant step in the degradation of work, whereas for Edwards (1979) new technology permits not only the more widespread application of technical control over the direction of work, but also the evaluation of worker performance through technical means. Relatedly, new technology has been seen by some writers as in itself being an important factor in the current level of unemployment. Through the application of microelectronics, management are able to remove labour from the production process, since its functions are increasingly assumed by the technology. Accordingly, the employer has need of fewer workers and so unemployment increases. In other words, not only is new technology new and hence may highlight changes in labour relations, but, in addition, it may constitute an important means by which employers change the pattern of labour relations.

Looked at from the perspective of an interest in new technology, the reasons for stressing the importance of union organization and the recession follow from the recent debates on the significance of new technology. Much of the early literature on the subject adopted a crude form of technological or economic determinism (Barron and Curnow, 1979; Evans, 1979): it was argued, for example, that new technology would increase unemployment and degrade jobs (e.g. CIS, 1979; Jenkins and Sherman, 1979). It has increasingly been recognized, however, that such approaches commit the same errors as earlier debates on automation (Blauner, 1964), the post-industrial society (Bell, 1974; see also Mallet, 1975; Touraine, 1974), and the convergence of industrial societies (Kerr et al., 1960; for critiques of these various approaches, see, e.g., CPRS, 1975; Dubois and Monjardet, 1978; Gallie, 1978; Kumar, 1978; Mann, 1973; Rose, 1979). Hence emphasis has been increasingly placed not only upon the social determinants of the development of new technology (e.g. Latour and Woolgar, 1979; Mulkay, 1979), but also upon the importance of social factors in shaping its precise impact when new technology is introduced into any particular situation (for a useful general review of the impact of new technology, see Council for Science and Society, 1981; for more specific studies on this theme see, e.g., Child et al., 1984; Sorge et al., 1983; Wilkinson, 1983; Willman and Winch, 1985). It follows that, in order to understand, say, the impact of new technology upon employment, we have to take into account not only the nature of the technology as such, but also the goals, interests and power of the various groups involved. Without a clear understanding of these factors, it is impossible to predict, or even comprehend, the effects of new technology.

Given this approach, clearly the issues that have been discussed above are likely to be of considerable importance in understanding how new technology affects labour relations and work organization. The recession, and the variations in its impact upon particular employers and unions, are likely to shape the resources which each can bring to bear upon the way in which new technology is introduced and hence the way in which it affects trade unions and their members. Similarly, we have argued that the nature of the workgroups covered by the union and the forms of union organization – in terms of scope and sophistication – are likely to affect both union power and the sorts of strategies which it pursues. Hence, for example, we would expect, given any type of membership, that more sophisticated workplace organizations would negotiate more actively and over a wider range of issues concerning new technology than a less sophisticated organization. Other things being equal, the same would be true of a workplace organization that was more strongly integrated with the larger union.

Our preceding discussion of trade union organization also indicates that variations in scope and sophistication would affect the types of issues of concern to a union. Where an organization is sophisticated and covers a large proportion of workers, then our previous arguments indicate that the union would seek to intrude into areas which in other cases would be accepted as the sole preserve of management. That is, such bodies would be more likely to try to influence not only the more immediate aspects of the wage–effort bargain, but also the broader features of management strategy, which serve to shape and constrain the nature of that bargain. Similarly, we would expect that, for example, a single-occupation union, particularly of craft workers, would place greater emphasis upon the preservation of skill and job territory, so that it would demonstrate a greater concern over such matters as training and work organization.

The pattern of negotiation over new technology and the impact of new technology are also shaped by employer strategy. Ideally, in order to understand this, we would need to know the rationale underlying management's decision on technical innovation: for example, the importance of labour considerations relative to marketing and purely technical factors. Although we are able to assess this in our case studies, we felt that a survey of shop stewards was not a very reliable means by which to investigate this issue. However, the way in which new technology impinges upon the work situation and the role of the unions is also shaped by the associated labour relations strategy which management develops. This will be indicated by management's readiness to negotiate with, and consult, the union. It may also be seen in the new techniques of labour relations and control which management develops: for example, we discussed earlier a variety of techniques by which management might seek to achieve greater flexibility in its use of labour. Hence, one interesting question is the extent to which the use of these methods is associated with technical innovation. Similarly, we can see the extent to which technical change is associated with changes in job requirements, effort levels and other aspects of the work situation. And, in doing so, we can assess the extent to which these changes came about through management being prepared to contest the demands of the union.

Although new technology may provide an opportunity to change the pattern of labour relations, such changes may be constrained by the existing pattern of management–union relations. This follows our previous argument that new companies are more able to exploit the current state of the labour market than are managements within existing plants. Hence we see two cross-cutting forces at work in relation to new technology. The first is the changes in relative bargaining power which may ensue from new technology itself and the state of the labour and product markets, along with associated changes in employer (and union) strategy. The second is the existing pattern of labour relations and work organization. Hence, although certain changes may be possible in new technology areas alone, other changes would have to be of a more general nature or might spread out into other areas. This may be extremely difficult if co-operation is to be maintained, with the consequence that management chooses to work within the confines of much of the existing structure (this also suggests that the scope for change will vary with the precise nature of technical change – whether it is relatively separate from continuing, older methods, for example).

The logic of our approach to the impact of new technology upon workplace trade unionism, then, can be broadly outlined in the following way. We need, first, to understand the general pattern of union organization and of labour relations; second, we have to see how far these have been changed as a result of changes in the product and labour market, and related shifts in management strategy. One such change may be the introduction of new technology. We then need to look at the scale and nature of union involvement in the implementation of new technology: for example, the issues over which it negotiated; the extent to which, and the areas over which, it contested management plans, and with what result. We can then go on to look at how technical innovation and the related patterns of bargaining affected the work situation of union members and the pattern of union organization more generally. The broad thrust of our argument is as follows. Where trade union organization is sophisticated, it will enjoy a considerable range of influence prior to the introduction of new technology. Such union strength will be reflected in the process of introducing new technology, with the result that more sophisticated organizations achieve more for their members than do the less sophisticated. As a result, union sophistication will be confirmed and, if anything, strengthened. But we have also to look at the extent to which changes in market conditions and management strategy, as well as possibly the inherent nature of the new technology, may change this general pattern. For example, to what extent does substantial job loss serve to reduce the range of bargaining over new technology and thereby weaken union organization? Or to what extent are such effects only found where management seeks to adopt a 'tougher' approach to the unions more generally, or to bypass them? In these ways, then, we look at the impact both of the recession and of new technology – for the two are intimately intertwined.

The Research

The research on which this book is based consisted primarily of a survey of over 1,000 stewards from a wide range of industries and trade unions. However, in our research we also undertook four detailed case studies; these are reported more fully elsewhere. Since we also make reference to our case-study findings at a number of points in the following chapters, it is necessary here to give some details not only of the survey, but also of the case studies. Fuller information on the methods employed is given in the appendix.

The Case Studies

Four case studies were undertaken: one in finance, one in small-batch engineering, one in brewing and one in chemicals. The selection of industries was due to our involvement in a larger, cross-national study of trade unions and the disclosure of information in relation to new technology. The larger project required that case studies be undertaken in these four industries (for details of the international project, see Levie and Moore, 1984). Here we will simply give a very brief account of certain key characteristics of the case studies.

The finance case study focused on the move from batch to on-line processing of personal lines (primarily car and household) insurance in a large multinational insurance company over the period from the mid-1970s to 1983. This meant that underwriters did much of their work with a VDU screen linked to a central computer, instead of filling out forms which were then sent to a central unit for in-putting. This reduced the amount of paperwork they had to undertake and was also associated with a streamlining of the range of policies offered by the company and some reduction in underwriting discretion. All of these changes reflected moves by the company to become more competitive in an area that was assuming increasing market importance. The changes led to some job loss, but also significant increases in job grading for many staff. The company employed nearly 4,000 staff, the majority of whom worked in a network of area offices. The change to on-line processing affected less than 10 per cent of the staff. About four-fifths of the staff were members of BIFU, the only union in the company. The members in the company formed a separate autonomous division within the union. Bargaining and consultation were highly centralized and the structure of the union within the company reflected this fact, although there was also a network of local representatives.

The second case study concerned the introduction of a number of computer numerical control (CNC) machines into a small-batch engineering works over the period 1979–84. By the end of our research, less than 5 per cent of the workers were working on new machines; although the changes in job requirements varied according to the precise nature of the machines, all programming was finally undertaken by the operators. They had therefore to become familiar with programming techniques as well as being able to conceptualize their traditional skills. Manipulative skills continued to be important in the setting up of the machines. The site was part of the spares parts division of a large, multinational company that manufactured highly sophisticated machines for the food and drink sector. All 350 manual workers were members of the AUEW, the only union representing manual workers at the site. Union organization was sophisticated. Annual negotiations over pay and related matters took place mainly at divisional level, but in addition there was a great deal of negotiation both at establishment and shop-floor levels.

The third case study investigated the construction of a new lager plant on the major site of a large multinational company, which had a wide range of interests other than brewing. Compared with the old brewery, the new lager plant was much more highly automated, much of this removing the more routine and unpleasant tasks. Furthermore, on the new plant – in contrast to the old – there was only one grade of worker, and the men worked as a team, rotating jobs amongst themselves. The period covered by the study was from the mid-1970s to the early 1980s. Some 1,500 workers were employed on the site in all, and of these only about 1 per cent worked on the lager plant. Manual union membership was 100 per cent. The TGWU represented all production and related workers, and four craft unions covered the relevant maintenance groups. Both inter- and intra-union organization were sophisticated, with annual negotiations over pay occurring at company level.

The final case study concerned a broader and earlier process of change in a chemical company, and focused in particular on the introduction of automatic process-sequence controls at the major site. The company was a large multinational employing over 50,000 staff in this country – the bulk of these, however, were not in the production division. Some 3,500 were employed on the site studied; of these, only 10 per cent worked on the chemicals plant, these being more or less equally divided between multi-purpose and dedicated plant. The major contrasts in work content were between dedicated and multi-purpose plant: in the latter, a larger proportion of the workers had a degree of autonomy and greater knowledge requirements, since they had to set up the plant in preparation for the manufacture of different products. There was, however, a general move to exert tighter controls over workers in an attempt to improve quality and output standards. In the automated plant, the range of skills became more polarized: for many workers, tasks became more routine and more closely supervised. However, the skill, knowledge and responsibilities of those working in the control room increased considerably. The automated plant employed less than one in five of the chemical workers. A variety of unions were recognized, but all manual production workers were members of USDAW. Union organization was only moderately sophisticated, and bargaining over pay and related matters was largely confined to divisional level.

The Survey

The aim of the survey was both to extend the coverage of the research and to test out a number of ideas and hypotheses which had informed our approach to the case studies and which had developed during the course of the work. In particular, we were concerned to extend the range of unions, industries and sectors beyond those covered by the case studies: we wished to include a greater variety of unions in order to test out the ideas outlined earlier in this chapter; we wished to include a wider variety of basic technologies and to consider variations between the private and public sectors. The analysis in subsequent chapters is based upon thirteen different samples: BIFU and ASTMS in finance; CPSA in mainstream civil service departments; the SCPS in similar departments; CPSA in Telecom; the POEU in Telecom; the NGA in the printing industry; TGWU in chemicals and the EETPU in the same industry; TGWU and EETPU samples in food and drink; AUEW and EETPU samples in small-batch engineering; and an EETPU sample from electrical engineering and electronics.

Given limited resources, the method adopted was to send postal questionnaires to samples selected from particular industries and unions. The samples were drawn from the individual unions, the exact methods by which this was done depending upon the nature of their records. In all, nearly 2,500 questionnaires were sent out along with letters from the relevant union; 1,035 had been completed and returned to us by the time we began to put the data on the computer. Although the response rate varied between the samples, overall it exceeded 40 per cent. When allowance is made for the fact that union records are inevitably out of date, due to the turnover of stewards and the demise of establishments, we estimate that the 'real' response rate is probably over 50 per cent. The survey was undertaken between July and October 1984.

It should be stressed that the survey was of an exploratory nature. The constraints of survey methods, particularly those employing self-administered questionnaires, are well known. However, it seemed to us that a survey of the kind we have undertaken could be of considerable use as a means of encouraging a more analytical approach to the study of technical change and as a counterbalance to the detail of the dominant, current approach of the case study. Certainly we have found the detailed analysis of the survey has not only been informed by our earlier ideas, but it has also been of considerable help in developing perspectives which inform our analysis of the case studies. In other words, both case studies and surveys have their weaknesses; the combination of the two techniques, therefore, may provide more reliable and interesting insights.

The Study Outlined

The subsequent chapters can be divided into two parts. The first looks at the pattern of union organization and influence, and the nature of management strategy in general terms. In doing so, it pays particular attention to the question of the extent to which changes in the economic and political context have affected union organization and labour relations. The second part focuses upon technical change. We first discuss the general characteristics of technical change, and then consider the role that the unions played in implementing those changes. Two subsequent chapters assess the changes in work experience associated with new technology and the way in which union organization was affected by technical change and associated developments. A final chapter seeks to draw the findings together and to relate them to the general discussion in this chapter. In addition, we seek to assess the more general utility of our approach to trade union organization by looking at questions of unemployment and technical change from a cross-national perspective.

Part I Union Organization and Patterns of Labour Regulation

2 Union Organization and its Context

In this chapter, we outline the nature of the establishments covered by our survey and consider in some detail the structure of trade union organization within the workplace. This provides a background to the discussion of technical change in part II, in addition to permitting us to assess a variety of debates concerning the way in which shop-steward organizations have been affected by the recession and the changed political atmosphere of the last five years or so.

The conventional wisdom argues that union power depends upon the state of the labour market. Hence, for example, the growth of shop-steward organization and of shop-floor power in the quarter century after World War II is often attributed primarily to full employment. When labour is scarce, then the balance of power shifts in favour of workers, since employers cannot effectively use the threat of unemployment to control the labour force. It follows from this argument, many would claim, that when unemployment increases, then the power of the union falls. So in the 1920s, for example, as unemployment increased, union density collapsed in many sectors and shop-steward organization was decimated. Moreover, this thesis appears all the more credible at the present, since government policy – directly and indirectly – is aimed at using the pressures of the market place in order to shift the balance of power in favour of employers.

However, as noted in chapter 1, there are a number of reasons for suggesting that, although market forces do play a role in shaping the power of trade unions, the argument just outlined is somewhat exaggerated. That is, the effects of high unemployment upon union organization are often less great than this thesis suggests. One reason for seeking to moderate the market argument is that it focuses upon the labour market and places insufficient emphasis upon the product market. Unemployment has increased in large part because of falls in output; the latter means that employers are in a weaker position and confront stronger competitive pressures. They may, therefore, often be loath to try to use the state of the labour market against the union for fear of inciting a strike, which would further weaken their position in the product market. In other words, employers have to decide to use the state of the labour market: otherwise, the extent to which high levels of unemployment affect labour relations is limited and largely due to the way in which workers' attitudes are affected. But rational employers will not seek a head-on confrontation with the unions, unless they can be very confident of winning or unless they have nothing to lose: that is, unless they find themselves in a desperate situation in the product market or have a generous or anti-union 'lender of the last resort' – notably, the government.

Two other factors are also likely to constrain the effects of the labour market upon labour relations and the role of the union. First, the market argument assumes that workers are highly substitutable so that the labour force can be changed with ease and considerable rapidity. In many companies this is not the case: it is simply not possible to man a large plant anew every day. Hence, the sanction of high unemployment may have less of an impact than is often assumed. Second, over the last two decades many employers have built up internal labour markets and a complex structure of worker rights, procedures and rules which approximate an internal state. In other words, they have sought to isolate their workers from the larger labour market. Structures of this kind cannot easily be transformed overnight. It follows, therefore, that the impact of the general state of the labour market upon labour relations is likely to be limited.

This is not to argue that high unemployment has no effect. Particularly where a company's position in the product market is weak, workers and their unions may be prepared to co-operate more fully with employers than they have in the past, in an attempt to maintain employment. This greater co-operation may also be directly encouraged by the employer through various techniques of consultation and employee involvement. In this case, union structures are likely to remain intact and the formal involvement of the union may actually increase. But the extent to which the union obstructs management may fall – because the main means of protecting workers is seen to be the preservation of as many jobs as possible.

Ironically, therefore, it may well be that the power of the unions is weakened more dramatically where product market forces do not operate so strongly. That is, political rather than market forces are the greatest threat to the position of the unions. In much of the public sector it is meaningless to talk of a product market; the level of demand for labour derives from political decisions. Even in the nationalized industries, the significance of market forces is limited by the fact that the government, if it so chooses, can subsidize the corporation. Hence it is no coincidence that the greatest challenges to union power and influence have taken place in the civil service, nationalized industries and other state-owned bodies that are dependent upon government financial support. In the public sector, the state is in a position to insist that its philosophy of labour is put into practice.

In the first section of this chapter, we briefly outline the characteristics of the establishments covered in the survey. First, we consider the nature of the labour force: in particular, we discuss the number of employees, skill levels and the importance of women and part-time workers. All of these factors have, in the past, been found to affect the strength of union organization. In larger establishments, union density is typically higher, and the number of stewards also tends to be greater: as a result, there more frequently exists a hierarchy of shop stewards and means by which the policies and actions of different stewards are co-ordinated: for example, joint shop-steward committees. Similarly, union organization tends to be more developed among skilled workers, whereas it has been found in the past that large proportions of women and part-time workers are generally associated with less sophisticated and weaker unions in the workplace (see, e.g., Daniel and Millward, 1983).

Second, we outline trends in output and employment in the establishments covered by the survey: these will constitute our two measures of the impact of market forces upon union organization and activity in subsequent chapters. It should, however, be noted that both measures reflect the way in which management reacts to market forces, particularly in multi-plant organizations.

Third, we look at management and company organization. Our pilot interviews indicated that shop stewards frequently had a limited knowledge of corporate structure and performance. Indeed, rarely could shop stewards even provide details of productivity trends or the profitability of their establishments. The amount of data we were able to collect was therefore fairly limited. The questions asked in the survey can be grouped under a number of headings. First, we asked respondents whether their establishment was the only one belonging to the company. Multi-plant organizations are likely to have more formalized patterns of management and labour relations; in addition, it has been found that other features of labour relations are often related to the characteristics of the company rather than the establishment. Second, we enquired about the existence of personnel managers: some studies have suggested that the existence of such specialists indicates that companies are committed to 'good' industrial relations. However, others have argued that the existence of personnel managers does not mean that the company places greater emphasis upon labour relations (Marsh, 1982) and, indeed, that such specialists can more meaningfully be seen as just one aspect of a broader pattern of specialist management and bureaucracy (e.g. Batstone, 1984a). Third, the survey covered matters relating to the distribution of power and authority within management. In the case of multi-plant companies, we asked about the degree of autonomy which plant management enjoyed; we also investigated how much freedom supervision had. In addition, we looked at how patterns of discretion had changed over the last five years. Where local management has more freedom, then – at least in the past – shop stewards at the workplace have typically had a greater influence. Where top management gives little discretion to plant-level management or to supervisors, then it is clearly more difficult for shop stewards to have much influence at workplace level. However, this picture may be changing. In parts of the public sector, there have been moves to decentralize authority within management, the aim being to permit greater flexibility in responding to local contingencies and in increasing efficiency. In this instance, therefore, greater autonomy for local management might be associated with a reduced role for trade unions. Some would also argue that high levels of unemployment, by weakening workers, permits management to decentralize and thereby impose greater control over the labour force.

In the second section of this chapter, we consider various aspects of management's approach towards the unions and the labour force. In the next chapter, we consider other aspects of management's approach towards its labour force. But it is useful to look at its policy towards trade unionism at this point, since we can then go on to see how far variations in management's approach affect the formal characteristics of shop-steward organization. Given this background, the subsequent sections describe the pattern of union organization found in the survey and attempt to explain variations in terms of a number of hypotheses relating to the 'size effect', the impact of job loss and the significance of management strategy. In doing so, we also attempt to assess how far union organization has changed over the last five years.

Context

The Labour Force

Table 2.1 shows the number of employees in the establishments covered by the survey. It can be seen that, in the main, our study

Table 2.1 Total establishment employment

	Percentage of establishments employing:					
	50 or less	51–100	101–250	251–500	501–1,000	1,001+
(a) Non-manual/public-sector group						
Finance	5	17	25	18	7	28
CPSA civil service	20	13	39	14	8	6
SCPS civil service	22	18	32	9	7	12
CPSA Telecom	7	—	17	17	24	35
POEU Telecom	—	1	28	29	22	20
(b) Production group						
Print	24	10	31	15	12	8
Chemicals	7	6	28	24	16	19
Food and drink	6	18	22	22	14	18
Engineering	5	11	31	27	14	12
(c) Maintenance group						
Chemicals	2	8	18	30	21	21
Food and drink	—	5	15	23	21	36
Engineering	10	2	20	18	25	25
Electrical engineering	4	—	18	27	16	35

covers large workplaces. With the exception of printing and the civil service, at least a third of the respondents in each sample say that over 500 people are employed in their establishment. Large plants are more common in the electrician samples than in their corresponding production samples, possibly reflecting the fact that in smaller plants there are often no electrician stewards. Large units are also very common in telecommunications and electrical engineering. A third or more of respondents are employed in plants with less than 100 workers in the printing sample and the two civil service samples. Overall, our clerical respondents are often employed in establishments that are as large as those of manual respondents.

The second characteristic of the labour force distinguished earlier was skill level. The concept of skill is a complex one and comparisons across different types of occupation are difficult. In the case of manual workers in the private sector, we simply asked how many manual workers were skilled. We were then able to calculate the proportion of the manual labour force that was skilled. Table 2.2 shows that the highest skill levels were found in printing and the various engineering samples: in these, over half the respondents said that more than half

Table 2.2 Occupational/skill distributions

	Percentage of establishments with X per cent in different occupations/skills:				
	10 or less	11–25	26–50	51–75	76+
(a) Non-manual/public-sector group					
Finance					
Managerial	37	34	21	5	3
Clerical	—	—	3	40	57
CPSA civil service					
EO/HCO	13	46	39	2	—
DP/SDP	92	5	3	1	—
CO/CA	2	8	16	57	17
Typists	87	9	—	2	2
SCPS civil service					
EO/HCO	18	41	34	2	4
DP/SDP	91	7	1	—	1
CO/CA	12	21	28	29	10
Typists	91	8	1	—	—
CPSA Telecom					
EO/HCO	78	22	—	—	—
DP/SDP	85	—	4	7	4
CO/CA	11	37	15	19	18
Typists	100	—	—	—	—
POEU Telecom					
T0	7	35	50	8	—
T1	18	77	5	—	—
T2A	1	5	45	48	1
Other manual	79	18	2	—	—

of the manual labour force was skilled. In the POEU questionnaire, we asked how many workers were in particular grades, which we listed by name. The T0 is an elite craftsman, and the T1 is also a highly skilled grade. If we take the proportion of workers employed in these two grades as equivalent to the classification 'skilled' in the other manual samples, then we can say that the POEU sample is also characterized by high skill levels.

In the non-manual samples, there are further problems in assessing skill levels. In terms of grading in the civil service, executive officers may be seen as more skilled than clerical officers, who, in turn, tend to be more skilled than typists. Data-processing grades are also skilled.

Table 2.2 (*continued*)

		Percentage of skilled workers				
		10 or less	*11–25*	*26–50*	*51–75*	*76+*
(b)	Production group					
	Print	—	6	21	35	38
	Chemicals	13	33	27	5	22
	Food and drink	21	41	25	9	5
	Engineering	5	22	24	25	24
(c)	Maintenance group					
	Chemicals	5	55	31	7	2
	Food and drink	20	58	18	3	1
	Engineering	2	22	23	32	22
	Electrical engineering	4	15	25	21	35

Given this crude guide, it can be seen that the SCPS civil service sample includes rather more highly skilled groups than the CPSA civil service sample. The Telecom clerical sample covers a wider variety of occupational groups and grades, so that no single grade is dominant. Finally, in the finance questionnaire we simply distinguished between managerial and clerical grades; the latter are dominant in virtually all cases. Indeed, to the extent that comparisons can be made with the available data, it seems possible that routine grades may be more common in the finance than in the public-sector samples. If we seek to make comparisons across the manual and non-manual samples, then it would appear that skill levels are higher in some of our craft-dominated manual samples than in some of our non-manual samples.

Two further characteristics of the labour force which, it was noted earlier, have often proved relevant to an understanding of union organization are the proportion of women in the labour force and the importance of part-time employees. Table 2.3 shows that women form a majority in the CPSA civil service sample, and are a significant proportion of the labour force in our other white-collar samples. Among the manual groups, they figure most importantly in food and drink, and to a lesser degree in electrical engineering. Telecom engineering and chemicals, on the other hand, are very much male preserves.

Table 2.4 provides data concerning the importance of part-time workers in our different samples. They are most common in food and

Table 2.3 Percentage of establishments with X per cent of female workers[a]

	10 or less	11–25	26–50	51–75	76+
(a) Non-manual/public-sector group					
Finance	3	—	46	43	8
CPSA civil service	2	1	16	63	19
SCPS civil service	9	9	28	48	7
CPSA Telecom	—	24	32	36	8
POEU Telecom	95	1	1	2	—
(b) Production group					
Print	42	30	15	9	4
Chemicals	75	10	10	3	2
Food and drink	26	24	13	16	21
Engineering	62	14	7	8	9
(c) Maintenance group					
Chemicals	72	16	3	2	7
Food and drink	32	16	14	14	24
Engineering	71	12	10	2	5
Electrical engineering	37	2	31	17	13

[a] Percentage of female manual workers for manual samples; percentage of female non-manual workers for non-manual samples.

drink. Otherwise, the differences between our manual and non-manual samples tend to be fairly small in this respect. In short, part-time workers are of little importance in most of our samples: in no case do a majority of respondents in a sample say that they account for more than 10 per cent of the labour force.

Trends in Output and Employment

Central to many recent arguments is the way in which union organ-ization and the general pattern of labour relations are affected by changes in activity and employment levels over recent years. Table 2.5 shows that output has generally increased over the last five years. This is the case in all the samples except the two engineering samples, where there have been net falls in output. The largest increases in output or activity are to be found in the non-manual and public-sector group.

In the private sector, changes in output are strongly related to changes in employment over the last five years. In the non-manual

Table 2.4 Percentage of establishments with X per cent of part-time workers

	10 or less	11–25	26–50	51–75	76+
(a) Non-manual/public-sector group					
Finance	83	11	3	3	—
CPSA civil service	92	7	1	—	—
SCPS civil service	95	5	—	—	—
CPSA Telecom	100	—	—	—	—
POEU Telecom	99	1	—	—	—
(b) Production Group					
Print	90	7	2	—	1
Chemicals	93	6	1	—	—
Food and drink	66	14	11	3	6
Engineering	94	3	1	—	2
(c) Maintenance group					
Chemicals	85	7	5	—	3
Food and drink	60	17	6	4	13
Engineering	96	—	2	—	2
Electrical engineering	86	4	4	—	6

Table 2.5 Change in output/activity over last five years

	Percentage of establishments where output has:				
	Risen a lot	Risen a little	No change	Fallen a little	Fallen a lot
(a) Non-manual/public-sector group					
Finance	53	32	—	13	2
CPSA civil service	63	16	8	8	6
SCPS civil service	59	16	10	8	7
CPSA Telecom	69	22	3	3	3
POEU Telecom	32	37	17	12	2
(b) Production Group					
Print	39	25	8	18	10
Chemicals	39	27	6	13	16
Food and drink	49	23	2	17	9
Engineering	19	23	9	12	37
(c) Maintenance group					
Chemicals	36	24	5	18	18
Food and drink	45	25	8	6	16
Engineering	25	8	7	18	42
Electrical engineering	34	20	8	12	26

and public-sector group, employment levels have fallen less dramatically than in the private manual samples (table 2.6); indeed, in many cases employment has actually increased over the last five years. In the manual manufacturing samples, job loss has often been substantial: over three-fifths of the establishments in engineering, for example, have cut employment by over a quarter in the last five years, and a fifth have more than halved their labour forces. Job loss is also substantial in chemicals and electrical engineering.

The major job losses in the private sector have been concentrated in establishments which, five years ago, employed large numbers of workers; this relationship is not found in the public sector. This also means that there is a tendency – although a relatively weak one – for job loss to be greater where union organization is more developed.

Organizational Structure and Ownership

We have seen in the preceding section that most of our respondents came from relatively large workplaces. In addition, the majority of them came from multi-plant companies. This is obviously so in the

Table 2.6 Changes in employment, 1979–84

	Percentage of establishments where 1984 employment is X per cent of 1979 level			
	<50%	51–75%	76–100%	101%+
(a) Non-manual/public-sector group				
Finance	—	6	48	46
CPSA civil service	3	11	55	31
SCPS civil service	4	8	61	27
CPSA Telecom	—	12	48	40
POEU Telecom	—	—	46	54
(b) Production group				
Print	7	18	57	19
Chemicals	16	30	34	19
Food and drink	9	13	49	30
Engineering	22	41	21	16
(c) Maintenance group				
Chemicals	15	34	34	17
Food and drink	14	33	35	18
Engineering	20	41	25	14
Electrical engineering	13	30	39	17

public sector, where ministries such as the Department of Employment have a large number of offices; it is also obviously so in the case of telecommunications. However, there are a small number of civil servants who say that theirs is the only establishment within their department. In the private sector, single-plant employers are most common in printing and engineering – a fifth to a quarter of the respondents in these samples say they work for such companies. Furthermore, the majority of respondents say that they work for British-owned companies: foreign ownership is most common in chemicals (one-third) and in food and drink (a quarter).

Personnel Management

Turning to questions of management structure, we asked respondents whether personnel specialists existed at establishment level and at some level above this. Table 2.7 shows the responses to these questions. Personnel specialists are most common at establishment level in the two Telecom samples and in the manual manufacturing samples with the exception of printing, which is characterized by small

Table 2.7 Existence of personnel specialists

	Percentage of establishments with personnel specialists at establishment level	Percentage of establishments with personnel specialists above establishment level
(a) Non-manual/public-sector group		
Finance	39	95
CPSA civil service	32	91
SCPS civil service	21	83
CPSA Telecom	72	91
POEU Telecom	78	97
(b) Production group		
Print	29	40
Chemicals	74	86
Food and drink	55	69
Engineering	53	59
(c) Maintenance group		
Chemicals	69	91
Food and drink	80	87
Engineering	64	69
Electrical engineering	72	84

plants. Establishment-level personnel managers are relatively rare in finance and the civil service. The detailed variations among the manual samples are primarily attributable to a size effect: that is, personnel specialists are more common where a large labour force is employed. In the non-manual samples (with the exception of Telecom), the infrequency of personnel specialists at office level is largely a reflection of the highly centralized pattern of collective bargaining.

A rather different picture appears when we consider the existence of personnel specialists above establishment level. These are virtually universal in the public and non-manual samples, and somewhat less common in manufacturing, even when we allow for the existence of single-establishment companies. In other words, in Telecom, personnel specialists are generally found at both the levels distinguished; within the finance and civil service samples, personnel managers are rarely found at establishment level, but are very common above this level. In manufacturing, the general picture approximates that in Telecom. More detailed analyses indicate that personnel specialists are more common where the labour force is larger, and where the establishment is part of a larger company (cf. Batstone, 1984a; Brown, 1981; Daniel and Millward, 1983).

The Distribution of Management Power

The extent and nature of union influence may also be affected by the distribution of power within management. As was noted earlier, the conventional wisdom is that stewards have more influence where supervisors have a good deal of autonomy. On the other hand, an established union may be able to achieve more solid and widespread gains from a more centralized management structure. Hence an important background to our discussion of union organization is the pattern of management discretion.

Table 2.8 shows that local management discretion tends to be highest in manufacturing, and lowest in the SCPS sample (the group most involved in policy formulation) and in finance. In the private sector, there is a tendency for local management discretion to be lower where the establishment has been doing less well over the last five years, as indicated by changes in employment or output. This suggests that when companies face severe problems, power is drawn to the centre in an attempt to achieve wide-scale economies, possibly through the exertion of tight controls and through plant closures or strategic workforce reductions. However, a stronger relationship is found between the pattern of local management discretion and the characteristics of the labour force: particularly in the manufacturing samples, local

Table 2.8 Level of discretion of (a) local managers and (b) supervisors

	Percentage of establishments where local management has:				Percentage of establishments where supervisors have:			
	Great deal	Fair amount	Not much	Virtually none	Great deal	Fair amount	Not much	Virtually none
(a) Non-manual/public-sector group								
Finance	9	37	45	9	34	42	24	—
CPSA civil service	24	46	21	9	27	55	16	2
SCPS civil service	9	39	42	10	28	51	19	2
CPSA Telecom	28	50	19	3	26	49	23	3
POEU Telecom	28	47	19	6	23	50	25	2
(b) Production group								
Print	25	40	28	7	25	38	27	10
Chemicals	43	29	23	5	20	36	31	12
Food and drink	42	26	30	2	30	52	16	2
Engineering	38	40	18	5	21	48	21	10
(c) Maintenance group								
Chemicals	36	34	23	6	28	42	24	6
Food and drink	33	43	18	6	28	39	28	5
Engineering	34	38	21	7	21	43	31	5
Electrical engineering	30	42	24	4	24	48	22	6

management discretion tends to be higher where more women are employed. In addition, high levels of autonomy on the part of local management are associated with stronger and more sophisticated workplace union organization.

A rather different picture is found, however, when we turn to the discretion of supervisors (table 2.8). The greatest freedom is found in the finance sample, but overall the variations among the samples are relatively small. The autonomy of supervisors does not appear to be very strongly influenced by trends in business activity or employment over the last five years. However, supervisors do have greater discretion where union organization is less sophisticated.

It is, of course, likely that the distribution of influence within an organization reflects many aspects of management structure and strategy that were not covered by our survey. And, as we have noted, it is traditionally argued that the structure of management has an important effect upon trade union organization. But although this may be true, this does not preclude the possibility that union organization affects the structure of management authority. Hence strong union organization is associated with a relative concentration of management authority at the level of the establishment. In other words, it may be that strong union organization tends to force local managers to seek some leeway from the larger organization and to impose constraints upon the freedom of action of lower management.

Given the dramatic changes in the economic and political climate over the last five years, it is also necessary to see how patterns of management authority have changed. As was noted above, some commentators have suggested that management would decentralize so that local management could maximize control over the labour force. On the other hand, a process of centralization would permit more thoroughgoing rationalization. These two patterns are not mutually exclusive: centralization may occur on some issues and the reverse on others. In addition, trends in discretion are likely to be related to previous levels of discretion. We did not feel able to investigate these two possibilities in the survey. We confined ourselves to asking about general trends in the discretion of local management and supervisors; the findings are shown in table 2.9.

Consistent with the declared policy of introducing so-called 'best practice', or, in other words, the principles of management organization believed to be found in the private sector, there has been a clear trend towards greater local management discretion in the public sector and particularly in Telecom (see Batstone et al., 1984, for a fuller discussion of this theme). In the other samples, the trend tends to be towards less autonomy for local management. In general terms,

Table 2.9 Trends in discretion of (a) local management and (b) supervisors, 1979–84

	Percentage of establishments where discretion of local management has:			Percentage of establishments where discretion of supervisors has:		
	In-creased	Not changed	Fallen	In-creased	Not changed	Fallen
(a) Non-manual/ public-sector group						
Finance	9	73	18	18	70	12
CPSA civil service	37	45	18	27	65	8
SCPS civil service	27	52	21	24	64	12
CPSA Telecom	50	31	19	34	54	12
POEU Telecom	47	38	16	42	45	13
(b) Production group						
Print	14	60	26	17	66	17
Chemicals	23	50	27	9	63	29
Food and drink	26	56	18	26	58	16
Engineering	23	53	23	14	65	21
(c) Maintenance group						
Chemicals	22	51	27	14	66	20
Food and drink	27	44	29	15	54	31
Engineering	15	63	22	16	63	21
Electrical engineering	12	60	28	16	63	21

the same pattern is found for the authority of supervisors, although here there has been a net increase in discretion not only in the public sector, but also in finance and the food and drink production sample. In the private sector, trends in output and employment are only weakly related to changes in the freedom of local management, although supervision has often achieved greater freedom where there have been large falls in employment or activity levels. The reverse tends to be true in the public sector. In addition, strong union organization is associated with increasing autonomy for supervisors in the private sector, but the reverse in the public sector.

In general terms, the findings can best be summarized by saying that there is a tendency towards the reversal of the traditional patterns of high centralization in the public sector and low centralization in the private sector. However, these trends have not – at least as yet – been sufficient to eradicate those traditional differences.

Management's Approach to Trade Unions

If the changed political atmosphere and the economic recession had provided management with the opportunity to reassert its power at the workplace, and this opportunity had been widely and eagerly grasped, then one would expect to find that employers were imposing a variety of constraints upon shop-steward activity within the workplace and in other ways reducing their support for trade unionism. In order to see how far this was indeed happening, we asked respondents about a number of indicators of management support for unions. The first was the extent to which management supported the closed shop, a key form of institutional security for many unions (although in some cases, notably the POEU, the union may itself be opposed to such an arrangement). Second, Batstone *et al.* (1977) have argued that an important feature of management support for stewards is the readiness to develop strong bargaining relationships. We chose to include this as another measure of management's approach, asking respondents about the frequency of off-the-record chats – a key feature of strong bargaining relationships – and whether these had become more or less frequent over the last five years. Third, we asked respondents about the extent to which management obstructed stewards going about their union business by imposing constraints upon them having time off; we also asked whether management had become more or less obstructive over the last five years. Fourth, we asked respondents a much more general question as to whether management's approach to unions and workers had changed over the last five years: responses to this question were grouped into three broad categories, indicating that management had become tougher, less tough or had not changed their approach. Finally, we asked our respondents whether management had imposed any sanctions, such as lock-outs, upon workers over the last twelve months.

Support for the Closed Shop

Table 2.10 shows that, in the view of respondents, there is little management opposition to the closed shop where it exists; the lowest level of support is found in the public sector – among clerical workers in Telecom. But even here 86 per cent of respondents state that management views the closed shop favourably. The overall picture,

Table 2.10 Support for closed shop (where it exists) by management

		Support for closed shop (%)
(a)	Non-manual/public-sector group	
	Finance	100
	CPSA civil service	—
	SCPS civil service	(100)
	CPSA Telecom	86
	POEU Telecom	—
(b)	Production group	
	Print	93
	Chemicals	94
	Food and drink	89
	Engineering	93
(c)	Maintenance group	
	Chemicals	88
	Food and drink	94
	Engineering	91
	Electrical Engineering	97

then, suggests little change from the late 1970s. Possibly of greater importance, however, is the effect which management's approach has upon the very existence of the closed shop. As will be seen below, the coverage of the closed shop varies considerably.

Off-the-record Chats

Table 2.11 shows respondents' answers concerning the frequency of off-the-record chats. These are very or fairly common in the majority of cases. Two points are, however, worthy of particular note. First, despite their strong support for the closed shop, printing employers are much less likely to have strong bargaining relationships with fathers of the chapel than are managers in the other manual samples. Second, off-the-record chats are relatively rare in the civil service. In the private sector, chats are more common the larger the number of union members and where personnel specialists exist.

The majority of respondents also state that the frequency of off-the-record chats has not changed over the last five years. Where changes have occurred, they have generally, or in 'net' terms, involved more

Table 2.11 (a) Frequency of off-the-record chats and (b) trends in off-the-record chats, 1979–84

	Percentage of establishments where off-the-record chats are:				Percentage of establishments where off-the-record chats have:		
	Very common	Fairly common	Not very common	Non-existent	In-creased	Not changed	De-creased
(a) Non-manual/public-sector group							
Finance	15	45	35	5	38	58	4
CPSA civil service	9	30	36	24	20	61	19
SCPS civil service	6	30	36	27	14	61	25
CPSA Telecom	8	47	36	9	11	69	20
POEU Telecom	10	52	32	6	10	75	15
(b) Production group							
Print	8	26	35	32	16	64	20
Chemicals	18	49	18	15	17	72	11
Food and drink	24	31	22	24	20	72	8
Engineering	14	51	17	19	22	68	10
(c) Maintenance group							
Chemicals	10	46	33	12	10	77	13
Food and drink	23	37	19	21	16	74	10
Engineering	12	44	23	21	18	67	15
Electrical engineering	18	38	30	14	22	58	20

frequent chats. This tendency is particularly marked in the case of finance. Indications of a weakening of bargaining relationships are, in 'net' terms, largely confined to the public sector. However, it should also be noted that at least one in ten of most of the samples say that bargaining relationships have become weaker.

Time off for Union Activities

Table 2.12 shows the extent to which management are said to interfere with stewards having time off for union duties. The vast majority of respondents say that they have little or no trouble in this respect, and well under a tenth state that there is a great deal of obstruction. This aspect of management opposition to union activity tends to be relatively common among white-collar groups and in the production groups. However, the most striking point is how little management has tried to obstruct steward activities.

The same picture is found when we turn to the question of whether or not management has attempted to impose greater constraints on stewards having time off over the last five years (table 2.12). With the exception of the CPSA civil service sample, the majority of respondents say that management has not attempted to prevent them taking time off. But there are substantial minorities who say that this has occurred. This is particularly so in the public sector, where over a third of respondents state that this has happened. It is also more common in the case of production than maintenance stewards. However, the significance of these trends should not be exaggerated: for, as was shown in the last paragraph, there are still remarkably few establishments where management interference with stewards has reached significant proportions (and, it should be remembered, some employers always have tried to impose controls upon the amount of time which stewards have for union duties).

Management's General Approach

It is quite possible that management maintains its support for the institutional position of the union and at the same time adopts strategies aimed at reducing the union's real influence. This may be so for a number of reasons. For example, management may be able to achieve its goals without resorting to a head-on confrontation with the unions; or the view may be held that a direct challenge to union organization would lead to major disputes, which might impose significant damage upon the company. It therefore seemed useful to ask not only about management support for the institutional position of the union, but also about changes in management's general approach towards the unions and labour force over the last five years. Table 2.13 gives a very different picture to that suggested by the preceding discussion. Overall, the responses are relatively evenly divided between those saying that there has been no change and those who state that management has adopted a tougher approach. Relatively few claim that management has become less tough. Again, we find it is in the public sector that managements are the most likely to be putting pressure on workers and their unions.

Management Sanctions

Despite the fact that a significant minority of employers are adopting a tougher approach in labour relations, very few have actually imposed sanctions upon workers (table 2.14). Certainly the use of lockouts and similar strategies on the part of the employer is still much rarer than the use of the strike and other sanctions on the part of workers and unions (see chapter 3). With the notable exception of the POEU, only about one in twenty say management has applied sanctions, although in some cases in manufacturing they have done so on several occasions.

The Overall Approach of Management

If employers were adopting a concerted strategy of weakening trade unions, then one would expect that they would be opposed to the closed shop, destroying strong bargaining relationships, imposing constraints upon stewards having the time off, adopting a tougher approach more generally, and, if necessary, imposing sanctions such as lock-outs. In other words, the responses to the questions just discussed would be strongly correlated.

In fact, the various dimensions are not, in the main, very strongly related to each other. In all three groups, there are only three relatively strong relationships: these are between the extent of management interference over time off and trends in this respect; between the frequency of off-the-record chats and trends in this factor; and between trends in management interference and management's more general approach. Most of the other relationships have a coefficient of less than 0.1 and very few more than 0.2. In other words, there does not appear to be any widespread and coherent management challenge to the unions.

It is possible to build the replies to these various questions into an index measuring management's approach towards trade unions. We do this by giving a score of one point for each of the following types

Table 2.12 (a) Management interference regarding time off for union activities; (b) trends in management interference regarding time off for union activities, 1979–84

	Percentage of establishments where management interferes				Percentage of establishments where management interference has		
	Great deal	*Fair amount*	*Not much*	*Not at all*	*In- creased*	*Not changed*	*De- creased*
(a) Non-manual/public-sector group							
Finance	—	13	30	57	18	63	20
CPSA civil service	6	19	53	22	54	32	14
SCPS civil service	3	7	53	37	43	53	4
CPSA Telecom	3	11	49	37	36	61	3
POEU Telecom	1	4	46	49	40	60	—
(b) Production group							
Print	7	11	30	52	35	58	7
Chemicals	4	9	52	36	34	59	8
Food and drink	4	10	43	43	26	67	8
Engineering	4	6	44	46	25	66	9
(c) Maintenance group							
Chemicals	—	8	41	51	18	74	8
Food and drink	1	5	40	54	12	82	6
Engineering	7	8	39	46	30	66	5
Electrical engineering	2	4	48	46	22	68	10

Table 2.13 Changes in management's approach, 1979–84

	Percentage of establishments where approach is:		
	Tougher	Same	Less tough
(a) Non-manual/public-sector group			
Finance	46	37	17
CPSA civil service	56	34	10
SCPS civil service	65	29	6
CPSA Telecom	78	22	—
POEU Telecom	83	17	—
(b) Production group			
Print	44	46	10
Chemicals	50	42	9
Food and drink	42	44	14
Engineering	41	43	15
(c) Maintenance group			
Chemicals	47	39	15
Food and drink	41	47	13
Engineering	40	55	5
Electrical engineering	38	56	6

of response: where management supports the closed shop, where it does not obstruct shop stewards at all as far as time off is concerned, where management has not become more obstructive on this count, where it has frequent off-the-record chats, where those chats have not become less common, where management's approach has not become tougher, and where management has not imposed sanctions upon workers. This provides an index with a maximum score of seven; such a score indicates a very supportive approach on the part of management, whereas a score of 0 would indicate a highly aggressive management strategy. Table 2.15 shows the scores on this index in the various samples. A number of points stand out. First, the bulk of respondents cluster in the middle range of the index: in other words, most managements provide a moderate amount of support for unions. Second, the toughest management approach is found in the public sector and particularly in the civil service – over a third of the civil service samples score less than three on the index. Third, in a third or so of the manual

Table 2.14 Percentage of establishments where mangement has applied sanctions

		No sanctions	One sanction	Two or more sanctions
(a)	Non-manual/public-sector group			
	Finance	100	—	—
	CPSA civil service	96	3	1
	SCPS civil service	98	2	—
	CPSA Telecom	100	—	—
	POEU Telecom	81	17	2
(b)	Production group			
	Print	92	7	1
	Chemicals	97	3	—
	Food and drink	96	4	—
	Engineering	95	2	3
(c)	Maintenance group			
	Chemicals	100	—	—
	Food and drink	93	3	4
	Engineering	93	3	3
	Electrical engineering	92	4	4

Table 2.15 Index of management's approach to trade unions (percentage of establishments)

		0	1	2	3	4	5	6	7
(a)	Non-manual/public-sector group								
	Finance	—	2	7	12	22	34	22	—
	CPSA civil service	—	10	24	25	21	11	9	1
	SCPS civil service	—	17	18	17	14	24	9	—
	CPSA Telecom	—	3	17	8	28	22	17	6
	POEU Telecom	2	6	9	24	25	19	14	1
(b)	Production group								
	Print	—	3	7	16	19	17	23	16
	Chemicals	—	2	8	12	21	28	19	10
	Food and drink	—	2	10	10	20	28	14	17
	Engineering	—	2	7	8	20	25	28	11
(c)	Maintenance group								
	Chemicals	—	—	3	13	20	33	27	5
	Food and drink	—	3	1	8	24	21	24	20
	Engineering	—	2	6	15	21	32	18	6
	Electrical engineering	—	2	4	20	18	26	22	9

private-sector samples, management demonstrates a relatively high degree of support for union organization within the workplace.

It is difficult to develop any strict comparison of the level of management support now as compared with, say, five years ago. In looking at certain dimensions of management's approach towards the unions, we have suggested that there appears to have been relatively little change, except in terms of management's general approach. Furthermore, in looking at the scores on the index, it has to be remembered that many companies have never provided a high degree of support for unions. But another interesting comparison is with a survey of personnel managers in large manufacturing establishments, which was undertaken in 1983. This suggested that between a fifth and a quarter of managements were adopting a tough approach towards the labour force (Batstone, 1984a). If we compare this with our respondents' assessments of changes in management's general approach, then it would seem that either stewards differ considerably in their view of management's approach as compared with personnel managers, or that over a period of a year managements have become considerably tougher. It does seem likely that personnel managers would tend to underestimate and stewards overestimate the toughness of management's approach. Certainly, although there were examples given by respondents of a very aggressive strategy on the part of management, there were also a significant number of cases where the hardening of management's approach appeared to be relatively minor. Such action might not be defined as getting tough by managers. On the other hand, in *Working Order* (Batstone, 1984a) part of the assessment of management's approach was based upon a more general assessment of managers' responses. This is therefore more comparable with the index created here. And in this instance, the differences between the two surveys appear less great. Certainly there is a consistency, in that the index we have created suggests that in the private sector very few employers have adopted a thorough and pervasive strategy of challenging the unions. In the next chapter, we turn to related questions of trends in union influence and control.

One factor that is clearly very relevant to an explanation of variations in management's approach towards the unions is the pattern of ownership. It is in the public sector, and particularly that part of it over which the government has the most direct control, that we find the least support for trade unionism. In other words, in general terms it would seem that political forces are a more potent inducement to an aggressive approach on the part of the employer than are market forces. However, the power of these political pressures is largely confined to the public sector: it does not appear to spread very widely into the private sector.

The index of management's approach towards the unions consists of two types of factor. The first is essentially static, in the sense that it concerns the actual level of management support; the second relates to trends. These are explained by different factors. Management has become less ready to support trade unions where union organization is more sophisticated and where falls in the level of activity have been greater. But these changes in management behaviour seem to have limited significance, since management support in absolute terms is still greater where union organization is more developed (we show below that union sophistication has been very stable over the last five years), and is not to be explained in terms of changes in employment or output.

Trade Union Organization at the Workplace

In outlining the nature of union organization at the workplace it is necessary, as was argued in chapter 1, to consider a number of dimensions. First, and most obviously, we have to look at levels of unions membership and density: union organization is likely to be stronger, the higher the proportion of workers represented. One factor promoting high levels of density is the existence of a closed shop. But, in addition, as was noted in chapter 1, the role which a union can play depends also upon the way in which its representation of members is organized. Relevant here is the question of the number of shop stewards. The greater the number of stewards per 100 members, then the more likely it is that the union will be able to represent the particular interests of different groups of workers. At the same time, the larger the number of stewards, the greater the need for some form of co-ordination. A number of different forms of co-ordination can be identified: the first of these is the existence of senior shop stewards, who have responsibilities not for specific small groups of workers, but for larger units such as whole departments or all the members within an establishment. Their role is both to pursue issues at higher levels of management and, perhaps most importantly, to co-ordinate the different actions and policies of various stewards. In addition, where the union has a large number of members and stewards, the workload at the centre may be such as to require one or more stewards working full-time. By committing themselves to union business in this way, they can better meet member demands and achieve a degree of co-ordination between different groups and stewards. In short, large numbers of members and stewards increase the workload and the need for some form of formal co-ordination: the development of a hierarchy of shop stewards is one means by which this can be done. Co-ordination may also be achieved by bringing stewards together on a regular basis to permit them to discuss issues and develop common policies: hence the existence of regular shop-steward meetings is another important feature of strong union organization. In smaller plants, however, there may be less need for a hierarchy of stewards or for formal meetings, since a degree of co-ordination can more easily be achieved informally. In the terms used in chapter 1, workplace sophistication varies by size.

There has been a relatively lengthy debate in recent years over the implications of formal steward structures of the kind just outlined. The tenor of the previous paragraph is that member interests can be more effectively pursued, at least in large establishments, where more complex formal structures are in place. The same line of argument can be found in a good deal of work on international variations in union organization and the efficacy of trade unionism. In this literature, considerable emphasis is placed upon high levels of mobilization or density, unity and centralization or other forms of co-ordination. Where these characteristics exist, it has been found that trade unions are generally more able to promote the interests of their members through solidaristic strategies and without resort to strike action. On the other hand, in Britain it has often been claimed that the formalization of shop-steward organization constitutes a 'bureaucratization of the rank and file'. This is associated with the development of an oligarchical leadership on the part of senior stewards, particularly if they are full-time, and the transformation of shop-steward organization from a vehicle for control on behalf of workers to one of control over them. That is, it is claimed that more formal shop-steward organizations adopt a managerialist approach and depend upon management rather than the membership for support. Hence, it is argued, bureaucratic organizations 'sell out'. Later in this section, we seek to assess how far formal shop-steward organization is associated with a centralization of power; in the next chapter, we will touch upon the question of whether such bodies demonstrate greater sympathy with management (for a fuller assessment of these arguments, see Batstone, 1984a).

The preceding discussion has concerned itself only with the individual union within the workplace. But very often there are a number of unions representing workers in the same establishment. The points we have raised concerning the organization of individual unions apply with possibly even greater force to the organization of trade unions generally at the place of work. That is, if there is a need for co-ordination where only one union exists, there is an even greater need for it where there is a multiplicity of unions. The existence of senior stewards and meetings or committees bringing the stewards from the various unions together are clearly of importance here.

Two other points also arise in the case of multi-union situations. The first is that the relationship between an individual union and the larger union organization within the workplace is likely to vary according to the proportion of total union membership held by that union. For example, a union representing production workers often has a very large membership both in absolute and relative terms, whereas a union representing a group of maintenance workers has a much smaller membership. In this case, it is likely that the production union will have a fairly formalized structure in its own right, and this may well become the basis for a more widespread formal structure. On the other hand, the small maintenance union is likely to have a less developed structure of shop stewards and may, for many purposes, be relatively dependent upon the formal structure of multi-union co-operation within the workplace. Second, it follows from this that there may well be tensions for a small union between seeking to defend the particular interests of its own members, on the one hand, and maintaining the unity of the unions within the workplace, which may be important for its own success, on the other.

A futher important feature of workplace union organization concerns its links with the larger union. Where links are weak, it is sometimes argued, there is a tendency for 'company unionism' to develop; indeed, some writers have suggested that many employers are seeking to achieve precisely this in the current recession. But, in addition, links with the larger union can be important not only in shaping the broader policies of the union, but also in providing support and expertise for union members within the workplace. Here our earlier arguments concerning the nature of the union nationally are relevant. Where a union deals with a single employer or a single industry and, to a lesser extent, where it covers a relatively homogeneous group of occupations, the more likely it is that there will be strong links between the workplace and the larger union organization. Or, in other terms, there will be a high degree of external integration.

In this section, then, we look first at the nature of the union membership, and then go on to consider the organization of shop stewards. In the next section, we discuss links between the workplace and the larger union, and finally we look at patterns of influence within trade unions.

Union Membership

We have defined union density – that is, the proportion of workers who are union members – in rather different ways for different samples. For manual groups, union density refers to the proportion of manual workers who belong to a union, and in the case of the non-manual samples the measure relates to the proportion of non-manual workers who are union members. Table 2.16 shows that union density is very high in all the manual samples: in at least four out of every five cases, more than 90 per cent of workers belong to a union. With the exception of white-collar workers in Telecom, levels of union density are lower in the non-manual samples. Less than half the finance respondents, for example, report that three-quarters or more of the staff are in a union. Union membership, then, tends to be higher among manual groups and in the public sector. Hence, density is very high among manual workers in the public sector (the POEU) and lowest among non-manual workers in the private sector (finance). The occupational variable, however, is more important than the sectoral. Moreover, the findings suggest that there has been no fall in union density in organized plants – at least in the industries covered by this survey.

Given this picture of high levels of union membership, there also arises the question of the relative importance of the different unions sampled. In finance, the respondents' union is the only one present in most cases, and in only two cases are there more than two unions in the workplace. In most of the public-sector samples, a variety of unions exist within the establishment. In the CPSA Telecom sample, nearly three-quarters of respondents say there are four or more unions, and typically in the civil service at least three are found. Among the manual samples, we find that the respondents' union is the only one representing manual workers in a majority of the production food-and-drink sample and in about a quarter of the AUEW and production chemicals samples. However, there are also substantial minorities of respondents in these samples who say that three or more unions exist within their workplaces. In the other samples, it is very rare for there to be only one union representing manual workers in the establishment.

Another factor that is important in explaining the relative numerical importance of a union within an establishment is the types of worker the union represents. As table 2.16 shows, the EETPU typically accounts for less than 10 per cent of union members where it covers only maintenance electricians, as is the case in three of our four samples from this union. With the exception of the EETPU and the SCPS – which tends to cover higher-grade civil servants – the respondents' own union generally accounts for the majority of union members within the establishment. But that union represents three-quarters or more of all union members only in the finance and the two TGWU samples. In brief, production unions tend to have the largest proportion of union members where no other unions cover this type of worker, and particularly where they also cover some indirect workers. This is most clearly seen in the TGWU samples. Where

Table 2.16 (a) Union density in relevant group; (b) relative importance of own union/total trade union membership

	Percentage of establishments where union density is:						Percentage of establishments where relative importance of own union/total trade union membership is:					
	25% or less	26–50%	51–75%	76–90%	91–99%	100%	10% or less	11–25%	26–50%	51–75%	76–99%	100%
(a) Non-manual/public-sector group												
Finance												
CPSA civil service	3	13	42	32	8	3	3	5	8	15	10	59
SCPS civil service	1	4	26	42	21	7	1	5	13	45	31	5
CPSA Telecom	—	8	33	36	17	6	7	19	52	12	6	4
POEU Telecom	4	—	9	30	26	30	4	33	7	26	22	7
	—	—	2	—	11	87	—	8	15	29	40	8
(b) Production group												
Print	1	1	5	8	5	80	1	14	28	30	10	17
Chemicals	—	1	9	11	7	73	3	—	5	31	33	29
Food and drink	—	2	2	10	7	79	—	—	—	10	19	71
Engineering	—	2	4	9	6	79	8	18	20	18	12	25
(c) Maintenance group												
Chemicals	—	2	2	6	7	83	84	16	—	—	—	—
Food and drink	1	1	3	5	—	89	91	5	4	—	—	—
Engineering	—	4	9	5	7	75	75	12	—	5	2	5
Electrical engineering	—	7	4	9	11	70	42	17	11	13	6	11

a variety of unions represent production workers, then the relative importance of the union, though still considerable, tends to be somewhat lower; examples are the AUEW and NGA samples. Similar points apply in the case of the non-manual samples. Finally, the EETPU samples rarely include production workers, and hence they account for only a small proportion of total union membership.

It is worth stressing the combined effects of size of establishment and the nature of the union membership upon the number of a union's members found within the workplace. As has already been noted, the EETPU respondents typically work in large establishments, but because the union generally covers only particular types of worker, the total membership is relatively small. Hence, although many of them work in plants with a labour force in excess of 500, in about 90 per cent of cases they have a membership of well below fifty. The same pattern is found with the SCPS. The NGA also often has fewer than fifty members, but this reflects less the nature of the occupations covered than the small size of many of the establishments in this sample.

A further factor affecting union membership is the existence and coverage of the closed shop. Table 2.17 shows that, with the exception of Telecom, where a large proportion of clerical (and Union of Communication Workers) members are covered, the closed shop is very rare in the non-manual/public-sector group. This is an important explanation of the relatively low levels of union density, except in the case of the POEU, where membership is extremely high (the union has on a number of occasions voted not to have a closed shop). In the private-sector manual samples, the closed shop exists in a majority of cases; generally, it plays a more important role among craft than other groups of workers. The closed shop is more common in larger establishments in these samples. (In this and subsequent tables, the term 'comparable' refers to manual unions in the case of manual samples, and non-manual unions in the case of non-manual samples.)

The Number of Shop Stewards

We consider first the number of shop stewards belonging to the respondents' own union; the relevant information is shown in the left-hand side of table 2.18. The Telecom and production unions have the largest number of stewards or equivalent workplace union representatives, and the lowest numbers are found in the maintenance samples. In the latter, the average number of stewards is two, except in electrical engineering, where the number rises to five. In the POEU sample, in

Table 2.17 Coverage of the closed shop: (a) own union; (b) all comparable unions

	Percentage of establishments where own union forms:			Percentage of establishments where all comparable unions form:		
	No closed shop	1–99%	100%	No closed shop	1–99%	100%
(a) Non-manual/ public-sector group						
Finance	97	—	3	97	—	3
CPSA civil service	100	—	—	100	—	—
SCPS civil service	98	1	—	97	2	1
CPSA Telecom	—	25	75	—	100	—
POEU Telecom	100	—	—	41	59	
(b) Production group						
Print	—	9	91	—	24	76
Chemicals	34	3	63	33	5	62
Food and drink	36	8	56	34	6	60
Engineering	30	2	68	30	3	67
(c) Maintenance group						
Chemicals	2	4	94	2	10	88
Food and drink	11	2	87	10	6	84
Engineering	41	2	57	41	5	54
Electrical engineering	35	4	61	35	14	51

contrast, the average number is 18. In most of the other samples, the number of stewards from the respondents' own union is about ten. These variations reflect the fact that the number of shop stewards is strongly related to the number of members of the union in an establishment. In the private sector, the greater the scale of job loss, the greater tends to be the number of stewards (this is not, of course, a causal relationship: it reflects, first, the fact that more stewards are found in large plants and, second, that it is in these plants that job loss has been greater); in the public sector, the reverse tends to be the case. In addition, in all the groups, the less supportive that management's approach is, the lower tends to be the number of stewards. However, both these effects are minor compared with the role that the size of union membership plays.

Table 2.18 Number of shop stewards in (a) own union and (b) all comparable unions

	Percentage of establishments where N shop stewards in own union					Percentage of establishments where N shop stewards in all comparable unions				
	1	2–5	6–10	11–25	26+	1	2–5	6–10	11–25	26+
(a) Non-manual/public-sector group										
Finance	15	28	25	23	9	15	28	25	18	14
CPSA civil service	19	32	32	13	5	9	29	23	29	11
SCPS civil service	24	39	22	7	8	11	33	21	23	13
CPSA Telecom	3	12	24	62	—	3	12	8	46	30
POEU Telecom	—	15	13	55	17	—	16	7	42	34
(b) Production group										
Print	7	41	34	18	—	4	29	25	28	15
Chemicals	2	31	30	30	8	2	26	24	29	23
Food and drink	2	47	18	20	12	7	41	17	22	13
Engineering	12	50	22	12	4	3	33	31	22	11
(c) Maintenance group										
Chemicals	59	36	5	—	—	4	18	26	44	9
Food and drink	49	45	6	—	—	3	23	17	41	16
Engineering	52	44	2	3	—	4	23	30	21	23
Electrical engineering	34	46	10	4	6	—	23	37	21	18

The size of steward constituencies does vary considerably between the unions. If we define the constituency in terms of the average number of workers per steward, then the largest constituencies are found in the finance sample; but this reflects the fact that union density in this sector is relatively low. However, if we define constituency size in terms of the number of union members (rather than workers), there is a very clear pattern with the exception of finance: the smaller the union membership, the smaller the size of the steward constituency. For example, the average for the electrician samples (with the exception of electrical engineering) is only 12; it is 11 in the case of the SCPS and 12 in the NGA. But in the other production samples, the average size of the constituency rises to about 25–30, and is even higher in the two Telecom samples.

When we turn to the total number of stewards in establishments, the variations between the maintenance and production samples largely disappear (right-hand side of table 2.18). Particularly large numbers of stewards are found in Telecom, the production chemicals sample, and two of the maintenance samples. In these, the average number of stewards exceeds 20, whereas in none of the samples is the average below ten. Again, these variations reflect the total number of union members in the establishment. The larger the number of union members, the larger the number of stewards. Again, we find little variation by the scale of employment change or by management's approach to the unions (see above).

The average constituency size of all stewards within the establishments also shows considerable variation. The smallest are found in the NGA and SCPS samples (15 and 16 respectively), indicating once more the importance of a size effect. In the larger manufacturing establishments, the number of members per steward rises to just under 30 in the chemicals and engineering production samples (the figures are rather higher for the corresponding maintenance samples) and to nearly 40 in food and drink. In Telecom, there are 33 workers per steward, whereas the number rises to 50 or more in the case of the CPSA civil service sample and the finance sample.

It is difficult to make strict comparisons between the number of stewards and the size of their constituencies as found here and in earlier studies. However, it is possible to make crude comparisons with the findings of a survey of private manufacturing establishments undertaken in 1978 (Brown, 1981). These suggest that the number of members per steward has not fallen over the six years between the two surveys, and may even have fractionally increased. In other words, as Batstone (1984a) found, although the number of stewards in manufacturing has fallen, it has not declined as fast as the number of jobs.

The Number of Senior Stewards

As was noted above, the existence of senior stewards (or equivalent officers) has been variously seen as a key mechanism for co-ordinating the activities of shop stewards and as a form of oligarchy and incorporation. The left-hand side of table 2.19 shows the number of such stewards – or approximate equivalents, such as branch chairpersons and secretaries – from respondents' unions. It can be seen that a significant minority of the finance and maintenance samples state that their unions have no senior shop stewards and rarely do they have more than one. At the other extreme, in Telecom there are always at least two senior stewards, and several are also often found in the civil service samples. In the production samples, several senior stewards exist in a substantial minority of cases, with the partial exception of engineering.

A variety of factors explain the variations in the number of senior stewards from respondents' unions. Most important is the number of stewards the union has: the larger the number of stewards, the larger the number of senior stewards. Second, senior stewards are more common in the public sector, even when we control for the number of stewards: this appears to be a reflection of the centralized structure of bargaining and the single-employer nature of these unions. It is also worth noting that, in the case of the NGA, the single-industry nature of the union has a similar effect. Third, the nature of management's approach towards the unions affects the number of senior stewards. Where the employer is less supportive, there tends to be fewer senior stewards. However, it does not follow that a tougher approach on the part of management over the last five years has led to a reduction in the number of senior stewards. Many employers have never given full support to the unions; and indicators of trends in management's approach towards the unions are not related to the number of senior stewards.

The right-hand side of table 2.19 shows the total number of senior stewards in the establishments covered by the survey. With the notable exception of finance, the majority of respondents in most of the samples state that there are at least two senior stewards. The largest number of senior stewards is again found in the public sector: in Telecom, the average figure is ten or eleven, and in the civil service the average is six. In most of the manual private-sector samples, the average number of senior stewards per establishment is three or four. The explanation for variations in the numbers is broadly the same as for the number of senior stewards from respondents' own unions. That

Table 2.19 Number of senior shop stewards in (a) own union and (b) all unions

	Percentage of establishments where N senior shop stewards in own union				Percentage of establishments where N senior shop stewards in all unions			
	0	1	2-5	6+	0	1	2-5	6+
(a) Non-manual/public-sector group								
Finance	21	55	24	—	21	55	24	—
CPSA civil service	2	30	51	16	2	17	48	33
SCPS civil service	2	34	56	8	2	26	40	33
CPSA Telecom	3	—	86	11	3	—	21	76
POEU Telecom	—	—	72	28	—	—	27	73
(b) Production group								
Print	1	46	46	7	—	15	66	19
Chemicals	7	49	37	8	7	35	35	23
Food and drink	6	62	26	6	6	46	37	11
Engineering	4	78	17	2	3	41	51	5
(c) Maintenance group								
Chemicals	38	58	5	—	16	15	51	18
Food and drink	42	53	5	—	13	21	50	16
Engineering	47	50	3	—	13	31	38	18
Electrical engineering	24	71	6	—	2	46	48	4

is, the larger the number of stewards, the larger the number of senior stewards. In addition, the larger numbers in the public sector and the NGA reflect union and bargaining structures. But in this instance, management's approach to the unions does not explain any of the variation. However, in the private-sector manual groups, falls in employment over the last five years tend to be associated with a larger number of senior stewards, once other factors are controlled for. That is, the number of senior stewards has fallen less rapidly than employment. The result is that equivalent sizes of establishment today have fractionally more senior stewards than they had five years ago.

The Number of Full-time Stewards

The second feature of steward bureaucracy noted above was the existence of full-time shop stewards. The left-hand side of table 2.20 shows that, with the exception of the Telecom samples, only a minority of respondents say that they have a full-time steward representing their union in the establishment. Full-timers are most rare in the maintenance samples, in the production engineering sample and printing. Only in a small minority of cases, with the exception of the POEU, do we find that the union has more than one full-time shop steward. In the non-manual public-sector group and in the production samples, the most important factors explaining the existence and number of full-timers are the number of members and the number of shop stewards that the union has. In the maintenance samples, the existence and number of senior stewards is a more powerful explanatory variable. Particularly, where union organization is less firmly embedded, notably in finance, the degree of management support for union organization also affects the existence of full-time shop stewards.

The second part of table 2.20 shows the number of full-time shop stewards from all the unions within the establishments. Again, it can be seen that, with the exception of the two Telecom samples, full-timers are found in only a minority of cases. However, except in printing and finance, this is a substantial minority, ranging from about a quarter to two-fifths of establishments. Moreover, it is frequently the case that if there are any full-timers at all, there are a number of them. The average number of full-timers in the different samples is as follows: none in finance and printing; one in the civil service samples, food and drink and engineering; two in chemicals and the non-manual areas in Telecom; and three in the case of the POEU.

The total number of full-time shop stewards is most strongly related to the number of stewards: the greater the number of stewards, the greater the number of full-timers. In addition, a more centralized

Table 2.20 Number of full-time stewards in (a) own union and (b) all unions

	Percentage of establishments with N full-time stewards in own union			Percentage of establishments with N full-time stewards in all unions		
	0	1	2+	0	1	2+
(a) Non-manual/ public-sector group						
Finance	78	18	4	78	9	13
CPSA civil service	62	30	8	60	25	15
SCPS civil service	70	20	10	67	20	13
CPSA Telecom	44	47	9	34	13	53
POEU Telecom	29	38	33	27	23	50
(b) Production group						
Print	86	7	7	88	4	8
Chemicals	63	24	13	63	12	24
Food and drink	57	31	12	57	31	12
Engineering	73	23	4	72	14	14
(c) Maintenance group						
Chemicals	91	8	1	75	10	15
Food and drink	91	8	1	58	25	17
Engineering	87	11	2	64	16	20
Electrical engineering	72	22	6	57	17	26

bargaining structure and a greater institutional security for the unions are associated with a larger number of full-timers. More detailed analyses indicate that in the private sector, although there has been a slight fall in the total number of full-timers, there are more of them per 1,000 union members than there were in 1978. That is, they have declined in numbers, but not as rapidly as employment has fallen.

Shop-Steward Committees and Meetings

The third feature of steward bureaucracy that has been emphasized in recent writing concerns the existence of various meetings and committees which permit the co-ordination, and some would say the control, of shop-steward activities. Here we asked three questions: these concerned, first, the existence of meetings of stewards from the respondents' own union within the workplace; second, whether a committee made up of stewards from different unions within the workplace existed; and, third, whether meetings of all the stewards within the workplace were held. Respondents were also asked how frequently these various bodies met.

Part (a) of table 2.21 shows that, with the exception of the maintenance samples (where typically the number of stewards is very small), the majority of respondents state that meetings of stewards from their own union do take place. In five of the samples – the two CPSA samples, the POEU and the two TGWU samples – these meetings are generally held at least monthly. The existence and frequency of these meetings is most strongly related to the number of union members and the number of stewards. In other words, as one might expect, where the union has a small number of members and few stewards, there is less need for such formal arrangements to ensure co-ordination of action. These findings appear to be broadly in line with the findings of Daniel and Millward (1983, p. 96).

Part (b) of table 2.21 shows that, with the notable exceptions of finance and, to a lesser degree, printing, some form of committee generally exists which brings stewards from the various unions together (where there is more than one union in the workplace). Moreover, in most cases these meet at least monthly in the private-sector manual samples, although less frequently in the case of the public sector. In other words, unions that have substantial memberships and have some clear identity (or are in competition with other unions) are less likely to co-operate with other unions on any regular basis. These unions also bargain at a more centralized level. The EETPU samples, however, are involved in such bodies, no doubt because their small membership in the plants covered by the survey mean that they cannot afford to be isolated from the majority of union members in the establishment. The finance case is therefore the most striking exception: this would appear to be due to high levels of inter-union competition, a reflection of the growth and relative newness of union organization in this sector. In the private-sector manual samples, the most important factor explaining variations in the existence of these committees and the frequency with which they meet is the number of shop stewards; in the public sector, it is the number of senior shop stewards that plays the most important explanatory role. Crude comparisons with the Daniel and Millward survey suggest that there has been little change in the existence of joint shop-steward committees and the frequency with which they meet since 1980 (1983, pp. 97–9).

The third type of shop-steward body we asked about was meetings of all shop stewards. The pattern found (part (c) of table 2.21) is broadly similar to that for joint committees. Hence these meetings occur in the majority of the samples, where more than one union

Table 2.21 (a) Frequency of meetings of stewards of own union; (b) frequency of committees of stewards of stewards from all comparable unions; (c) frequency of meetings of stewards from all comparable unions

	Percentage of establishments where meetings of stewards of own union are held:			Percentage of establishments where committees of stewards of two or more comparable unions are held:			Percentage of establishments where meetings of stewards of two or more comparable unions are held:		
	At least monthly	Less often	Never	At least monthly	Less often	Never	At least monthly	Less often	Never
(a) Non-manual/public-sector group									
Finance	34	51	15	4	11	85	—	26	74
CPSA civil service	57	28	15	42	35	23	30	34	36
SCPS civil service	27	35	38	29	44	26	23	31	45
CPSA Telecom	64	6	30	20	72	8	26	44	30
POEU Telecom	72	21	7	18	61	21	19	58	23
(b) Production group									
Print	37	36	27	25	24	51	16	28	56
Chemicals	62	24	14	44	17	39	35	29	36
Food and drink	66	19	15	61	22	17	31	42	27
Engineering	37	20	43	64	14	22	38	23	38
(c) Maintenance group									
Chemicals	19	11	70	49	23	28	36	41	23
Food and drink	18	16	65	48	23	29	28	28	44
Engineering	21	12	67	71	12	17	40	20	40
Electrical engineering	36	10	54	73	13	13	52	16	32

exists, except in finance and printing. However, the frequency with which they meet tends to be greater in the manual manufacturing samples than in the public sector. Again, meetings of this kind are more common where there are large numbers of stewards and where bargaining occurs at establishment level among unions with large memberships and weak occupational/industrial identities. It again appears that there has been little change in the importance of joint shop-steward meetings since 1980 (cf. Daniel and Millward, 1983, pp. 97–9).

Joint Negotiation

Another factor relevant to inter-union co-operation within the workplace is the structure of bargaining. Where unions negotiate jointly, there is a greater need to co-ordinate policy. Hence, the extent to which there is joint negotiation is closely related to the existence of joint shop-steward committees and meetings. Table 2.22 shows the responses to questions concerning the extent to which joint negotiation occurs: the first part of the table concerns the extent to which, for example in the case of manual respondents, different manual groups negotiate together; non-manual respondents were asked about negotiation with other non-manual groups, and in the finance sample no distinction between manual and non-manual groups was made, since unions typically cover all grades. This last point explains the high level of joint negotiation in finance. Joint negotiation among comparable groups is most common in the various engineering samples; at the other extreme, the various groups rarely bargain together in printing and, to a lesser degree, in food and drink, and chemicals. The public sector sits between these two extreme groups. However, in all the samples, the majority of respondents state that at least some groups negotiate together. On the other hand, it is rare for manual and non-manual groups to do so (see the second part of table 2.22). This is particularly true in the case of manual private-sector groups. It is more common in the non-manual and public-sector groups, particularly in Telecom.

Steward Co-ordination

The preceding discussion has focused upon structures that facilitate co-ordination within an individual union and across trade unions within the workplace. In addition, we investigated this question more directly by asking respondents: 'Which of the following best describes the way union representatives operate in this establishment: senior stewards

Table 2.22 (a) Percentage of establishments where joint negotiation with comparable groups takes place; (b) frequency of joint negotiation by manual and non-manual groups

	Percentage of establishments where joint negotiation with comparable groups takes place			Percentage of establishments where joint negotiation by manual and non-manual groups takes place:				
	All groups	Some groups	All individually	Often	Some-times	Hardly ever	Never	Not applic-able
(a) Non-manual/public-sector group								
Finance	59	16	24	27	16	5	27	24
CPSA civil service	40	52	8	2	13	10	19	56
SCPS civil service	47	50	3	5	5	8	24	58
CPSA Telecom	20	71	9	29	51	11	3	6
POEU Telecom	52	40	8	14	64	12	11	—
(b) Production group								
Print	13	39	49	7	9	10	52	23
Chemicals	40	36	24	3	9	13	60	16
Food and drink	51	23	26	4	13	8	48	27
Engineering	72	15	14	1	14	13	53	18
(c) Maintenance group								
Chemicals	37	54	10	5	23	18	47	8
Food and drink	17	50	33	3	18	14	61	5
Engineering	69	19	11	3	19	19	52	7
Electrical engineering	58	23	19	8	20	27	41	4

typically play the leading role and other representatives follow; *or* senior stewards do not play a leading role: all stewards collectively decide on policy which is binding on them all; *or* individual stewards and work groups decide on their own course of action?' The last option indicates a lack of co-ordination, whereas the first two options simply distinguish between different types of co-ordination. Table 2.23 shows that the majority of respondents believe that the shop-steward body acts collectively. This is least true of the food and drink, and chemicals maintenance groups and, to a lesser degree, of the corresponding production groups and printing. Co-ordination of some kind, then, is relatively high in the various engineering samples and in the non-manual and public-sector group. However, what is striking is that the means of co-ordination vary quite markedly. Among the manual production groups, and particularly in some of the maintenance samples, the steward collectivity plays this role. In the public sector, the senior steward (or equivalent) is the means of co-ordination. The key explanatory factor is a size variable: the larger the number of stewards and members, the greater the role of the senior steward(s).

The Sophistication of Trade Union Organization within the Workplace

The preceding sections have outlined various characteristics of trade union organization within the workplace. The discussion has been structured to a large extent by the question of the degree of bureaucracy, along with the density of union membership. In summarizing this section, and as a useful index in the ensuing discussion, we have built up two general indicators of what we term the sophistication of trade union organization at establishment level. The first of these concerns the respondents' own unions and is termed 'intra-union sophistication'; the second covers inter-union organization and we have termed this measure 'inter-union sophistication'. Before looking at the scores on these indices, it is necessary to say something about the way in which they were constructed.

The inter-union sophistication index consists of seven dimensions. The first is the coverage of the closed shop: where this is 100 per cent of the union's members, then a score of 1 is given on the index. Second, if there are five or more shop stewards belonging to the union, then a further score of 1 is given (in the case of the electricians, the point was given if there were two or more stewards). Third, a point was scored where a senior steward existed and two points were scored if there were two or more senior stewards. Fourth, the existence of a full-time shop steward gave another score of 1. Fifth, if the stewards

Table 2.23 Patterns of decision-making

	Percentage of establishments where:			
	Senior shop stewards lead	Shop stewards decide together	Shop stewards and groups go own way	Only 1 shop steward/other
(a) Non-manual/public-sector group				
Finance	45	30	5	20
CPSA civil service	74	20	4	2
SCPS civil service	58	36	5	1
CPSA Telecom	72	22	6	—
POEU Telecom	69	27	3	2
(b) Production group				
Print	43	42	15	—
Chemicals	45	44	10	1
Food and drink	32	54	14	—
Engineering	37	59	5	—
(c) Maintenance group				
Chemicals	15	48	34	3
Food and drink	19	48	33	—
Engineering	31	59	10	—
Electrical engineering	41	53	6	—

from the union met at least monthly, then a further point was added to the index. In short, the scores on the intra-union sophistication index can range from 0 to 6. However, in order to facilitate subsequent analyses and comparison with other indicators, such as inter-union sophistication, the scores were adjusted to a maximum of 10. A score of 10, then, indicates that the union is strongly organized, at least in formal terms, within the workplace.

The first section of table 2.24 shows the scores on the intra-union sophistication index. It can be seen that the highest scores are found in Telecom, the lowest in finance and the maintenance samples. The relative newness and weakness of trade unions in banking and insurance is the cause of the low scores in finance; in the maintenance samples, it reflects the small numbers of electricians typically found in the establishments covered by the survey.

The key factor explaining a high degree of intra-union sophistication is the size of the union's membership; but – and this is an important point for our subsequent analysis – the level of union membership in 1979 is more strongly related to the index scores than is the level in 1984. Indeed, changes in union membership over the five-year period are inversely related to the degree of sophistication. That is, the greater the fall in membership, the more sophisticated the union organization. This is not a direct causal relationship. Rather, it is due to two things: first, job reductions have been disproportionately concentrated in large establishments, where union sophistication is typically greater. Second, union organization as measured by this index is very stable, despite cuts in jobs. Moreover, only in finance – where union density is lowest – is the degree of sophistication affected by the approach adopted by management. These indications of the stability of union sophistication are very important in the subsequent analysis, where we use the current degree of union sophistication as an indicator of union sophistication in the past: these findings suggest that, in the vast majority of cases, this is a reasonable thing to do.

The inter-union sophistication index consists of seven dimensions. The first of these is union density: for the manual groups, if density is 100 per cent, then a point is given. In the case of the non-manual samples, union density rarely achieves this level, and so the cut-off point for scoring was varied: in finance density had to be over 70 per cent, in the civil service over 80 per cent, and in the clerical telecommunications sample over 90 per cent. Second, a point was scored where there were five or more shop stewards. Third, a point was given if there was a senior shop steward, and an additional point if there were five or more. Fourth, the existence of one full-time steward gained a point, and a further point was given where there were

Table 2.24 (a) Intra-union steward sophistication index; (b) inter-union steward sophistication index (percentage of establishments)

	Intra-union index					Inter-union index					
	0/2	3/4	5	6/7	8+	0/2	3	4	5	6	7+
(a) Non-manual/public-sector group											
Finance	29	29	29	10	2	31	15	37	12	—	5
CPSA civil service	14	21	22	28	16	13	17	15	22	16	18
SCPS civil service	25	23	24	17	10	13	14	20	17	13	22
CPSA Telecom	3	—	6	31	60	11	3	14	17	28	28
POEU Telecom	—	7	14	36	42	18	14	8	21	23	17
(b) Production group											
Print	3	18	33	27	19	30	29	20	8	6	7
Chemicals	8	14	23	26	29	15	14	21	26	19	6
Food and drink	11	18	22	26	24	15	20	20	26	14	6
Engineering	15	29	22	19	15	8	14	22	25	21	11
(c) Maintenance group											
Chemicals	41	27	14	14	5	27	11	25	20	9	8
Food and drink	35	20	30	10	5	25	14	23	16	14	9
Engineering	45	21	18	15	2	11	11	19	24	11	24
Electrical engineering	21	28	18	24	10	13	8	20	26	16	18

two or more full-timers. Further points were given where meetings or committees of stewards from the various unions were held at least monthly, where the unions generally negotiated together, and where decisions were made collectively by the stewards or by the senior stewards, rather than individually by stewards and work groups. This gives a range of scores from 0 to 9; they were adjusted, as with intra-union sophistication, to a base of 10.

The right-hand part of table 2.24 shows that the highest levels of inter-union sophistication are to be found in the public sector and the various engineering samples. Printing and finance achieve the lowest scores: the former reflects the small size of establishment and the tendency for the various craft groups to negotiate separately, whereas the finance score reflects the institutional insecurity of the unions.

As in the case of the intra-union sophistication measure, we find that scores on the inter-union sophistication index are higher the larger the total union membership in the establishment. Again, the relationships are stronger with the 1979 level of membership than with the 1984 level, indicating a high degree of stability. In addition, there is once more an inverse relationship between the degree of inter-union sophistication and the scale of job loss. In this instance, the approach of management is only important in the finance sample.

It is useful to illustrate the measures of sophistication – and certain of their limitations – by looking at our case studies. Union organization in two of these scored very high on the sophistication measure. Both had 100 per cent union membership and closed shops; both had a full-time steward, and in both cases union officers met together regularly. These meetings constituted an important means by which sectional problems could be raised and, at the same time, provided an opportunity for formulating more general policy. The full-time steward played an active role in both respects, but was supported and constrained by the other stewards and, in the case of the brewery, the branch. Furthermore, in both cases, stewards acted within the structure provided by plant-level or branch-level decisions. In the case of the brewery, where a number of manual unions existed, there was also a very high degree of inter-union co-operation: representatives of the various unions met together regularly and on plant-level issues negotiated jointly. At this level, all issues had to be agreed upon unanimously.

However, our case studies also indicate a number of other points concerning the measurement of sophistication. The first of these is the importance of steward–member links, which we simply assumed to exist in the survey (although see also the later discussion of democracy). In both the cases cited, there were opportunities, through shop-floor meetings or through the branch, for members to influence union policy and steward behaviour. In addition, there was close day-to-day interaction between stewards and members in the course of work. Second, our case studies indicate the importance not merely of the number of stewards, but also how they are distributed. In both our brewing and engineering case studies, the steward collectivity was careful to ensure that the pattern of steward constituencies represented key interest groups within the plant, and, of equal importance, that all steward positions were filled. Although in our other two case studies the pattern of steward constituencies broadly reflected different interests, it was noteworthy that a number of steward constituencies remained unfilled. This weakened the extent to which particular interests could be fed into the union and reflected the nature of the work situation. In both chemicals and insurance, these gaps in representation were in part attributable to the importance of internal labour markets: these were also important in our other two case studies, particularly brewing, but here they were controlled much more closely by the union. In addition, in the chemicals case study it was noteworthy that the gaps in steward representation were most marked in the dedicated plants (including the automated ones we concentrated upon). This appeared to be due to a number of factors. One of these was that on dedicated plants work was of a far more routine nature (the reorganization of pipework, etc., which was required on multi-product plant was not necessary), and so the dominant definition of the role of the union here at shop-floor level – in terms of the provision of information to shape individualistic mobility strategies – assumed less significance.

This definition of the role of the union was related to the broader nature of union organization. Of particular relevance here was the extent to which steward action was co-ordinated at plant level. This example indicates the major importance of regular steward committees or similar bodies. In the chemicals company, a full-time steward was responsible for all the plants within the manufacturing division; at this level, there was also the union side to the annual negotiations. But this only met prior to the negotiations and played no role in the day-to-day events of the company or plant. At plant level, there was no means of co-ordination: the only formal institution at this level was the branch, but this played little role – and no role in strategic terms – as far as issues within the plant were concerned. There were, however, meetings of stewards from various sections, but generally these met only on an irregular basis. The result, therefore, was that individual stewards were relatively isolated and could not work within a structure that gave them some significant basis for action. For this very isolation from the centre meant that there were few pressures upon the centre to develop adequate frameworks; the negotiating committee and the full-time steward confined themselves largely to the bread-and-butter issues of wages and related matters. The same weaknesses were found as far as co-operation between the various unions on the site was concerned. A plethora of negotiating units existed at the site, but the unions had no contact with each other that would permit the discussion of common issues. The result of these structures was not only that there was little pressure from the centre to fill the gaps in steward representation, but, in addition, the structure of union organization encouraged the representation of sectional interests (albeit incompletely), without providing the means by which these different interests could be shaped into a coherent whole. The bifurcation of activity at company and shop-floor level which resulted from this encouraged a limited conception of the role of the union on the part of many members.

A not dissimilar situation arose in the case of the insurance company studied. Here, stewards within individual offices were often relatively isolated, and this weakness was all the greater due to the nature of the work situation. Even where there were a larger number of stewards – as in the head office – co-ordination was limited. The primary focus of union organization was at company level: here organization was sophisticated, with the union within the company having its own annual conference, an executive which met regularly, and an active full-time secretary. Hence at company level the union developed policies and played an active role: but the significance of such activity was constrained by weaknesses at lower levels of organization. Although the union was seeking to encourage stewards to play a more active role, its own impact was constrained – it did not receive sufficient information from local stewards, and, even when agreements were made at company level, which provided a base from which local stewards could raise issues, our evidence indicates that they frequently failed to do so. These points are expanded upon more fully in our forthcoming volume. The relevance of our case-study data to our present purposes is both to indicate the significance of our measure of sophistication and also to point to some of its limitations.

Links with the Larger Union

A great deal of recent discussion of shop stewards has paid scant attention to the question of the links between the unions at the workplace and the larger union. Where this has been discussed, it has often been suggested that these links have been weakened and that there may even be a growth of 'company unionism'. Certainly we have just seen that many shop-steward organizations have a degree of organizational sophistication that is probably comparable with that of many early trade unions nationally. But it does not follow from this that links with the larger union are of no importance. Indeed, our survey suggests quite the reverse.

In looking at this question, we will consider, first, the extent to which the basic unit of the wider union – the branch – overlaps with workplace union organization. Where this is the case, then clearly there are institutional links between the workplace and the larger union: union communications are more likely to go directly to the place of work; the collectivity that bargains at the establishment can also put forward proposals to the larger union through branch-related mechanisms. Second, we asked respondents how important they felt the role of the larger union was in negotiations relating to the establishment. Third, we asked a question about the influence of different groups in deciding union policy as far as the establishment was concerned: the replies to this question are discussed more fully in the next section, but for our present purposes replies relating to the influence of the wider union are of relevance. Fourth, we asked respondents whether the larger union generally ratified major agreements. Fifth, we asked whether there were any meetings between stewards from the respondents' workplace and their counterparts in other parts of the organization. This question has often been treated in other surveys as referring to combine committees: in practice, however, the majority of such meetings appear to be at the initiative of the union or to involve full-time union officials. In any event, the existence of such meetings indicates a linkage with the wider union movement. Finally, we build up an indicator of what we call 'external integration': the extent to which the workplace organization is linked with the larger union.

Table 2.25 shows that company-based branches are common: this is particularly so in the public sector, except for the non-manual sample in Telecom, and in finance and the TGWU. The first reflects the single-employer nature of the unions; the TGWU pattern reflects a union policy of trying to integrate the workplace into the union and ensure that the branch maintains a certain degree of vitality. Company-based branches are least common in the (ex-)craft unions outside the public sector, reflecting their traditional strategy of controlling the local labour market for their trade.

Branch organization is not the only, or even the primary, link between the workplace and the larger union. We therefore asked

Table 2.25 Branch organization (percentage of establishments)

	Own employer	Mainly own employer	Mainly other employers
(a) Non-manual/public-sector group			
Finance	59	15	27
CPSA civil service	75	16	9
SCPS civil service	76	10	14
CPSA Telecom	42	56	3
POEU Telecom	62	38	—
(b) Production group			
Print	14	7	79
Chemicals	71	18	12
Food and drink	54	32	14
Engineering	10	16	74
(c) Maintenance group			
Chemicals	13	3	84
Food and drink	17	1	82
Engineering	16	5	79
Electrical engineering	11	15	74

about the role of the larger union in negotiations concerning the establishment. Perhaps the most surprising finding in table 2.26, in view of recent arguments concerning workplace isolationism, is the importance attached to the larger union by respondents. In most of the samples, at least three-quarters of the respondents rate the union as very or fairly important. Moreover, the variations between the samples are relatively small. It might have been expected, for example, that the larger union would be seen as more important in craft, public-sector and non-manual unions. But the data provide remarkably little support for this view.

However, it is possible that the criteria employed by respondents in replying to this question vary considerably. The constraints of a postal questionnaire and the nature of our primary interest precluded us from going into this question further. However, other questions do help to throw further light on this matter.

One possibility is that the larger union is significant as a source of identity and legitimacy. This is indicated strikingly in our insurance case study. Until the late 1970s, a staff association had existed, but a merger with another company (where a different form of collective

Table 2.26 Role of larger union

	Percentage of establishment where larger union role is:			
	Very important	Fairly important	Not very important	Un-important
(a) Non-manual/public-sector group				
Finance	46	34	20	—
CPSA civil service	41	41	14	4
SCPS civil service	29	31	29	10
CPSA Telecom	33	53	14	—
POEU Telecom	40	41	18	1
(b) Production group				
Print	34	36	24	6
Chemicals	45	33	18	4
Food and drink	35	54	11	—
Engineering	39	43	12	6
(c) Maintenance group				
Chemicals	38	41	13	8
Food and drink	37	31	19	13
Engineering	39	28	26	7
Electrical engineering	43	27	18	12

organization existed) and financial and administrative pressures led to the merging of the staff association with BIFU. This move, stimulated by the beginnings of large-scale changes within the company, led to an expansion in the range of union activity and in the conception of the role of the union on the part of the membership. In addition, management began to change its approach to industrial relations in recognition of the involvement of a larger union. Important in these changes appeared to be the recognition on the part of all parties that association with a wider organization changed the situation considerably. For company activists, in particular, affiliation with a larger organization provided a legitimation for demanding a wider range of influence (see also Batstone *et al.*, 1977). That the larger union constitutes a source of legitimacy and, if necessary, of support is important, we would argue, in most workplace organizations; hence, trends towards company unionism are likely to be of limited significance. But the larger union may also have a more direct influence upon the activities of shop stewards at the workplace. Here our questions concerning actual influence over union policy and the ratification of agreements are relevant.

Table 2.30 shows respondents' models of the patterns of influence over workplace union policy. Generally speaking, the larger union is seen to have about the same amount of influence as the other groups identified. If we compare the ratings of the larger union and senior stewards (who tend to have the highest score), a slight pattern is discernible. The wider union is seen as more influential among three groups: the public sector, particularly in the case of Telecom; non-manual groups, for example finance; and craft organizations. The clearest examples of the last are printing and to a lesser extent the AUEW. But when we allow for the fact that the role of the union tends to be greater in larger establishments, its importance in the maintenance samples is also striking. In short, then, as the discussion in chapter 1 suggested, where the union is heterogeneous in terms of sector and occupation, its influence over workplace decisions is less.

The pattern is rather different when we turn to the question of the ratification of major agreements (table 2.27). In all the samples, only a minority state that the wider union is engaged in this process. However, those minorities are very substantial in some cases. In two craft unions – the POEU and the NGA – almost half the respondents say that the wider union ratifies agreements; this is also relatively common in the rest of the public sector and in finance. Such ratification is very rare among the manual private-sector samples, with one exception, which is, again, a craft union – the EETPU in chemicals. The level of bargaining as well as the nature of the union affect the role of the larger union in this respect.

The final aspect of the link between workplace union organization and the wider union which we investigated was whether stewards met other stewards working for the same employer. Table 2.28 shows that there are considerable variations in this respect. Such meetings are very common in the non-manual and public-sector samples; and in the POEU these meetings are often held at least monthly. But among the private-sector manual samples these meetings are less common. Meetings of stewards from different establishments are especially rare in multi-plant organizations in printing and the various engineering samples. In all the groups, however, inter-establishment meetings are more common where there are full-time shop stewards and where bargaining is more centralized.

In an attempt to summarize these findings and facilitate subsequent analysis, we constructed a further index, which we call external integration: this measures the closeness of the link between the workplace

Table 2.27 Ratification of major agreements (percentage of establishments)

	Any rati-fication	Ratification of agreements by:				
		Branch	Mass meeting	Ballot	Shop stewards	Larger union
(a) Non-manual/public-sector group						
Finance	100	7	2	71	17	24
CPSA civil service	99	36	27	42	2	28
SCPS civil service	100	23	22	31	4	39
CPSA Telecom	100	22	22	56	3	31
POEU Telecom	100	58	—	—	4	46
(b) Production group						
Print	98	15	17	38	4	48
Chemicals	98	53	29	26	12	7
Food and drink	100	26	40	40	20	10
Engineering	100	1	58	21	27	10
(c) Maintenance group						
Chemicals	98	3	48	18	21	30
Food and drink	100	4	54	28	20	6
Engineering	100	2	63	24	18	7
Electrical engineering	100	—	61	35	28	2

Table 2.28 Frequency of meetings of stewards from different establishments of the same employer

| | Percentage of establishments where meetings held: | | | |
	Monthly	Less often	Never	Only one establish-ment
(a) Non-manual/public-sector group				
Finance	12	72	15	1
CPSA civil service	17	63	19	1
SCPS civil service	9	52	38	1
CPSA Telecom	20	64	16	—
POEU Telecom	53	41	6	—
(b) Production group				
Print	6	21	61	12
Chemicals	8	32	57	3
Food and drink	8	43	41	9
Engineering	13	18	55	13
(c) Maintenance group				
Chemicals	8	39	37	16
Food and drink	9	34	51	6
Engineering	9	25	51	15
Electrical engineering	12	27	55	6

and larger union. The index gives a score of one point for each of the following: where the role of the wider union is said to be very important; where the larger union ratifies agreements; where the wider union is said to have a great deal of influence over workplace policy; and where stewards meet their counterparts from other parts of the employing organization. The index has then been adjusted to provide a maximum score of 10.

Table 2.29 shows the scores on the external integration index by sample. The highest scores are in the non-manual/public-sector group, which is characterized, in the main, by single-employer and single-industry unions and centralized bargaining. The single-industry NGA also scores high on the index, despite the fact that its concentration of members is low. With the exception of electrical engineering, the other craft and ex-craft unions also tend to score relatively high on the index. Again, this is especially worthy of note in view of the small numbers of electricians in many of the samples.

Table 2.29 External integration index (percentage of establishments)

	0/1	2/4	5/6	7+
(a) Non-manual/public-sector group				
Finance	5	37	39	20
CPSA civil service	6	38	38	18
SCPS civil service	9	43	24	23
CPSA Telecom	3	39	36	22
POEU Telecom	1	30	24	45
(b) Production group				
Print	29	30	24	17
Chemicals	27	43	23	7
Food and drink	35	43	16	6
Engineering	39	32	21	8
(c) Maintenance group				
Chemicals	30	36	23	11
Food and drink	29	38	26	8
Engineering	40	36	23	2
Electrical engineering	33	51	14	2

There is a weak relationship between the degree of external integration and union sophistication. Union organizations that are more sophisticated tend to have closer links with the larger union: in the non-manual, public-sector and the production groups, intra-union sophistication is important, whereas in the maintenance group inter-union sophistication plays the more important role. Size of establishment is not related to the degree of external integration. The most important factor in explaining variations in the degree of external integration is the level of bargaining. The more centralized bargaining is, the greater is external integration. In addition, the nature of the union is important: single-employer and single-industry unions tend to have closer links between the workplace and the larger union.

Patterns of Influence within the Workplace

The discussion of union bureaucracy has been closely linked to arguments concerning patterns of influence within trade unions: as was noted above, some writers have claimed that bureaucracy means oligarchy. In this section, we turn to a consideration of this question.

But in doing so, we will also consider the impact of other factors upon patterns of influence within unions. Some of these relate to the structure of the union itself: for example, it might be argued that although some form of 'primitive democracy' is possible where a union has small groups of members, this is impossible where the membership totals several thousand. Hence member influence is likely to be less and senior steward influence greater, the larger the number of members. Second, it might be expected that the influence of members within the establishment is lower where ties with the larger union are stronger (although the union's membership as a whole might still have considerable influence); member influence will vary between different union types. It would follow that where bargaining is more centralized, there is rather less scope for member influence over union policy relating to the workplace. Other factors are also relevant. It is conventionally argued that more skilled workers play a more active role in the union; conversly, women, part-time workers and non-manual groups tend to be less active and therefore, in effect, leave decisions to stewards and officials.

It is also necessary to consider two other factors which run throughout this study. The first is the effect of job loss upon the distribution of influence within the union at workplace level. It might be expected, for example, that where there have been large reductions in employment or membership, stewards can be less confident of winning concessions from management and of members being prepared to engage in industrial action. As a consequence, the influence of stewards declines and the role of the membership increases. However, the impact of changes in employment is likely to be mediated by the strategies of management: they may try to win the co-operation of the union and so build up the influence of union officials and key stewards. On the other hand, an aggressive approach on the part of the employer might lead to shifts in influence away from senior stewards in favour of both the larger union and the membership.

The preceding discussion, and the general debate concerning the impact of steward bureaucracy, operates on an implicit assumption that power within trade unions is zero-sum: that is, if group A has a lot of power, then group B can only have a little – it is not possible for both to have a great deal of power. Such assumptions may have some validity where the interests of different groups are fundamentally opposed. But such a picture does not fit the general run of trade unions. This argument should not, of course, be taken too far, but it does seem sensible to look at the power and influence of different groups, rather than simply to assume that if one group has power, another cannot. Furthermore, in the survey we were to a large extent dependent upon the assessment of respondents about the distribution of influence, although we did ask a number of more objective questions. The analysis of their replies indicates that they did not in the main espouse a zero-sum model of power and influence.

In seeking to identify patterns of influence – or, more strictly, respondents' models of those patterns – we asked a number of questions, several of which have been touched upon already. These concerned the question of who ratified major agreements; the influence which different groups had upon the behaviour of the union in the workplace; and, third, whether stewards led or followed the membership.

Respondents were asked whether major agreements were ratified by any of the following groups or bodies: branch meetings, mass meetings, ballots, meetings of shop stewards and the wider union. Table 2.27 shows, first, that in nearly every case somebody ratified agreements. The branch generally played a limited role in this respect, except in the POEU and the production chemicals sample. In addition, substantial minorities in the other public-sector samples and in food and drink said the branch ratified agreements. The branch tended to play an important role where it was based at the place of work. Mass meetings were most common in the manual private-sector samples, particularly where the branch did not ratify agreements. In a minority of white-collar public-sector samples, mass meetings were also used to put agreements to the membership. The alternative to the mass meeting and the branch – the ballot – is again widely used, particularly by non-manual groups. But it is also common in three other samples: print, production food and drink, and electrical engineering. All three of the methods so far discussed are widely used, and provide opportunities for all members to influence decisions. By comparison, ratification of agreements by shop stewards and by the larger union is rare. The shop stewards play the most active role in the private-sector samples except printing, whereas, as was noted in the preceding section, the larger union most frequently plays a role in the public-sector and non-manual group, and in printing and the maintenance chemicals sample.

The second question we asked respondents concerning patterns of influence was the following: 'Generally speaking, how much influence would you say each of the following have in deciding union policy as far as this establishment is concerned?' Respondents were asked to assess the influence of members, the wider union, senior shop stewards and other stewards on a four-point scale ranging from a great deal to none. Table 2.30 can be considered in two ways. The first is by looking at the degrees of influence attributed to different groups, the second by comparing the relative influence of different groups.

It can be seen that in most samples the membership is attributed at least 'a fair amount' of influence. Members are seen to have more influence in the manual than in the non-manual samples. Stewards other than senior stewards are generally said to have less influence than the membership; indeed, if we compare the scores for these two groups, there are only two samples where the stewards are rated as more influential, and then by only very small margins (the clerical telecommunications sample and electrical engineering). In the main, however, and particularly among manual groups, with the exception of engineering, the differences in scores are quite substantial. In the three engineering cases, the distinctive pattern is due to the greater influence of other stewards.

Senior shop stewards are generally seen as having more influence than other stewards, except in two of the maintenance samples. The influence gap is much greater in the public than in the private sector, reflecting the centralized pattern of bargaining. Similarly, senior stewards are seen as having more influence than members in the public sector, finance and in production and electrical engineering. In most of the private-sector manual groups, and particularly among the 'pure' maintenance samples, members are attributed considerably more influence than senior stewards. These patterns reflect variations in the assessments of both senior steward and member influence.

Finally, we can briefly look again at the influence attributed to the larger union; in general terms, in the private sector the wider union is seen to have less influence than any of the other groups considered (except in print, where centralized bargaining is common, and in the maintenance sample from chemicals). In the public sector, on the other hand, the impact of the wider union is typically rated as second only to that of the senior steward. In other words, where the union is of a single-employer or single-industry nature and, relatedly, where bargaining is centralized, the larger union and the senior steward are typically seen as having a good deal of influence. In other cases, the key groups tend to be the membership and the senior stewards.

This pattern is largely consistent with the findings of table 2.23 concerning the role which stewards play. In the public sector, the senior steward is often seen as playing the leading role. In production samples and in all the engineering samples, the steward collectivity is more likely to be seen as making decisions. In the non-engineering maintenance samples, individual stewards and workgroups are more often described as acting autonomously.

Table 2.30 Patterns of influence: (a) member influence; (b) larger union influence; (c) senior steward influence; (d) other stewards' influence (percentage of establishments)

	Member influence				Larger union influence				Senior steward influence				Other stewards' influence			
	Great deal	Fair amount	Not much	None	Great deal	Fair amount	Not much	None	Great deal	Fair amount	Not much	None	Great deal	Fair amount	Not much	None
(a) Non-manual/public-sector group																
Finance	35	33	30	2	31	36	31	2	42	40	10	8	25	49	13	14
CPSA civil service	31	40	27	2	27	47	23	4	48	47	5	1	11	54	26	9
SCPS civil service	13	40	44	3	41	37	21	2	41	48	10	1	10	43	31	16
CPSA Telecom	28	39	33	—	36	53	11	—	61	36	3	—	28	47	22	3
POEU Telecom	47	31	21	1	49	34	15	2	52	45	3	—	12	51	26	12
(b) Production group																
Print	49	27	17	7	29	40	25	6	33	55	9	2	21	47	21	12
Chemicals	59	27	13	2	17	40	31	13	54	33	11	2	30	53	10	6
Food and drink	63	29	8	—	13	36	39	13	48	42	7	2	35	53	8	5
Engineering	53	31	15	1	21	39	30	10	50	46	3	1	29	61	5	5
(c) Maintenance group																
Chemicals	61	21	16	2	19	38	36	8	16	46	23	14	18	53	18	12
Food and drink	53	24	17	6	22	19	45	15	22	41	23	14	15	41	29	16
Engineering	36	53	5	7	7	48	35	11	40	33	14	12	27	53	14	7
Electrical engineering	44	32	20	4	5	48	38	10	53	31	13	2	31	58	9	2

In addition, we asked respondents the following question: 'Which of the following best describes the behaviour of the union organization in this establishment in relation to the membership: it acts as the leader of the membership, stirring them to action or calming them down as the occasion requires; *or*, it simply tries to carry out the expressed wishes of members?' Table 2.31 shows a strikingly simple pattern. In all the non-manual and public-sector samples, the majority of respondents describe the stewards as adopting a leadership role, whereas this view is expressed in only a minority of cases in the private-sector manual samples. Here substantial majorities state that the stewards simply do as the members wish.

In order to facilitate discussion, we have created two indices to summarize these findings. The first seeks to measure the degree of centralization within the union organization at the workplace. This index gives a score of 1 for each of the following: where senior steward influence is rated as greater than that of both members and other stewards; where the senior steward is said to have a great deal of influence; and where stewards are said to lead rather than follow members. The second index concerns the level of member influence, and again has a maximum score of 3. In this case, one point is given

Table 2.31 Steward leadership

	Percentage of establishments where:	
	Stewards lead members	Stewards follow members
(a) Non-manual/public-sector group		
Finance	65	35
CPSA civil service	72	28
SCPS civil service	55	45
CPSA Telecom	67	33
POEU Telecom	54	46
(b) Production group		
Print	42	58
Chemicals	48	52
Food and drink	34	66
Engineering	41	59
(c) Maintenance group		
Chemicals	28	72
Food and drink	35	65
Engineering	39	61
Electrical engineering	37	63

for each of the following: where members ratify agreements in some way; where they are said to have a great deal of influence; and where stewards follow members' wishes. Clearly, in part this measure is the inverse of the centralization measure: but the one is not the total obverse of the other.

Table 2.32 shows the average sample scores on these two measures. Centralization is marked in the public sector and is often particularly low in the maintenance samples. The average member-influence scores are the reverse of this pattern, although it is worth noting that the scores for member influence tend to be higher than those for centralization. The crucial question, however, is how we explain differences in the scores, and, in particular, how they relate to the two measures of union sophistication and the degree of external integration.

We can usefully look at the impact of the three indicators of union organization in turn. The inter-union measure of sophistication is positively associated with centralization in all three groups, although the relationship is not very strong in the non-manual/public-sector group. On the other hand, the relationship between sophistication and member influence is either very weak or does not operate consistently in the expected direction: that is to say, it is not the case that as sophistication of inter-union organization increases, there is a steady decline in member influence. When we turn to intra-union sophistication, it is only in the case of the production unions that there is a strong relationship with centralization: that is, centralization rises with sophistication. There is no relationship in any of the groups between the degree of intra-union sophistication and the level of member influence. Finally, external integration is not significantly related to the degree of centralization in any of the groups; there is, however, a weak relationship between closer ties with the larger union and lower member influence in the case of the non-manual/public-sector group. But this pattern is not found in the manual production samples.

Three other factors play a small role in explaining patterns of influence in workplace union organizations. The first of these is changes in employment: in the private sector, member influence is marginally greater where job losses have been substantial; in the production samples, centralization also tends to be less where employment has fallen dramatically. Second, in the public sector a tough approach on the part of management reduces the degree of centralization within the union, but with no corresponding increase in member influence. In the manual production group, a tougher approach on the part of management is associated with greater member influence. Third, in the production group, establishment-level bargaining is related to greater

Table 2.32 (a) Centralization index; (b) member-influence index (percentage of establishments)

	Centralization index				Member-influence index			
	0	1	2	3	0	1	2	3
(a) Non-manual/public-sector group								
Finance	37	39	7	17	10	54	22	15
CPSA civil service	19	35	22	25	12	48	34	6
SCPS civil service	25	34	18	22	21	42	34	2
CPSA Telecom	11	39	25	25	19	39	33	8
POEU Telecom	21	30	29	21	21	38	32	9
(b) Production group								
Print	37	42	16	6	14	36	33	18
Chemicals	38	31	22	9	4	30	40	26
Food and drink	49	26	20	6	4	26	37	33
Engineering	39	33	17	11	8	27	41	25
(c) Maintenance group								
Chemicals	77	16	3	5	11	27	33	30
Food and drink	65	25	6	4	6	21	46	26
Engineering	55	15	18	13	3	37	37	23
Electrical engineering	39	33	12	16	2	33	33	31

member influence and a lower degree of centralization. However, these factors play a very small role compared to formal union structure.

In sum, then, there are some relationships between the structural characteristics of union organization and patterns of assessed influence within the union at the workplace. But, in the main, these relationships are neither as strong nor as significant as one might expect from a good deal of the literature.

Conclusions

In this chapter, we have considered the nature of the establishments from which our respondents come and key features of union organization. It was found that in the manual private-sector samples there have been substantial job losses over the last five years, and these have been concentrated in larger establishments: those where union organization has been strongest. However, despite this and the general level of unemployment, there are few signs that employers have developed a concerted attack upon trade union organization. It is certainly the case that many have become less supportive of trade unions in a number of respects; but the evidence indicates that the absolute level of support has not changed substantially. Trends over the last five years have been more hostile to trade unions in the public sector, reflecting the policies of the government. In the private sector, management has adopted a somewhat tougher approach towards the unions where levels of business activity have fallen and where union organization is stronger. But this has not been on a very significant scale so that absolute levels of support in these establishments generally remain higher than in other workplaces.

In part as a result of this, there appears to have been little change in the formal structure of trade unions at the place of work. Union density remains high, as does the coverage of the closed shop; the absolute numbers of stewards, senior stewards and full-time stewards have fallen, but less fast than employment, with the result that in formal terms union organization is often stronger now for any given size of establishment than it was five years ago. Hence the measures of internal union organization which were developed – intra-union and inter-union sophistication – are generally more strongly related to the size of union membership in 1979 than in 1984. Moreover, the impact of job loss and management strategy upon the degree of sophistication appears to be very small.

It was also found that the links between workplace union organization and the larger union are generally relatively strong; in part, the strength of this relationship varies with the degree of sophistication. But more important are the nature of the larger union – whether it is a single-employer or single-industry union and, to some degree, its degree of occupational heterogeneity – and the level at which bargaining occurs.

Finally, in this chapter we have looked briefly at patterns of influence within the union at the workplace. This is partly related to the degree of organizational sophistication; in some cases job loss and the nature of management policy also play a small role.

It is useful, in concluding this chapter, to highlight a theme that was stressed in the introduction to this study: the relationship between the nature of the larger union and its formal structure within the workplace. We can divide the unions in the survey into three types, concerning the range of employers and industries which they cover. The public-sector unions can all be classified as single-employer unions, in that their membership is confined – or was at the time of the survey – to the public sector. Two other unions – BIFU and the NGA – cover specific industries. The other unions in the survey cover a wide range of industries and employers. As we move from single-employer to single-industry to multi-industry unions, we find that the degree of external integration declines. Moreover, for any given size of membership, internal union organization tends to be more sophisticated the more the union is confined to a particular sector or employer.

We also find the same pattern when we consider the occupational homogeneity of unions: that is, once size of membership is controlled for, the craft and ex-craft unions tend to have somewhat stronger links with the larger union and are more sophisticated internally. In contrast, multi-industry, multi-occupation unions have lower levels of external integration, but high levels of sophistication within the workplace: this reflects the large numbers of members which they typically have within any one workplace in the survey.

More generally, the size of the union membership is an important factor affecting the degree of sophistication. Another factor shaping union organization, and the degree of external integration in particular, is the level at which bargaining formally occurs. However, there is a relationship, as will be seen in the next chapter, between the nature of the union and the level at which bargaining occurs. In single-employer and single-industry unions, bargaining tends to be more centralized. It might therefore be argued that the nature of the union is less important than the bargaining level. However, it seems more useful to think of the relationship between bargaining level and union structure in a more complex way: unions that deal with a single employer or industry are more likely to want to bargain more centrally.

At the same time, an employer who seeks to bargain centrally may often be more keen to shape the nature of the unions with which it deals: this was certainly the case historically in the parts of the public sector covered by this study. In effect, other employers may be seen as seeking to develop a single-employer union organization by giving support to inter-union co-operation (as well as by bargaining at workplace or company level).

3 Labour Relations and Trade Union Influence

The preceding chapter has described the structure of union organization in the establishments covered by the survey and the general context within which the unions operate. In this chapter, we move on to consider the types of labour relations policies that management pursues, and how these relate to patterns of bargaining and trade union influence. This discussion cannot be seen as exhaustive: as we are only too fully aware, there are significant constraints upon the extent to which issues can be investigated through a postal questionnaire. Furthermore, since one aim of this chapter is to provide a backdrop to the analysis of the effects of technical change, no reference to relationships between new technology and the various factors that form the subject of this chapter are discussed here: they are taken up in subsequent chapters.

Although there has been a great deal of interest in management strategy towards labour, the characterization of strategies has been far from adequate. Indeed, there appears to be a growing consensus that simple categorizations are empirically invalid (e.g. Deaton, 1985). Accordingly, in this chapter we will start by looking at different elements of management strategy and then go on to see how far they are interrelated. More specifically, we will consider the following features of management's approach towards labour; first, the extent to which management has shifted the way in which it meets its labour requirements over the last five years. Here we will be concerned with the extent to which employers have made increasing resort to different types of secondary labour: that is, labour that is treated less favourably than key groups within the more permanent labour force. It has been widely argued, for example, that British employers are seeking to reduce their commitments to, and dependence upon, a primary labour force as a result of the recession. This can be variously attributed to the need to increase efficiency and reduce costs or to an attempt to weaken the power of the primary labour force. Second, we will consider the extent to which employers have attempted to adopt an individualistic strategy towards workers. Again, it has been widely claimed that employers are seeking to bypass the union and develop a more individualistic relationship with employees in an attempt to win their support for management strategies and an intensification of effort. Third, we will look at the nature of payment systems. In the last decade or so, there has been a good deal of discussion of the effects of different sorts of payment system. One aspect relevant to this chapter is whether employers have shifted away from individual incentive payments, which foster a calculative approach to the wage–effort bargain, and towards collective systems of payment linked to more general performance indicators. Such moves would indicate an attempt to use the payment system to foster employee identification with corporate goals and performance. This type of approach might be more common where companies have suffered falls in output and employment over recent years. Fourth, we consider the extent to which employers make use of scientific management techniques. These have assumed significance in a great deal of the labour process and industrial relations literature. We will seek to assess how far the recession has affected their application. Fifth, the shift in the balance of power associated with high unemployment and workforce reductions might induce employers to adopt a simple and direct strategy of intensifying effort levels and achieving large-scale changes in the way in which work is done. We will consider each of these aspects of management's labour relations strategy in turn, and then see how far they are related to each other and to the approach which management adopts towards the unions. We then go on to look at the pattern of bargaining in the workplace and the extent to which these different strategies have affected the role that the union plays.

Trends in the Use of Secondary Labour

We asked respondents whether, over the last five years, management had made more or less use of the following types of labour input: part-time labour, subcontract labour, casual labour, contracting work out, overtime and shiftworking. The question is very crude and simple: most obviously, we do not know the exact importance of these different types of labour. It is possible, for example, that an employer has reduced his or her dependence upon most types of secondary labour, but has increased the use of one or two types dramatically. We cannot tell from our data how often this is so. Similarly, it is possible that our respondents are unaware of changes in the use of different kinds of labour – for example, where this has been done 'behind the backs' of stewards. Hence the findings have to be treated with a good deal of caution. However, we felt it was worth including this crude question, given the widespread discussion of this topic and the rarity with which any hard evidence is put forward. The length constraints of a postal questionnaire and the nature of our primary purposes precluded any more detailed questions.

As has been noted elsewhere (Batstone, 1984a), one of the ironies of the recent discussion of employer labour-market strategy is that it flies in the face of traditional dual labour-market theory. This argues that employers use secondary labour to give them flexibility. that is, they will use it in boom periods and will not employ it when markets are slack. The current discussion, however, reverses this argument. It is claimed that in the recession employers have made more, rather than less, use of secondary labour. Most writers appear to demonstrate little awareness of this contradiction. The arguments can, however, be made compatible quite simply. It is plausible that the depth of the recession has led employers to rethink their definition of the 'normal' level of output and/or to seek greater flexibility more generally. Hence, for example, if they believe that the normal level of output is likely to be lower in the future than it was in the past, then it is logical for them to reduce the size of the primary labour input and, if output is currently above the new 'norm', to make greater use of secondary labour. But in fact there are likely to be considerable variations between employers in this respect. They will vary because of the nature of the labour process itself; because of differences in the actual and predicted state of demand; and because they are likely to be at different stages in the process of adjusting the balance between different types of labour. The first stage of adjusting to a fall in demand is likely to be a reduction rather than an increase in secondary labour. In addition, it is possible to meet any demand above the norm by extending the hours of work of primary workers: notably by resort to overtime or shiftworking. This is the reason for including these two types of labour input in the questionnaire.

Table 3.1 shows how employers have changed their use of different types of labour over the last five years. The patterns vary between samples and the different types of labour. In finance, for example, there have been relatively few 'net' changes, except on two counts: a much more widespread use of part-time labour and of overtime. In other words, in this case employers have sought to adjust their labour input both through primary and secondary labour. In the civil service, greater resort to most of the types of labour distinguished has been made in the last five years, with the exception of shifts. The most marked increases are in part-time and casual labour, although in the SCPS sample subcontract labour and contracting work out are also common. In Telecom, there has been much greater use of overtime and, to some degree, of contracting work out. Casual labour is more widely used in non-manual areas, whereas subcontract labour has become more important on the engineering side. It should be noted, however, that part-time workers may be treated as primary rather than secondary labour.

In printing, more work has been contracted out and, to a lesser extent, shiftworking has increased. In the other manufacturing samples, there has generally been little change in the use of casual or part-time labour, but there has been widespread resort to more over-time and shiftworking. There have also been increases in sub-contracting of both work and labour. This is especially true in chemicals and on the maintenance side in food and drink. In other words, employers in manufacturing have typically increased labour input through greater or more intensive use of their primary labour force rather than widespread resort to secondary labour. In order to tap the latter, they have sought the services of other employers. In contrast, employers of non-manual labour have been much more prepared directly to employ secondary labour.

The preceding discussion has been concerned with 'net' trends. In fact we find considerable variations within the various samples. It is conceivable that these different movements reflect a shift towards common levels of dependence upon particular types of secondary labour in different industries. Our data are not of a kind to test this possibility, but it does seem rather unlikely. However, it should be noted that if the use of secondary labour remains constant while the number of primary workers is reduced, then – both at the level of the economy as a whole and within individual establishments – secondary labour will account for a growing proportion of total employment. To the extent that some employers make use of more secondary labour – and this outweighs any reductions by other employers in its use – then, of course, it increases in importance in absolute terms. It is therefore possible that secondary labour assumes greater importance both in absolute and relative terms, even if only a minority of employers are making greater resort to such types of employment.

In none of the groups of samples are there significant relationships between the trends in the use of secondary labour and changes either in total employment or in the membership of the respondent's union. However, there are some relationships between trends in the use of

Table 3.1 Changes in the use of different types of labour input over the period 1979–84: (a) part-time labour; (b) subcontract labour; (c) casual labour; (d) contracting work out; (e) overtime; (f) shifts (percentage of establishments)

	Part-time labour			Subcontract labour			Casual labour:		
	Increase	No change	De-crease	Increase	No change	De-crease	Increase	No change	De-crease
(a) Non-manual/public-sector group									
Finance	52	22	26	14	72	14	9	75	16
CPSA civil service	28	61	11	10	84	6	45	26	29
SCPS civil service	32	63	5	26	73	1	40	52	8
CPSA Telecom	14	50	36	8	78	14	50	31	19
POEU Telecom	5	90	5	27	66	7	3	94	3
(b) Production group									
Print	13	72	15	11	80	9	12	73	15
Chemicals	19	55	26	41	50	9	15	69	16
Food and drink	24	60	16	20	64	16	38	46	16
Engineering	16	53	31	28	53	19	20	63	17
(c) Maintenance group									
Chemicals	38	41	21	53	36	13	15	68	17
Food and drink	30	32	38	60	28	12	24	53	23
Engineering	18	63	19	40	41	19	10	75	15
Electrical engineering	10	52	38	26	48	26	12	56	32

	Contracting work out			Overtime			Shifts		
	Increase	No change	De-crease	Increase	No change	De-crease	Increase	No change	De-crease
(a) Non-manual/public-sector group									
Finance	11	73	16	58	21	21	14	79	7
CPSA civil service	22	73	5	37	37	26	3	88	9
SCPS civil service	37	62	1	31	55	14	3	92	5
CPSA Telecom	24	64	12	64	28	8	17	72	11
POEU Telecom	37	48	15	73	14	13	10	78	12
(b) Production group									
Print	33	56	11	38	28	34	23	68	9
Chemicals	42	45	13	50	28	22	22	62	16
Food and drink	28	50	22	50	20	30	32	60	8
Engineering	36	46	18	38	29	33	31	50	19
(c) Maintenance group									
Chemicals	61	28	11	41	28	31	15	60	25
Food and drink	66	25	9	44	25	31	37	44	19
Engineering	34	51	15	37	27	36	36	46	18
Electrical engineering	36	42	22	42	30	28	36	38	26

secondary labour and trends in the hours worked by primary workers. For example, in two of the three groups, overtime has increased where more casual labour has been used. These patterns suggest that generally employers may be using secondary labour as a supplement to their existing/remaining labour force rather than as a direct substitute for it. In other words, it seems possible – and we can put it no more confidently – that employers typically resort to secondary labour and the extension of the hours of primary labour to meet increases in demand which they fear may not be permanent. In three of our four case studies there were examples of this: in the chemical plant, for example, manning had been reduced several years ago when demand had fallen. Subsequently demand had unexpectedly increased, but, it was thought, only temporarily – accordingly the company recruited temporary labour to meet production requirements. Similarly, in the engineering plant a large and unusual job had to be undertaken – temporary workers were employed for a short period to undertake this work (on the other hand, contracting work out was reduced with the introduction of the CNC machines). In the insurance company, temporary labour was also employed for a period to permit the continuation of normal working levels when certain departments were being transferred from an old building to a new location (although, in addition, the catering in the new offices was subcontracted).

There are weak relationships between trends in the use of different kinds of secondary labour: for example, between casual labour and part-time labour. However, this may in large part be misleading. In the examples cited, it may be that the casual labour tends to be part-time. Such relationships may also be due to the fact that respondents did not recognize the distinctions we were trying to make; this may be an important explanation of the close relationship found between trends in the use of subcontracting and contracting work out. But even with these associations, we find that overall there are few cases where trends in the use of different kinds of secondary labour are all in the same direction. The strongest trends of this kind, such as they are, are found in the civil service, in chemicals and in food and drink (particularly for the maintenance samples; this, however, may reflect disagreements between management and union concerning the relaxation of craft demarcations or other conditions – this, for example, was the case in our brewing case study). The strongest overall trend towards reducing the use of various kinds of secondary labour is reported in the two Telecom samples and in electrical engineering.

More detailed analyses indicate that the use of secondary labour varies within the different groups of samples. In the public sector it is used more widely in strongly organized establishments, where local management has little autonomy; it may even be the case that (potential) jobs of union members have been lost as use is made of secondary labour. Among the production samples, secondary labour is used more widely where the discretion of local management has fallen over the last five years; it has increased less where union organization is more sophisticated. In the maintenance group, we again find that the sophistication of union organization affects trends in the use of secondary labour. In the public sector and in the production group, then, we find that more centralized management structures or trends in this direction are associated with greater use of secondary labour. However, although union sophistication appears to check this sort of strategy on the part of management in the private sector, it is in the areas of strongest union organization that secondary labour has become more important in the public sector. Except in the latter, however, these relationships are fairly weak – this is possibly a reflection of the crudity of our measures.

Inidividualistic Labour Strategies

A second theme, which has been widely discussed in the last few years, concerns attempts by employers to bypass trade unions by introducing techniques that, it is claimed, foster a direct relationship between the worker and management. In the management literature, these are often seen as methods that can improve productivity and efficiency both directly and indirectly: directly by permitting workers to take greater initiative, and indirectly by increasing the legitimacy of management and management action in the eyes of the workforce. In the late 1970s, two forms of this approach were widely introduced. These were, first, a number of techniques designed to permit workers a greater variety in their work and even some increase in autonomy: hence we saw some companies experimenting with job enrichment or enlargement and with semi-autonomous workgroups. Second, many more companies began to introduce joint consultative committees, although generally these were union-based. More recently, however – as indicated by a good deal of literature coming from the CBI – employers have shown greater interest in techniques that are aimed at 'involvement' rather than 'participation'. Important among these have been briefing groups and quality circles. Unlike semi-autonomous workgroups, neither of these permits workers to apply their own ideas directly to the work process (for a fuller discussion of these developments in Britain, see Batstone, 1986).

In the survey, we asked respondents whether the following techniques currently existed, and whether they had done so five years earlier: quality circles, briefing groups, autonomous workgroups, union-based consultation and non-union-based consultation. Table 3.2 shows responents' answers. The first point to note is that union-based systems of consultation were, and continue to be, the most widely used of the participative techniques investigated. Far from declining in use, they have been more widely introduced in the last five years. In contrast, non-union-based consultation was relatively rare in 1979 and is still not very common. In only two samples has it been more widely introduced than union-based consultation in the last five years, and in both cases the difference is very small. In brief, then, union-based consultation is four or more times as common as non-union-based systems, and, far from showing a declining popularity, its usage has increased far more than that of non-union-based consultation.

If we turn to more direct participative techniques, we find that autonomous workgroups are the least widely used and also show the least increase over the last five years. There appears to be no distinctive pattern as far as the existence of these groups or their recent intro-duction are concerned, other than their relative popularity in the POEU sample. Indeed, it is in this sample that all of the direct participation techniques are most common and have seen the greatest increase over the last five years. This reflects a fairly long-standing commitment on the part of Telecom management to adopt a labour relations philosophy that is deemed to be more consistent with a strong orientation to the market (see Batstone et al., 1984) – a strategy that had probably been encouraged by the movement towards privatization at the time of the survey. The result is that Telecom outdoes the practice of companies that are already privately owned. The contrast between Telecom and the other public-sector samples is also striking: in the civil service, the adoption of participative techniques is very limited.

In the private sector, participative techniques are most common in the finance sample, where they have increased dramatically in the last five years. Within manufacturing, quality circles are relatively popular in the engineering samples, where skill levels tend to be higher, whereas briefing groups find more favour in chemicals and food and drink. The printing employers seem to be as unconvinced of the advantages of these techniques as the civil service.

Direct participation is more common in larger establishments and where the proportion of women is higher. Briefing groups are also associated with the existence of personnel specialists. There is no systematic relationship between the use of these techniques and the scale of job loss.

Table 3.2 Individualistic labour strategies in 1984 and 1979: (a) quality circles; (b) briefing groups; (c) autonomous workgroups; (d) union-based consultation; (e) non-union-based consultation (percentage of establishments)

	Quality circles		Briefing groups		Autonomous workgroups		Union-based consultation		Non-union consultation	
	1984	1979	1984	1979	1984	1979	1984	1979	1984	979
(a) Non-manual/public-sector group										
Finance	24	7	41	17	9	9	81	64	9	7
CPSA civil service	6	3	23	13	8	6	93	81	11	10
SCPS civil service	3	1	9	7	5	2	83	74	5	4
CPSA Telecom	12	3	23	9	11	3	91	85	9	—
POEU Telecom	34	4	60	15	23	10	84	83	4	2
(b) Production group										
Print	6	5	21	11	2	1	69	56	6	8
Chemicals	13	9	33	18	10	5	79	70	11	7
Food and drink	6	6	29	16	6	6	71	63	8	8
Engineering	23	13	23	12	5	5	75	74	6	7
(c) Maintenance group										
Chemicals	7	2	32	15	5	7	81	63	9	17
Food and drink	15	12	41	20	11	3	65	60	15	13
Engineering	25	13	21	8	5	7	54	53	5	3
Electrical engineering	29	10	27	10	8	2	82	78	16	10

In all the sample groups, the use of the three direct, individualistic techniques – that is, autonomous workgroups, quality circles and briefing groups – are related: that is, where one technique is used, then the others are also likely to be used. This may, however, reflect problems of nomenclature, with the result that respondents are referring to the same, sole technique (which is possibly called something different in their companies) when they reply in the affirmative to each of the questions. But it is also possible that some employers are prone to experiment with the latest trends in involvement techniques and hence multiply the various methods they employ (this, for example, was the case in our engineering study).

In none of the groups of samples, however, was the use of these techniques associated with non-union-based consultative systems; indeed the few relationships which were found with systems of consultation were with union-based schemes. Furthermore, these individualistic techniques are more widely used the more sophisticated union organization is. This suggests – particularly given the stability of union sophistication – that these techniques have done little to weaken the position of the unions (cf. Batstone, 1984b). Finally, in the private sector, these techniques have been more widely adopted where the scale of job loss has been smaller rather than larger.

Payment Systems

Pay is probably the primary means of control at the disposal of an employer, and the precise type of payment system is important for that very reason. Individual incentives embody a model of the economic person, rationally calculating how much effort he or she should put in and guided by the priority of the size of the pay packet. Individual piece-work, however, shifts a great deal of control of work effort to the individual worker, and defines the link between worker and employer in a calculative manner. At the other extreme, the payment system can be used as a means of fostering worker identification with the employer. This is the rationale underlying the use of plant or company-wide bonuses; to a lesser degree, such a strategy may underlie group-based incentive schemes. But particularly in the former case there can be little relationship between the effort the worker puts in and the level of rewards he or she receives. With bonuses, the worker's income depends upon the performance of the unit as a whole: the aim, therefore, is to encourage co-operation and a realization on the part of the worker that his/her future is bound up with that of the employing unit. Although it is still an incentive, its rationale is therefore dramatically different to that of individual piece-work payment.

Table 3.3 shows that individual incentives are rare in the vast majority of samples; only in finance, where such incentives are often of a more indirect nature (in the form of merit-based increments) and hence do not embody simple models of the economic individual, are they common. Individual incentives are virtually unknown in the public sector, but they are relatively common in the engineering samples, where piece-work has a long tradition. Individual incentives have been introduced a little more widely in the last five years in finance and in electrical engineering. The general picture, however, is that there are few signs of any dramatic changes in the use of individual incentives and, such as there are, they indicate a declining popularity. The same picture is found in the case of group incentive schemes, although the trends vary considerably between the samples. In the public sector, incentives of this kind are again virtually unknown, but they are relatively common in finance, printing and engineering. In chemicals, and food and drink, there are marked differences between the main-tenance and production samples; these are largely attributable to the

Table 3.3 Payment systems: (a) individual payment by results; (b) group payment by results; (c) bonuses

	Individual PBR (%)		Group PBR (%)		Bonuses (%)	
	1984	1979	1984	1979	1984	1979
(a) Non-manual/public-sector group						
Finance	56	49	21	17	58	33
CPSA civil service	3	3	5	2	19	5
SCPS civil service	1	1	1	—	9	3
CPSA Telecom	9	6	—	3	3	6
POEU Telecom	1	—	—	2	1	1
(b) Production group						
Print	10	17	27	25	23	31
Chemicals	4	9	25	27	31	31
Food and drink	16	18	10	16	53	35
Engineering	30	38	29	33	45	34
(c) Maintenance group						
Chemicals	2	2	8	5	52	44
Food and drink	3	5	23	19	48	33
Engineering	20	30	28	23	41	44
Electrical engineering	25	20	22	25	43	49

fact that we asked respondents about the payment systems of their own members. But what is intriguing is that, in chemicals, group incentives are more common among production than among maintenance groups, whereas the reverse is the case in food and drink.

Company or plant bonuses are more common than the other two types of payment system investigated, although they are very rare in the public sector. They are most common in finance, food and drink, and the various engineering samples. These types of bonus are the area of greatest change in payment systems over the last five years: they have become more common, particularly in finance and food and drink.

It was suggested above that these different forms of incentive indicated quite different philosophies on the part of management. To the extent that this is the case, we would expect that employers would seek to ensure that a dominant 'message' was embodied in the payment system. But, in fact, this is often not the case: hence, for example, the different types of payment system are often to be found in the same plant or office. This is particularly true in the finance sample, although here individual incentive payments include merit awards. But it is also the case that plant bonuses are sometimes paid along with individual piece-work. Other evidence indicates that such confusion of British payment systems is one of their most noticeable characteristics, reflecting the ad hoc reaction of employers to different short-term pressures, including incomes policies (White, 1981).

Overall, it seems that very few employers have totally committed themselves to using the payment system as a means either of fostering company loyalty or highlighting the link between effort and pay for the individual in the short term. Those industries where the payment system is most widely used to foster company identity are finance, food and drink, and the various engineering groups. This approach is least common in the public sector. There are few systematic relationships between such an approach and other factors across all the samples, even within the private sector. There are no relationships between the scale of job loss or management's approach to the unions and the extent to which the payment system is used as a means of fostering employee identification with the employer. Nevertheless, local management discretion tends to be lower where these techniques are employed.

Scientific Management

Closely related to systems of pay is the use of techniques designed to measure work and responsibilities. More generally, it has often been argued that the use of so-called scientific management techniques is an important method of management control over labour. In the survey we could not investigate these issues in detail, but we did ask about the use of two common techniques – work study and job evaluation. Table 3.4 shows that work study is most widely used in finance and engineering; it is particularly rare in non-manual areas in telecommunications, in printing and among maintenance workers in chemicals. Again, trends in the use of work study vary between samples; its use has declined in telecommunications for clerical grades, but has increased for engineers. It has also fallen in popularity in printing, but has been more widely adopted in electrical engineering and the civil service. However, only in finance does a majority of respondents say that work study is used. Job evaluation, like work study, is widely employed in finance; but it is also common, according to respondents, in the civil service and for production workers in chemicals, and food and drink. This technique has shown a somewhat greater growth in popularity than work study over the last five years – except in the case of maintenance groups in chemicals, where its use has actually fallen.

Table 3.4 Scientific management: (a) work study; (b) job evaluation

	Work study (%)		Job evaluation (%)	
	1984	1979	1984	1979
(a) Non-manual/public-sector group				
Finance	61	56	81	76
CPSA civil service	35	24	50	38
SCPS civil service	33	30	45	38
CPSA Telecom	14	20	26	26
POEU Telecom	32	26	29	16
(b) Production group				
Print	10	18	11	5
Chemicals	27	23	43	37
Food and drink	29	27	49	47
Engineering	41	42	29	21
(c) Maintenance group				
Chemicals	13	14	23	29
Food and drink	24	23	33	31
Engineering	28	31	21	21
Electrical engineering	49	39	35	35

In all of the sample groups, the use of work study and of job evaluation are interrelated: where one is used, so also tends to be the other. Such commitment to scientific management is most common in larger workplaces in the private sector. There is no systematic relationship between the use of such techniques and job loss or the nature of management's approach to the unions. In large part due to the size effect, however, scientific management is more common in the private sector where union organization is more sophisticated.

Intensification of Work

The final aspect of management strategy which we discuss in this chapter is a simple intensification of work. It might be expected, for example, that, given the state of the labour market, and particularly where large number of jobs have been lost, employers would be able to require higher levels of effort from workers.

Certainly there has been a good deal of change in working practices over the last five years. For example, we asked respondents whether they had negotiated any changes in working practices over this period. Nearly two-thirds said they had; the proportion varied from a peak of four-fifths in the chemicals production sample to 44 per cent in finance. However, it is possible that some changes in working practices have been introduced without negotiation, particularly perhaps in finance. Thus there have been substantial changes in the past five years. It should be remembered, however, that the reorganization of working methods has been a constant feature of the industrial scene for well over two decades. In other words, it is not entirely clear that there has been an increase in such changes as unemployment has increased.

Moreover, it is possible that changes in working practices do not lead to an intensification of effort: management aims may be frustrated, or the changes may be of a technical kind with no implications for the exertion of the workforce. We therefore asked respondents a more direct question about work intensification: 'Over the last five years, have effort levels here: increased to very high levels; increased, but still at reasonable levels; not changed much; fallen?' Table 3.5 shows that in every sample a majority of respondents say that effort levels have risen. No change, or a reduction of effort, are most common in private-sector craft areas – printing, maintenance and production engineering. At the other extreme, a substantial number of respondents state that effort levels have risen to very high levels. The largest numbers – just under a third – stating this are in the non-manual and

Table 3.5 Changes in effort levels, 1979–84 (percentage of establishments)

	Increase, very high levels	Increase, reasonable levels	Little change	Fall
(a) Non-manual/public-sector group				
Finance	31	46	18	5
CPSA civil service	28	45	24	3
SCPS civil service	29	48	20	3
CPSA Telecom	33	56	6	6
POEU Telecom	32	58	8	2
(b) Production group				
Print	19	51	25	5
Chemicals	25	56	16	3
Food and drink	20	52	24	4
Engineering	16	51	22	11
(c) Maintenance group				
Chemicals	8	52	24	16
Food and drink	20	49	20	10
Engineering	21	39	31	8
Electrical engineering	18	49	18	14

public-sector samples. But even in the other samples, with the exception of maintenance groups in chemicals, about a fifth of respondents state that there has been such an intensification of work. However, effort intensification is not related to the scale of job loss in any of the groups of samples. The one contextual factor which does consistently appear is changes in output over the last five years: but it is not the case that effort rises in the face of declining output. Rather, effort levels have increased, where output levels have risen. This suggests two possible explanations: first, that management have been able to avoid recruiting extra workers, even when output increases. The other possibility is that the workforce has agreed, willingly or unwillingly, to effort intensification in exchange for the concentration of production at their establishments and hence some degree of job protection and/or for increased pay (see chapter 6).

Patterns in the Labour Relations Strategy of Management

The preceding discussion has considered different aspects of management's approach towards labour. Our indicators, it should be stressed, are necessarily crude. But they do permit us to look at the extent to which different aspect of management's approach are related. Before looking at the actual findings, however, it might be useful to outline briefly the sorts of relationships one might expect to find, if employers had adopted a full-blown strategy of the kind suggested by combining the arguments found in a good deal of recent discussion. First, the score on management's support for the unions would be very low; related to this, trends in the use of secondary labour would be upwards, since employers would be seeking to meet their labour requirements through secondary rather than primary workers. Third, these strategies might be supplemented by attempts to bypass the unions and win the hearts and minds of workers through individualistic participation techniques. Fourth, payment systems would be used to foster employee identification. Fifth, scientific management techniques would be more fully adopted; and finally, there would be an intensification of effort.

When we look at the relationship between the various aspects of management's approach towards labour, the most striking point is how few relationships exist and how weak most of them are. In other words, very few employers have adopted a strategy of the kind outlined above. Moreover, the extent to which they have even adopted a very coherent policy – by the standards of the crude model – seems remarkably limited. It is perhaps useful to detail this point a little more fully.

Turning first to trends in the use of secondary labour, we find no significant relationships with the other aspects of strategy discussed in this chapter (other than, as already noted, with trends in the working patterns of primary labour). Nor are such trends related to changes in employment, nor to management's approach towards the unions. All of these points equally apply to trends in the use of overtime and shiftworking.

Second, individualistic involvement techniques are related to payment systems – that is, the use of various kinds of incentive – only in the finance and maintenance samples. They are, however, rather more strongly associated with the use of scientific management techniques: but these relationships are primarily attributable to a common size effect. Other than the relationship (already noted) with union-based consultation, there are no relationships between individualistic involvement techniques or patterns of consultation and management's more general approach towards the unions.

Third, turning to payment systems, we have already noted a number of relationships. In addition to these, incentives of various kinds are related to the greater use of scientific management – this is particularly true of work study, which is especially common where payment-by-results systems are used. In the private sector, there is also a weak positive relationship between the use of work study and the payment of bonuses. Again, neither payment systems nor the use of scientific management are significantly related to changes in employment or in management's approach towards the unions.

Finally, trends in effort levels are not significantly related to any of the other aspects of labour relations investigated here. As noted above, they are not related to changes in employment; neither do they vary significantly with management's approach towards the unions, except in the case of the maintenance groups. But here increases in effort are associated with greater management support for the union.

Attempts were also made to categorize the various combinations of strategies into different types, which could then be used in subsequent analyses. However, it was found that by far the largest concentrations were in those categories where few of the tactics distinguished were employed. It is possible that, with a great deal of work, some useful categorizations could be developed; we have not pursued this further because, first, the quality of the data is not good enough. Moreover, to do so means either employing purely statistical criteria in cluster analysis (a somewhat dubious operation) or dropping certain of the dimensions for at least some of the categories – and we had no clear criteria by which to do this. Accordingly, in the subsequent analyses we investigated the impact of each aspect of management's labour relations strategy separately.

It should again be stressed that our data are extremely crude and that we have been focusing upon a rather dubious stereotype of what would constitute a 'modern' management approach. It is possible that more adequate indicators would give a rather different picture, or that employers are adopting rather different strategies to that suggested in our model. But with these very important cautions in mind, the evidence suggests that few employers have developed and successfully applied a coherent strategy designed at weakening the unions and instituting a strategy of effort intensification along with attempts to foster worker identification with the company or employer. If nothing else, these findings will perhaps serve as a caution against the claims of some grand overarching strategy on the part of management, at least on any very widespread scale.

The Level and Range of Bargaining

The most important level of bargaining over pay has been widely seen as a key factor shaping the pattern of industrial relations. More centralized systems, for example, within multi-plant companies are seen as encouraging a broader perspective on the part of union representatives and, possibly, at the same time serving to limit the role unions play on the shop-floor (although we have questioned this, arguing that it may equally facilitate multi-level bargaining). On the other hand, more decentralized systems have recently been seen as permitting management to pay different rates in different plants and making it more difficult for trade unions to intrude into management's strategic plans. A rather different emphasis is to be found in the Donovan tradition (for a discussion of this, see Batstone, 1984a): this stressed the need for some correspondence between the location of power and formal bargaining structures. Similarly, there has been a good deal of debate concerning the level at which bargaining should occur in the public sector. More recently, the question of the impact of the recession upon bargaining levels has been widely discussed. It has been argued, for example, that high unemployment shifts the balance of power in favour of employers and, in order to maximize this advantage, they will decentralize bargaining. The interests of the union are seen to be the reverse of this: with their power on the shop-floor and within the individual workplace weakened, it is argued, they will have an interest in centralizing bargaining so that the strong can support the weak. In this section, we look at the most important level of bargaining over pay.

It is common for bargaining to occur at a number of levels. Although pay may be settled at one level, other issues may be negotiated at another. For example, it is widely recognized that centralized negotiations cannot adequately handle detailed issues concerning work organization, which may vary from plant to plant and from workgroup to workgroup. In addition, supplementary bargaining is common. For example, a centralized agreement may formally permit more detailed bargaining locally over its precise interpretation and implementation. Even where this possibility is not formally recognized, supplementary bargaining may occur: particularly where unions are strong at lower levels, they are likely to negotiate over the applicability and interpretation of agreements and over matters not covered by those agreements; in other words, bargaining will develop and be based upon a body of local 'case law', which may diverge significantly from formal agreements. For these reasons,then, it is also necessary to look at bargaining at a variety of levels. Here it might be expected that where there have been major job losses, and where management has adopted a less supportive approach towards the unions, the amount of multi-level bargaining will be less.

The discussion of variations in bargaining levels between different issues raises the further question of the range of bargaining itself. This is clearly of crucial importance. For although the degree of influence which unions achieve through bargaining clearly varies, bargaining over an issue is generally a pre-condition of influence. This is not, of course, always the case: a union may have some degree of unilateral control, but typically its significance is limited. Other forms of union influence, such as joint consultation, are also generally of limited importance. In short, the range of bargaining is a fairly good indicator of the frontier of control, or the extent to which the unions impose constraints upon management's freedom of action. Again, those who espouse the view that high unemployment seriously weakens unions would predict that the range of bargaining has declined substantially over the past five years or so, particularly where job loss has been substantial and where management has sought to exploit the labour-market situation.

The Formal Level of Bargaining over Pay

Over the last two decades or so there have been substantial changes in the level of bargaining over pay. In the private sector, there have been moves, particularly as far as manual workers are concerned, away from industry or multi-employer bargaining to establishment- and more recently to company- or divisional-level negotiations (see, e.g., Brown, 1981). In the public sector, a variety of trends are to be found, but in the areas covered by our survey there has been a good deal of talk, and even effort, put into decentralizing many aspects of bargaining.

Table 3.6 shows the most important level at which pay was bargained over in the different samples. The patterns are both clear and predictable. In the public sector, according to respondents, 'company'-level bargaining is virtually universal. In finance, the company also tends to be the most important bargaining level, although a third say that multi-employer bargaining is. The latter is the most important in the printing industry, according to our survey. But for the remainder of the manual samples, the distinctive feature is the importance of establishment-level bargaining; in chemicals, food and drink, and electrical engineering, however, single-employer bargaining above the level of establishment is also relatively common.

Although comparisons with previous surveys are difficult, due to differences in the size distribution of establishments covered and the mix of industries, it would appear that multi-employer bargaining in manufacturing may have declined since 1978, except in printing. In addition, there may have been a slight increase in company-level bargaining in engineering. The former point is consistent with the 'management' hypothesis outlined above. The latter, however, is not, for the sector most hit by the recession in the survey has actually

Table 3.6 Most important levels of bargaining over pay (percentage of establishment)

	Multi-employer	Com-pany	Establish-ment	No nego-tiations	Other
(a) Non-manual/public-sector group					
Finance	36	61	—	—	3
CPSA civil service	2	98	—	—	—
SCPS civil service	1	99	—	—	—
CPSA Telecom	—	100	—	—	—
POEU Telecom	—	100	—	—	—
(b) Production group					
Print	54	13	31	1	1
Chemicals	11	28	57	3	2
Food and drink	12	35	43	—	10
Engineering	15	25	58	—	2
(c) Maintenance group					
Chemicals	13	42	36	3	6
Food and drink	3	44	42	8	4
Engineering	5	7	79	8	2
Electrical engineering	2	44	54	—	—

centralized bargaining. There is also one further point which is worthy of note: to the extent that multi-employer bargaining is a sign of employer solidarity, then it would appear that this has declined in the private sector over the last five years (cf. Batstone, 1984a, on falls in the membership of employers' associations).

Areas of Bargaining

We asked respondents whether they bargained over four issues – manning, redeployment, grading and earnings. These were selected to cover aspects of pay and work organization. Part (a) of table 3.7 shows that a large majority of respondents say that they negotiate all four issues investigated. The proportion stating this is especially high in the non-manual/public-sector group, with the exception of SCPS, suggesting the importance of bargaining level and union structure. Bargaining range is lowest in food and drink; in some cases the range of bargaining for maintenance groups is rather lower than that for the corresponding production groups. This may, however, reflect the fact that some of the issues investigated simply are not relevant to them.

The question asked not merely whether these four issues were negotiated, but also whether they were negotiated at shop-floor, establishment and/or company level. We wished to know how bargaining over these areas related to the most important level of bargaining over pay and the extent to which issues were bargained over at more than one level. Parts (b) – (e) of table 3.7 show that in the non-manual and public-sector group bargaining is strongly concentrated at company level, reflecting the formal structure of bargaining over pay. In addition, there is also a substantial amount of negotiation at establishment level. Bargaining is rare, however, on the shop- or office-floor. In the manual, private-sector samples – with the exception of printing – little bargaining occurs at company level; negotiations are concentrated at the establishment, along with a considerable amount of bargaining on the shop-floor, particularly in engineering. In printing, negotiations are spread more evenly across the three levels, reflecting both the importance of centralized or multi-employer bargaining and also the close links between different levels of bargaining (a hallmark of the classic strategy of the craft union).

The overall picture, then, can be summarized as follows: the pattern of actual bargaining is strongly influenced by, or related to, the most important formal level for bargaining over pay. But this level does not monopolize negotiating activity. There tends to be a substantial amount of bargaining at one level below this key level. Hence shop-floor bargaining is common, but company bargaining rare, among the private-sector manual samples, whereas the reverse is the case for the non-manual, public-sector samples.

Two further questions arise from these findings. The first is what issues tend to be negotiated at what levels; the second is what issues tend to be negotiated at more than one level. Table 3.7 shows that bargaining is particularly centralized in finance; on no issue does a majority of respondents state that bargaining takes place anywhere other than at company level. However, for all the non-manual and public-sector groups there is a fairly clear pattern: grading and pay are very much issues for company-level bargaining, whereas issues relating to work organization – that is, manning and redeployment – are frequently negotiated at establishment level rather than more centrally. This is especially true in telecommunications. The most even distribution of negotiations across the three different levels is found in printing: in part, this reflects the variations in the level at which pay is formally negotiated. But what is particularly noteworthy in this instance is the amount of bargaining that occurs at shop-floor level, over grading in particular. In all of the production samples, however, shop-floor bargaining over work-organization issues is only slightly

Table 3.7 Range and level of bargaining: (a) number of issues negotiated; (b) level of negotiations for manning; (c) level of negotiations for redeployment; (d) level of negotiations for grading; (e) level of negotiations for earnings; (f) extent of multi-level bargaining over issues

	Number of issues negotiated (percentage of establishments)					Percentage of establishments negotiating manning at:				Percentage of establishments negotiating redeployment at:			
	0	1	2	3	4	Shop-floor level	Estab-lish-ment level	Com-pany level	Any level	Shop-floor level	Estab-lish-ment level	Com-pany level	Any level
(a) Non-manual/public-sector group													
Finance	—	3	—	3	94	16	40	75	100	9	34	76	94
CPSA civil service	—	—	2	3	95	8	48	72	98	9	72	34	95
SCPS civil service	5	3	4	12	76	5	49	57	94	12	54	32	89
CPSA Telecom	—	3	—	8	89	11	86	14	97	3	53	53	100
POEU Telecom	—	—	—	1	99	10	83	32	100	6	89	21	100
(b) Production group													
Print	7	2	3	8	87	38	47	19	92	44	44	16	92
Chemicals	2	7	2	3	82	41	59	4	88	37	57	2	84
Food and drink	2	6	10	8	75	34	52	10	90	32	54	6	82
Engineering	2	9	4	6	80	41	48	8	89	45	44	4	86
(c) Maintenance group													
Chemicals	5	5	8	6	77	32	58	10	86	27	61	3	81
Food and drink	4	5	8	9	75	32	49	17	86	25	58	7	80
Engineering	7	5	8	10	71	45	47	7	85	40	42	2	79
Electrical engineering	6	4	—	2	88	34	64	6	90	26	70	9	90

	Percentage of establishments negotiating grading at:				Percentage of establishments negotiating earnings at:				Percentage of those establishments that negotiate, negotiating at two or more levels on issues of:			
	Shop-floor level	Establishment level	Company level	Any level	Shop-floor level	Establishment level	Company level	Any level	Manning	Redeployment	Grading	Earnings
(a) Non-manual/public-sector group												
Finance	7	26	83	94	2	2	98	98	20	15	13	3
CPSA civil service	3	30	84	100	1	3	98	100	23	15	14	2
SCPS civil service	2	31	66	88	1	3	80	80	17	8	11	3
CPSA Telecom	—	12	85	92	3	—	97	97	11	8	—	—
POEU Telecom	3	23	83	100	3	5	98	99	20	13	7	5
(b) Production group												
Print	47	36	24	96	29	48	42	98	11	11	7	17
Chemicals	29	63	5	86	19	55	26	90	10	7	5	4
Food and drink	20	62	10	84	18	48	32	90	4	10	7	7
Engineering	25	55	17	84	26	58	19	95	5	5	9	5
(c) Maintenance group												
Chemicals	23	59	15	84	20	47	40	94	7	4	9	7
Food and drink	23	56	16	83	24	49	35	96	9	6	9	8
Engineering	27	50	8	76	43	48	15	93	11	2	9	10
Electrical engineering	35	70	9	88	16	59	27	94	4	4	13	2

rarer than at establishment level, and even on earnings and grading about a fifth to a quarter of respondents state that bargaining takes place at shop-floor level. The pattern is broadly similar for the maintenance samples, although in this case bargaining over redeployment is more likely to occur at establishment level than on the shop-floor. The overall pattern, then, indicates that work-organization issues tend to be negotiated at lower levels than grading and earnings. This difference is more marked, however, in the non-manual and public-sector group than it is in the private-sector manual samples.

The second question which was raised above concerned the extent of multi-level bargaining over issues; that is, how often is the same issue negotiated at a number of levels. Part (f) of table 3.7 shows that multi-level bargaining is most common where the formal level of bargaining over pay is centralized, that is, above the level of the establishment, and hence primarily in the public-sector and non-manual samples. However, the table also shows that even in these situations multi-level bargaining is far from the norm; in no sample do more than a quarter of respondents say that they bargain over the same issue at more than one level. With the notable exception of printing and electrical engineering, multi-level bargaining is more common over work-organization than pay-related issues. However, it is probable that these figures are an underestimate of multi-level bargaining: the table that we asked respondents to complete was fairly long and tedious, so that respondent exhaustion may have occurred in a number of cases.

The key factor affecting the range of bargaining in the private sector is the sophistication of union organization; more sophisticated organizations negotiate a wider range of issues. Job loss appears to have no effect upon the range of bargaining, although some aspects of management strategy are of relevance. The use of scientific management techniques, for example, is associated with a wider range of bargaining and with bargaining at a greater number of levels. The degree of support which management gives to the unions is also relevant, but in an unexpected way. A less supportive role on the part of management is associated with a wider range of bargaining among the private-sector manual groups. It would appear that managements have withdrawn their support mainly where union organization is sufficiently strong to bargain over a wide range of issues, but have not thereby been able to reduce the range of issues in which the union is involved.

In the public sector, the sophistication of union organization does not explain the range of bargaining, since negotiations are so concentrated above the level of the establishment. More sophisticated organizations are, however, more likely to bargain over issues at establishment and shop-floor levels. Moreover, there is a tendency for lower levels of management support for the unions to be associated with a smaller range of bargaining in this group. Again, trends in employment appear to play no role and other aspects of management policy are relatively insignificant.

These findings on levels of bargaining suggest a further conclusion: that formal agreements at the level at which pay is negotiated frequently include only a limited range of issues. In other words, the extent to which agreements cover a wide range of issues, thereby removing a great deal of bargaining at lower levels, appears fairly limited.

It is also possible crudely to assess the extent to which the range of bargaining has changed in the recession, by comparing our findings with those of earlier studies. A survey of personnel managers in 1983 suggested that the extent of bargaining in large private-sector plants may have declined since 1980 (Batstone, 1984a). However, when we compare the present survey with earlier surveys, a very different picture appears – that bargaining has actually increased dramatically. This rather surprising finding needs to be treated with some caution for two reasons. First, previous studies have suggested that shop stewards generally claim a wider range of bargaining than do managers, the latter possibly differentiating more strongly between consultation and negotiation – although this pattern does not appear to be sufficient to explain the large variations found between the present survey and the 1983 study. Second, the question we asked was a much broader one than is generally employed, since it stressed bargaining at different levels. In other words, relatively few shop stewards may themselves negotiate particular issues, but at some other level senior stewards or full-time officials might. But, given the extraordinarily high levels of bargaining found in this survey, it is difficult to believe that there has been any substantial or indeed significant decline in bargaining activity in the vast majority of establishments. However, workers may now gain less from negotiations than they did in the past: bargaining may be less regular and/or less influential. The significance of local bargaining may also reflect management's attempts to give greater local discretion in order to permit changes in working practices, etc., without any formal negotiation. If this were so, individual shop stewards would be forced to bargain locally with little support: in other words, the scale of shop-floor bargaining and, where bargaining is more centralized, of establishment-level bargaining, might reflect the relative weakness of the unions. However, the data support neither of these findings. For example, in the non-manual/public-sector group, a wide range of bargaining at establishment level is associated with greater control over management. In the private-sector manual groups, a greater range of bargaining at shop-floor level is associated with an increase, rather than a decrease, in union influence over the last five years.

The variety of levels at which bargaining occurs also raises the question of the significance of formal agreements. Part of the reform of industrial relations over the last two decades, it is often claimed, has involved the formalization of agreements and their tighter application. Others, however, have suggested that management has an interest in formalizing agreements on pay issues, thereby reducing the scale of bargaining, while carefully avoiding agreements on work organization in order to maximize management flexibility and freedom of action (for a critique of this view, see Batstone, 1984a). There also arises the question of the way in which the recession and the changed political atmosphere have affected the role of agreements. If negotiations were tightly constrained by agreements in the past, then it might be expected that management would seek to weaken their hold in order to exploit changes in the labour market. But if agreements had played a limited role in the past, and informal bargaining had worked to the advantage of the unions, it might be expected that employers would seek to apply agreements more strictly.

Table 3.8 Role of agreements (percentages of establishment)

	Not very important	Basis for negotiation	Restricts negotiation
(a) Non-manual/public-sector group			
Finance	22	56	22
CPSA civil service	18	69	13
SCPS civil service	29	50	21
CPSA Telecom	3	89	9
POEU Telecom	8	81	10
(b) Production group			
Print	15	68	17
Chemicals	6	75	19
Food and drink	6	71	24
Engineering	5	83	12
(c) Maintenance group			
Chemicals	9	66	25
Food and drink	13	70	18
Engineering	15	75	10
Electrical engineering	8	82	10

Given these alternative scenarios, we asked respondents the following question: 'Which of the following best describes the role of formal agreements in this establishment: they do not play a very important role; or, they provide the basis for a good deal of negotiation; or, they effectively restrict and limit the amount of day-to-day negotiation?' Table 3.8 shows that in the majority of establishments formal agreements do play a significant role: that is, very few respondents say that they are not very important. A limited role for agreements is most marked in the civil service, finance, printing and the maintenance samples. At the other extreme, relatively few respondents state that agreements restrict negotiation, although this view is generally more common than the first view. A restrictive role is found in finance, the higher grades of the civil service, and two of the manufacturing samples. However, in every sample, a majority of respondents state that agreements form the basis for a good deal of bargaining. This suggests that a considerable amount of fractional bargaining occurs, despite the changes in the economic and political context.

Trade Union Influence

It is useful at this point briefly to recap the main findings so far. We have found that although some employers are adopting a tougher approach towards the labour force and the unions, this strategy is rarely on a wide and coherent scale. The approach of management tends to be significantly tougher in the public than in the private sector. In institutional terms, management support for trade unions remains considerable in the private sector. Hence we find that although the number of shop stewards has generally fallen where employment has declined, it has fallen less rapidly than the number of jobs. As a result, for any given size of plant, union organization now is often formally stronger than it was five years ago. The evidence also suggests that the degree of sophistication of union organization, as measured by the indices we built up, has remained remarkably stable over the last five years. Furthermore, the extent to which changes in the labour market have constrained bargaining, both of a formal and informal kind, or have reduced the significance of agreements as a basis for fractional bargaining, appears to be fairly limited. In formal terms, then, little appears to have changed, and the impact of job loss and tougher approaches on the part of management seem limited. It might, however, be argued that although there has been little change in formal terms, there have been substantial changes in real terms. In other words, the rituals of bargaining continue, but unions are achieving less through those negotiations. This could be so for a number of reasons. For example, managements may have little need to engage in a head-on attack on trade unions or increase their use of secondary labour, because they are perfectly able to win concessions from the unions. Relatedly, employers may prefer to win the support of unions – and employees through participative techniques – rather than risk incurring the heavy costs which might result from creating a major confrontation (with the corollary that where the employer could carry those heavy costs – as in the public-sector – they would be more prepared to 'try it on').

To assess the actual degree of union control through a postal survey is obviously difficult; indeed, as soon as one tries to specify what exactly union control or influence means, it is clear that a large range of issues would have to be investigated and complex conceptual problems arise. We were therefore forced to content ourselves with asking two simple questions. The first of these was: 'How far would you say your union in this establishment affects and limits management's freedom of action over working practices and effort levels?' Second, we sought to investigate the trend in union influence by asking: 'Over the last five years, has union influence over working practices and effort levels in this establishment increased or decreased?' Respondents' answers are shown in table 3.9. We are, then, dependent upon very crude, subjective assessments. It is quite possible that the exact meaning of answers varies between respondents. Hence, the findings should be treated with care and caution.

The first part of table 3.9 shows that very few respondents believe that their union has no influence within the workplace; with the exception of SCPS, it is striking how few respondents in the public sector express this view. Only in two samples do more respondents say that they have no influence than say that they have a great deal. And in all the samples, except finance and the SCPS, a clear majority of respondents state that they have either a great deal or a fair amount of influence.

Although respondents generally indicate that the role of the union within the workplace remains substantial, the second part of table 3.9 shows that sizeable minorities believe that the influence of the union has declined over the last five years. There are, however, marked variations between the samples. The greatest decline in the role of the union is in Telecom and two of the maintenance samples. On the other hand, the proportions expressing this view in the relatively less strongly organized finance sector and in the strongly organized printing sample are remarkably low. The latter is of considerable interest, in view of the opinions of some commentators that the combination of the use of the law by some employers and new technology would seriously

Table 3.9 Union control over management: (a) current degree of control; (b) trends in union control, 1979–84

	Current degree of control (percentage of establishments)				Trends in union control (percentage of establishments)		
	Great deal	Fair amount	Not much	None	Increased	No change	Decreased
(a) Non-manual/public-sector group							
Finance	2	47	42	9	42	47	11
CPSA civil service	14	61	23	2	52	30	18
SCPS civil service	8	39	41	11	32	43	26
CPSA Telecom	17	64	17	3	31	28	42
POEU Telecom	18	72	9	1	27	29	44
(b) Production group							
Print	40	49	6	5	38	45	17
Chemicals	33	51	11	6	37	34	30
Food and drink	28	39	26	8	43	29	28
Engineering	20	56	16	8	19	51	30
(c) Maintenance group							
Chemicals	16	50	28	6	16	56	28
Food and drink	22	48	22	9	20	39	41
Engineering	10	49	31	10	21	30	49
Electrical engineering	14	55	20	10	29	41	31

undermine this craft union. Equally surprising in many respects are the relatively small number of civil service respondents who believe that the influence of the union has declined, despite the approach of the government.

In a number of the samples, there are more respondents who believe that the power of the union has increased than say it has fallen over the last five years. This is the case in all the non-manual samples, with the exception of Telecom. It is also true in printing and in the two TGWU samples. 'Net' losses of union influence tend to be more marked in the maintenance than the production samples. These findings are somewhat surprising, but a pattern is suggested by the 'net' figures. With the notable exception of a union – the NGA – that continues to pursue a classic craft strategy, union influence has tended to decline among those groups where union organization within the workplace is more traditional: maintenance groups, engineering and Telecom. Where workplace union organization has less of an active and influential tradition, the reverse tends to be the case: over the last five years these groups – in finance, the civil service and in food and drink, and chemicals production – have tended to increase their influence. However, one cautionary note should be added, which is of particular relevance to the civil service: the question may have been interpreted as relating solely to union influence within the place of work. It is therefore quite possible that respondents would argue that, although influence had increased within the workplace, it had fallen in overall terms, because the union centrally was less able to win concessions from the employer. That is, power has shifted to some degree from the national to the local level within the civil service. Moreover, as the next section suggests, in that process the nature of union influence may have begun to change.

The actual level of union control and influence is partly related to trends in influence; where respondents say that union influence has declined over the last five years, then they are also likely to say that the union does not have a 'great deal' or 'fair amount' of control at present. But, in addition, a number of other factors are important in explaining the influence wielded by the union. Most important in the private sector is the level of union sophistication: the more sophisticated union organization, the greater the level of influence. In addition, the higher the level of external integration, the more influence the union tends to have. Multi-level bargaining is also associated with greater union control.

Changes in private manual employment and union membership play no role in explaining the power of the union, nor does management's approach towards the unions. The other aspects of management's labour relations policy discussed in earlier sections of this chapter only have a very limited effect in the case of the production samples; moreover, they do not all operate in the expected direction. Rather surprisingly, when other factors are taken into account, union influence tends to be greater where effort levels have increased in the case of the maintenance samples.

Turning to the non-manual public-sector group, we find, first, that the greater union sophistication, the greater is the influence wielded by the union. No aspects of management policy appear to be significant, but changes in employment are. Where job losses have been smaller or where employment has increased, the influence of the union tends to be greater. But the strongest relationship is a size effect: the greater the labour force in the establishment in 1979, the greater the control the union is said to have currently over management.

The factors explaining trends in union influence, however, are rather different. In all three groups, the less union membership has fallen (or the more membership has increased), the more likely it is that union influence has grown over the last five years. Multi-level and shop-floor bargaining are also associated with more favourable trends in union influence in the private sector, but union sophistication is not. In the public sector, the influence of more sophisticated organizations is less likely to have fallen. In the private sector, however, closer links with the larger union appear to act as a check upon reductions in the power of the union in the workplace. In all three groups, falls in employment (as well as union membership – see above) are associated with declining union influence, and a tougher approach on the part of management has the same effect. Other labour relations policies on the part of management play a very minor role: the most important of these are effort levels in the maintenance group – union influence rises with effort.

In the production samples, loss of members (as an indication of loss of jobs rather than falls in union density) plays the greatest role in explaining trends in union influence, and features of union organization and bargaining are more important than the policies pursued by management. In maintenance, the unexpected relationship with effort levels is the most important explanatory factor; job loss is the second most important. At first sight, a factor not so far mentioned plays the most crucial role in the public sector: where a large proportion of the labour force are women, the influence of the union is most likely to have increased. However, this reflects the fact that fewer women are in the POEU than in the civil service; nevertheless, it does suggest that government policies have served to mobilize groups where women are more strongly represented.

We can usefully illustrate some of the preceding points by briefly discussing some of the findings of our case studies. Elsewhere we discuss the role of the unions in the various plants at length and here we can only briefly summarize the main points. The first of these is that in three of our four plants employment had been reduced in recent years: however, this had not adversely affected the formal role of the unions, who continued to negotiate over the same range of issues. Indeed, in the brewery case study, redundancies occurred as part of a productivity deal and rationalization plan in the face of declining sales of the plant's main product. However, although the range of bargaining did not expand (it had previously been substantial), its depth did increase. That is, stewards at local level became increasingly involved in the negotiation of issues, and this continued even after the details of the productivity deal had been agreed upon and implemented (hence, in this case, and contrary to a good deal of accepted wisdom, productivity bargaining involved decentralization). In the insurance case study, job loss was associated with a considerable expansion in the role of the union, although this was in part due to the merger of the former staff association with BIFU, which occurred at about the same time. In effect, the rationalization programme was the vehicle by which the union began to intrude into traditional areas of management prerogative (although it should be stressed that this was not strongly opposed – indeed to some extent it was encouraged – by management).

More generally, the case studies clearly illustrate the link between union sophistication, the range of union influence and the importance of multi-level bargaining. The linkages between these three factors can be summarized as follows:

	Engineering	Brewing	Chemicals	Insurance
General influence: Shop-floor	high	high	low	low
Establishment/ company	high	high	moderate	growing
Multi-level bargaining	high	high	low	low
Union sophistication	high	high	medium	medium

The detailed reasoning underlying the classification of the various union organizations in terms of general influence are outlined more fully in our associated volume: essentially, they relate to the areas over which bargaining occurred and the extent to which union activity imposed constraints upon management action. It can be seen that there is a close relationship between union influence and the degree of sophistication. An important factor linking the two, however, is multi-level bargaining, which is co-ordinated through sophisticated union organization. As was noted in chapter 2, for example, in the chemicals company, a major weakness of organization was the lack of co-ordination among stewards: as a result, local and central levels tended to focus upon different sorts of issues. The lack of integration meant that stewards individually exercised little influence at shop-floor level, since framework agreements either did not exist or tended to constrain management action to only a limited degree. Conversely, and relatedly, there were few means by which local pressures could feed into and extend union influence centrally. This is in marked contrast to the situation in the brewing and chemicals case studies.

Industrial Action

Very often the use of the strike weapon and other types of collective sanction is seen as an indication of union strength. This is correct in the sense that some form of collective identity and organization is a precondition of strike action; it requires that individual union members be prepared to incur costs in order to pursue a collective goal. On the other hand, it can equally be argued that the absence of collective sanctions can indicate considerable union strength: unions do not engage in strike action because they have no need to, being able to achieve their ends merely because of the possibility of their imposing sanctions. In other words, the absence of collective action may be a sign of strength or of weakness.

Despite this considerable problem, it is obviously important in a survey of the kind we have undertaken to investigate patterns of collective action. Previous surveys have indicated that the use of the strike weapon, for example, is far more widespread than official statistics suggest (since these ignore strikes below a certain size and because there are severe administrative difficulties in collecting relevant information). But the market model of labour relations would lead one to expect that high levels of unemployment would lead workers to resort less often to the strike weapon (although possibly engaging in longer strikes when they did go out). If this were the case, then one might also expect that strike action would be rarer where managements had adopted a tougher line towards workers and the union. On the other hand, unions might contest management strategies of this kind, with the result that strike action increases. Indeed, this possibility would appear to be in the minds of the majority of employers who have not engaged in 'macho' tactics, depending rather upon winning the consent and support of trade unions and workers. However, again one would expect substantial differences between the private and public sector. In the latter, we have seen, managements have adopted a tougher approach towards the unions and the workforce. But, on the other hand, market pressures – both in terms of job loss and in terms of product markets – are less strong, with the consequence that union organization is less weakened through market forces than in the private sector (or, although weakened, still remains relatively strong). In this situation, the public-sector unions might be more prone to engage in industrial action than their private-sector counterparts.

Table 3.10 shows the patterns of industrial action in the establishments covered by the survey in the last twelve months. We asked respondents about three types of industrial action: strikes of at least a day or a shift; shorter stoppages; and the use of other sanctions such as overtime bans. It can be seen from the table that in the private sector the majority of establishments have experienced no strikes in the year before the survey. Strikes have occurred, however, in a substantial minority of establishments, particularly in the maintenance group. In the manufacturing samples as a whole, strikes have occurred in about one-third of establishments. This figure corresponds quite closely to that found by Batstone for 1983, and suggests that in the private sector strike action is less common among manual workers than it was five years ago. However, compared with 1983, it seems that strikes may have become rather longer in duration.

Among non-manual workers and in the public sector, the picture is rather different. Nearly a third of the finance sample, for example, state that a strike of some kind had occurred in the twelve months prior to the survey. In other words, these workers have a level of strike action that is comparable with that of manual workers (except that very few say there has been more than one strike, whereas a number of strikes are often reported in the manual samples). Of even greater interest is the pattern of industrial action among the public-sector respondents. The level of strike action in the POEU sample is broadly comparable with that found among other manual groups, but the strike rate among white-collar public-sector groups is extremely high. In all, over four in every five say that they have had some form of strike action in the last twelve months, and a significant minority say that strikes have occurred on several occasions. These levels of strike action are extremely high. It is clear that in a very large number of situations unions have been prepared to challenge the tougher approach declared by the government (although, of course, many of these cases of industrial action were probably not confined to individual establishments, but were parts of broader stoppages).

Sanctions that are short of strike action are generally about as commonly used as the strike. The overall pattern is also similar to that found in the case of strikes, although it is rather less marked. That is, sanctions such as overtime bans tend to be more common in the public-sector white-collar samples.

If we look at the final part of table 3.10 we find that over the last twelve months some form of industrial action has occurred in all but a handful of white-collar public-sector establishments covered by the survey. In all samples, about a half of the respondents say some form of industrial action has taken place; this is least often the case in finance, the POEU, and two of the private-sector manual samples. Again, the picture for the private-sector manual samples broadly corresponds with that found by Batstone in 1983 (Batstone 1984a). This indicates a decline in the use of sanctions by workers over the last five years in manufacturing. Nevertheless, this fall has to be kept in perspective: it is still the case that in over half the establishments from manufacturing covered by the survey some form of industrial action has taken place. Moreover, against this decline in the use of sanctions among private-sector manual groups has to be set the rise in strike-proneness of white-collar workers and the public sector. In finance, the level of industrial action is not very different to that found among manual groups. The rise in strikes in the public sector can only be described as astronomical.

The factors that explain variations in strikes and the overall level of industrial action are basically the same. In the private sector, indicators of the size of the labour force or of union membership are the most important. The larger the group, the higher the level of industrial and strike action. A tougher management approach towards the unions plays a small role in discouraging collective action, whereas the use of scientific management techniques encourages it. Indicators of union sophistication and widespread bargaining activity are also relevant in the private sector. In the public sector, the degree of union sophistication and multi-level bargaining are more strongly related to the level of strike action; but the second most important factor at first sight appears to be the proportion of women in the labour force. The more women, the more strikes and other forms of industrial action. This relationship is due to variations in the importance of women as a proportion of the labour force in different samples. That is, it reflects the relative importance of women in the civil service samples. If we

Table 3.10 Industrial action over preceding twelve months: (a) strikes of one day/shift or more; (b) stoppages of less than one day; (c) other sanctions; (d) all strikes; (e) all sanctions (percentage of establishments)

	Strikes of day/shift or more				Stoppages of less than day				Other sanctions			
	0	1	2/3	4+	0	1	2/3	4+	0	1	2/3	4+
(a) Non-manual/public-sector group												
Finance	87	13	—	—	80	20	—	—	77	23	—	—
CPSA civil service	33	35	23	9	32	42	23	3	47	46	6	1
SCPS civil service	41	40	18	1	38	46	13	2	67	28	4	1
CPSA Telecom	61	30	6	3	39	46	15	—	34	53	13	—
POEU Telecom	73	26	1	—	86	13	1	—	74	24	2	—
(b) Production group												
Print	83	10	6	2	79	14	6	2	70	19	7	4
Chemicals	84	11	4	1	84	11	4	2	52	32	15	1
Food and drink	81	10	6	2	69	21	4	6	73	25	—	2
Engineering	85	9	7	—	72	12	14	3	57	16	19	9
(c) Maintenance group												
Chemicals	81	8	8	3	88	5	5	3	64	19	9	8
Food and drink	74	21	3	3	71	14	8	7	63	27	8	1
Engineering	75	18	5	2	66	21	9	5	63	20	11	7
Electrical engineering	79	15	4	2	65	8	21	6	56	35	4	4

Table 3.10 (*continued*)

	All strikes				All sanctions			
	0	*1*	*2/3*	*4+*	*0*	*1*	*2/3*	*4+*
(a) Non-manual/public-sector group								
Finance	70	27	3	—	61	26	13	—
CPSA civil service	6	37	35	22	3	26	43	29
SCPS civil service	11	45	36	7	11	35	38	15
CPSA Telecom	22	53	22	3	7	42	36	16
POEU Telecom	66	24	10	—	57	21	22	—
(b) Production group								
Print	66	24	6	4	48	26	19	7
Chemicals	71	18	7	4	43	24	26	7
Food and drink	63	19	13	6	50	29	13	8
Engineering	66	15	13	7	44	19	19	19
(c) Maintenance group								
Chemicals	75	13	6	6	58	17	8	17
Food and drink	58	19	15	8	47	19	19	15
Engineering	49	32	11	9	32	30	21	16
Electrical engineering	52	19	21	8	33	33	21	13

consider only the civil service samples, no such variation is found. In addition, although changes in employment and union membership play no role in explaining variations in the level of collective action in the private sector, they are relevant in the public sector. The greater the scale of job/membership loss, the greater is the level of industrial action. Compared with the role of these sets of factors, the significance of variations in the strategy of the employer is very limited (at least in terms of variations within samples). Finally, it is worth noting that the size of the establishment or of union membership at the time of the survey do not play a very important role in the public sector; however, strike action does tend to be lower, the larger the labour force of the establishment was in 1979.

These findings are rather surprising for a number of reasons. The first is that the scale of job loss does not appear to affect strike activity in the private sector; and, even more significantly, high levels of collective action are more common in the public sector, the greater the reduction in employment. Second, strike action in the public sector tends to be concentrated in the smaller establishments. Third, the strike-proneness of parts of the public sector where large proportions of women are employed is worthy of particular note. In short, the policies that the state has adopted in the public sector have served to mobilize those groups that are traditionally the least likely to engage in such action: those in small establishments, women, and those that have seen job losses in their places of work (those policies have also led to severe problems of recruitment and retention of staff according to the Civil Service Commissioners, see the *Financial Times*, 25 April 1985).

Conclusions

In this chapter we have looked at the labour relations policies pursued by management, and the extent to which these have shaped bargaining activity and the influence exerted by the unions. It has been seen that few employers appear to have made widespread resort to the secondary labour market, at least in terms of a wide range of different types of secondary labour. More common has been the adoption of participative techniques aimed at the individual worker, as well as consultation with trade unions. There does not appear to have been a substantial growth in the use of scientific management techniques, but there has been a growing use of the payment system in an attempt to win worker support and commitment to the company. All of these patterns are found in the private sector; in the mainstream civil service, however, managements have made no resort to participative techniques or to payment systems to win worker support (although the situation is different in Telecom). In the civil service, and also in Telecom, managements have sought to intensify effort levels more than they have in the private sector. In the main, however, it appears that few employers have combined these various labour relations techniques in a manner which might be inferred from some recent discussions: from the standard of the ideal type outlined, it appears that few employers are adopting a coherent and sophisticated strategy of weakening the labour force and the unions.

The picture is supported by the fact that there have been few changes of any significance in the formal level of bargaining over pay. More importantly, the range of bargaining remains remarkably high in all the samples. Despite this, however, a significant number of respondents state that union influence over management in the workplace has fallen over the last five years; in many samples, however, that influence is said to have increased. Moreover, the majority of respondents believed that the union continued to have a significant degree of influence over management. Relatedly, we find that, although the level of industrial action has fallen somewhat among manual workers in manufacturing, there has been a trend in the reverse direction among non-manual workers and in the public sector. This pattern is not only of considerable interest in indicating that there is a further spreading of the strike habit, but also because of the way in which groups traditionally seen as the least ready to engage in strikes are now showing the highest levels of strike action.

Finally, it is useful to highlight the variations in bargaining between different types of trade union. As was suggested in chapter 1, the number of issues bargained over tends to be higher in single-employer/industry unions: averaging across the sample totals, we find that about twice as many respondents from the multi-industry as from the single-employer/industry unions said they did not bargain over all the issues investigated. Moreover, the former were less likely than the latter to claim that they had a great deal or a fair amount of control over management.

Part II The Case of Technical Change

4 The Nature of Technical Change

In part II of this study we turn to the question of technical change and the way in which this was affectd by, and affected, trade unions in the workplace. Throughout this section we will be concerned with a number of key themes, which were outlined in chapter 1. It is perhaps useful to repeat them here. The first of these is that different types of union will adopt different approaches to the question of new technology; we pointed to the importance of the nature, size and density of the membership; the nature of the membership represented; and certain features of union organization. More specifically, we suggested that unions that were more organized within the workplace and/or had closer relations with the 'external' union were more able to develop and pursue policies in relation to new technology. However, in addition, we recognized the importance of the nature of the employer, and in particular the differences in the nature of industrial relations between the private and public sectors.

The second set of hypotheses concerned the market position of the establishment: it was pointed out that many have argued that adverse product and labour-market conditions will shift the balance of power against unions. It follows from this argument that under such conditions unions will be less able to influence the way in which technical change is introduced. It may also be the case that, realizing their limited power and the nature of the labour market, unions will modify their demands. We suggested that this market model was too simple: adverse product-market conditions may also weaken the position of the employer. Conversely, an employer who does not face a declining market may choose to exploit the general slackness of the labour market; in the public sector, which is guided by the 'political contingency' rather than by direct market forces, management may adopt a tougher approach towards labour, even though immediate market pressures are relatively weak. Hence, it follows that we need to look directly at the sorts of strategies that management adopts towards the labour force. It could therefore be argued that where management has provided them little support, the position of the unions is weaker and they will be less able to influence the process of technical change. Against this argument, however, one could hypothesize that the adoption of such aggressive strategies, particularly where jobs are not insecure, will lead to resentment on the part of the workers and increase their readiness to challenge management action. Finally, we need to look at the nature of the technical change itself. Although we have cautioned against the adoption of technological determinism, the nature and scale of technical change can constitute a means by which management seeks to shape, either directly or indirectly, the power of workers and their unions.

These, then, are the themes that will run throughout the analysis in part II. In this chapter, we look at the general characteristics of technical change, and its effects upon employment. In chapter 5, we consider the role the union played in relation to technical change. Chapter 6 investigates how technical change has affected the wage-effort bargain, and finally, in chapter 7, we consider how technical change has affected union organization.

In considering the nature of technical change, there are a number of themes which we pursue. The first concerns the extent to which there has been technical change in the past. This is important for a number of reasons. Current patterns of change are likely to be related to traditions of technical change; although the significance of such change may clearly vary, it is likely that unions will be more acquainted with how to handle change where this has been common in the past.

On the other hand, it is sometimes argued that new technology tends to have a greater effect as time passes. Some claim that management will introduce only marginal changes initially, in order to win the consent and support of the workforce and unions; having achieved this, management will gradually exploit the potential of the technology more fully to the detriment of employees. But any greater effect of new technology over time may be due to a learning curve: that is, over time management begin to see the full potential of new technology and build up confidence and experience. It will thereby be more able to use advances in technology more fully. In addition, particular types of production system may by their very nature be more amenable to technical change and may have been so for many years. Hence there will be both a tradition of technical change and a great deal of current change; accordingly, new technology will have a more widespread effect.

These hypotheses, then, suggest the need to look at the history of technical change. But they equally indicate the utility of looking at the time at which the current phase of technical change began, which is the second main topic we consider. Hence the arguments just outlined would indicate that the earlier the current phase of technical change began, the greater its impact. However, there might in this case be an additional consideration. The greater impact of technical changes that began earlier may be attributable less to management strategy or the nature of the technology as such, than to the changing state of the market. Companies that planned to introduce technical change earlier may have been hit less by the recession and therefore may be more able to introduce widescale changes. Those that planned such changes more recently may have confronted greater financial and market problems, thereby inducing them to introduce more moderate changes in technology. Against this view, one might hypothesize that more recent and advanced technologies may have a greater effect on the workforce than older ones.

The third aspect of technical change which we take up relates in part to the market argument outlined in the preceding paragraph. For as well as looking at changes that have been introduced, it is useful to consider changes that have not yet got beyond the planning stage. We therefore look at the question of planned changes that have not as yet been introduced. Here we can expect a number of reasons to figure importantly. Most obviously, changes may still be in the process of implementation: we therefore have some picture of the likely extent of technical change in the future. Second, as we have already mentioned, there may be market or financial constraints upon the extent of technical change, and it is important to see how far the recession has imposed checks upon the introduction of new technology. Third, through this question we can develop some idea of the degree to which technical problems exist in the process of implementation. Finally, we can see how far union activity has imposed constraints – temporarily or permanently – upon technical change.

The precise nature of both the 'core' production process and of the technical changes that have been introduced may also be relevant to an understanding of the effects of technical change. As has already been suggested, it is likely that particular types of production process are more amenable to technical change than others. In addition, it is likely that the nature of the core production process will be associated with the particular types of innovation that have been introduced. A related issue concerns the extent to which a variety of technical changes are associated with each other: that is, is it possible to identify general patterns or clusters of technical innovations?

Related to the characterization of the precise nature of technical change is the question of whether or not the changes include 'new' technology. Most of the recent debate on technical change has focused almost exclusively upon technologies that incorporate microelectronics; such change is seen as having particularly dramatic effects upon employment and work experience. But technical change may also occur which does not incorporate such technology, and the question arises of how far 'new technology' does in fact have distinctive effects.

It should, however, be remembered that in a survey of the kind we have undertaken it was impossible to investigate in any great detail the precise nature of the many hundreds of cases of technical change. We have therefore been forced to characterize types of technical change in a fairly broad manner. When we talk about the effects of particular types of technical change, therefore, we are referring to relatively broad categories rather than to the effects of specific types of equipment. Hence our arguments concerning the impact of particular types of technical change have to be treated with some caution. However, we believe that our findings are still of some significance, if only because more detailed case studies – including our own – indicate that the precise effects of a particular piece of equipment can vary quite widely (e.g. Noble, 1979; Sorge et al., 1983).

There is, however, a very real risk that one places excessive emphasis upon the precise nature of the technology. As we found in our case studies, equally important is the question of other changes that occurred with the new technology. Put at its most obvious, in engineering a good deal of attention has focused upon the introduction of numerically controlled machines. But the impact of such machines is likely to be related to their relative importance within the workplace. Obviously, where only 1 per cent of the machines have been changed, this is less likely to have much impact than if 100 per cent of the machines have been changed. Similarly, the effects are likely to vary with the extent to which plant capacity has changed with the new technology, and also whether the product or service has been changed. In other words, as we have stressed, technical change has to be seen as part of a package of changes, and the characteristics of the rest of this package are likely to have a significant effect upon the precise impact that technical change has. For example, where technical change is associated with a large increase in capacity, then it is likely, other things being equal, to have less adverse effects upon union strength than where it is associated with a reduction in capacity. And, of course, the question then arises of whether it is the change in capacity that is more important than the change in the precise nature of the technology (if indeed it is possible to distinguish between the effects of the two).

Finally, and perhaps most importantly for our purposes, it is necessary to look at how many workers are affected by the new technology. This has two aspects. The first is the employment effect of technical change: that is, how many jobs have been created or lost as a result of technical change, or, more strictly, the package of changes with which new technology is associated. The second dimension concerns the proportion of workers working with the new technology. For our purposes, these are the two most important features of technical change, since they are most likely to concern the unions. In chapter 6, we look at other important characteristics relating to the wage-effort bargain.

In the preceding discussion we have pointed on a number of occasions to the total package of changes associated with new technology. There is, then, a need to have some idea of the nature of management strategy in relation to technical change. We felt unable to investigate this through the survey, since our pilot interviews indicated that in many cases shop stewards were unclear as to the reasons underlying the changes. It is perhaps useful, therefore, to consider briefly the evidence from the case studies, if only to provide examples of the complex of reasons underlying technical change.

The four case studies illustrate the diversity of reasons for technical change. In the insurance case study, we can characterize the change as being stimulated by tough market competition. In this case, the company decided that it needed to rationalize the range of policies it offered and at the same time to streamline the administration associated with those policies, in order to reduce costs and thereby achieve greater competitiveness. The introduction of on-line computerized systems was seen as a central feature of this process of rationalization. Although it is conceivable that the process of rationalization could have occurred without the introduction of new technology, the potential of the latter figured centrally in management thinking and made the proposed rationalization that much more attractive. In this case, then, we have a market stimulus to change where new technology figured centrally within the strategy.

In the brewing case study, the situation was rather different. Here, the main beers produced by the company were suffering from a long-term decline in sales. Lager was, however, becoming increasingly popular; the company had been involved in a co-operative venture to brew lager, but there was now a need for increased capacity. For a variety of reasons the joint venture broke up and so the company decided to construct its own lager plant. In this instance, then, the nature of the market was the central factor in the decision. But, in contrast to the insurance case, management wished to avoid employing the latest technology, since it wished to begin lager production as soon as possible and feared encountering 'teething' problems if it used untried equipment. Microelectronics were incorporated into the new plant simply bcause it was included in what now constituted 'standard' plant. Moreover, the lager plant that was finally constructed did not incorporate the new technology to its full potential, simply because the company was eager to maintain certain functions for workers. In this case, then, we have a market-driven technical change in which the new technology as such played a minimal role as far as management was concerned.

In our chemicals case study we have, yet again, a rather different situation. Here, market and technical factors both figured, but were less intimately related than in the case of the insurance company. In this instance, the decision to install a new plant reflected the success of a relatively new product. This had achieved high and stable sales and so, in line with general company policy, it was decided to build a dedicated plant for its manufacture. This provided the occasion for the engineering specialists within the company to put forward their ideas. Indeed, in this company there had been a long tradition of seeking technical solutions to problems of handling materials and controlling quality. In the years prior to the construction of the new plant that we studied, the engineers had seen the possibilities of improving quality standards and reducing waste by using microelectronics in the weighing out of raw materials and controlling the production process. This was merely a further incremental stage in a long history of technological innovation. Moreover, these technical ideas developed largely independently of the particular plant in which they were finally introduced. That is, the need to construct a new plant provided the opportunity for the engineers to implement their latest ideas. Technical considerations figured importantly in the change; but whereas in insurance they were intimately associated with the decision to introduce changes, in the chemicals case the need to install new equipment was simply an occasion or opportunity to introduce the latest technical developments.

In our fourth case study – a manufacturer of spares in machine tools – the market played some role in the decision to innovate. The demand for the company's product was declining as the sales of its customers fell. However, this increased the importance of an efficient spares and servicing function for the company, and CNC machines were seen as a means of speeding up the production and delivery of parts. But the introduction of numerically-controlled machine tools and machining centres can also be seen as the knock-on effect of earlier technical innovation. The latest generation of machines had been built in a different part of the company using numerically controlled machines. It was then found that it was difficult to make spare parts for this latest generation of machines using conventional equipment. The solution was therefore to introduce into the spares plant numerically-controlled machines. Thus the use of such machines had gradually been extended as the company realized their potential.

We would not wish to argue that our four case studies exhaust the reasons for technical change. They clearly do not: for example, in telecommunications, certain changes in technology have taken place because they provide more reliable services and permit the introduction of new services. In the civil service, certain changes are not market-driven: they reflect the desire of the government to reduce the costs of certain services and functions. But what is clear is that there can be a wide variety of reasons for the introduction of change: what our case studies illustrate is that the importance or centrality of technical considerations may vary significantly and that the extent to which they are related to market and cost considerations will also differ. But it follows that the precise impact of technical change upon workers and their unions is likely to differ significantly. We take this theme up below.

The History of Technical Change

As was argued above, we need first to look at the history of technical change within our survey. We asked respondents, 'During the 1970s had there been much technical change in this establishment which affected groups covered by your union?' Table 4.1 shows that such change had been widespread. In Telecom, nine out of every ten respondents said that technical change had been considerable, and about three-quarters of respondents in all but three of the other samples stated the same. In these three groups – both civil service groups and the production engineering sample – about half of the sample respondents said that there had been little technical change over this period. In the latter case, there is a marked contrast with the maintenance sample, where nearly three-quarters said that there has been a good deal of change. This difference is attributable to two factors: the first of these is that maintenance workers are more likely to be affected by technical change than production workers, where such changes have been small; second, establishments tend to be larger in the electrician than in the AUEW sample, and it is in larger plants that a history of technical change is more frequently found. Indeed, this pattern of greater technical change in larger plants is found in the

Table 4.1 Percentage of establishments in which there had been previous technical change

	Good deal of change (%)
(a) Non-manual/public-sector group	
Finance	81
CPSA civil service	56
SCPS civil service	49
CPSA Telecom	92
POEU Telecom	92
(b) Production group	
Print	80
Chemicals	79
Food and drink	74
Engineering	43
(c) Maintenance group	
Chemicals	71
Food and drink	85
Engineering	71
Electrical engineering	68

survey as a whole. It is also more common in multi-establishment organizations.

The variations are, however, rather less marked between the different samples when we turn to the question of technical change affecting union members in the last five years (table 4.2). But it is still the case that those samples where significant proportions say that there was little technical change in the 1970s are also more likely to say that there has been no technical change in the last five years. More generally, there is a very strong association between a history of technical change in the 1970s and the experience of recent technical change: that is, the changes that have occurred in the last five years are often part of a longer process of change. Recent experience of technical change is again more common in large than in small establishments.

We also asked respondents when the recent phase of technical change had actually started. Table 4.3 shows that the recent spate of technical change tended to start earliest in telecommunications (for both engineering and clerical samples) and also in electrical engineering: that is, the two sectors whose products are so intimately related to the growth of new technology. Changes have been much more recent in the two civil service samples and, again, in engineering. That is, those sectors where technical change started most recently tend also to be

Table 4.2 Percentage of establishments in which there has been technical change in the last five years

	Establishments that have experienced technical change (%)
(a) Non-manual/public-sector group	
Finance	95
CPSA civil service	75
SCPS civil service	62
CPSA Telecom	97
POEU Telecom	93
(b) Production group	
Print	73
Chemicals	73
Food and drink	78
Engineering	60
(c) Maintenance group	
Chemicals	81
Food and drink	87
Engineering	68
Electrical engineering	70

those where, as yet, there has often been no previous technical change and where there is little history of technical innovation. Larger establishments are more likely to have started their most recent phase of technical change earlier than smaller establishments.

Planned Technical Change

We now turn to the question of the extent to which management has plans for introducing new technology, but has not as yet done so. We asked respondents: 'During the last five years, has management ever proposed introducing any changes in plant, machinery or equipment in this establishment and not (as yet) actually done so?' Table 4.4 shows that there are a significant number of establishments where this is the case. About three-quarters of respondents in the POEU and CPSA civil service samples say that planned changes have not as yet been introduced, and about half say this in the finance and production samples. There is no relationship between such planned change and

Table 4.3 Start of the technical change

	Percentage of establishments in which change started:		
	Before 1979	1980–1	1982–4
(a) Non-manual/public-sector group			
Finance	39	46	15
CPSA civil service	23	35	42
SCPS civil service	17	27	56
CPSA Telecom	48	40	12
POEU Telecom	61	23	16
(b) Production group			
Print	32	39	29
Chemicals	34	39	27
Food and drink	40	41	19
Engineering	23	30	47
(c) Maintenance group			
Chemicals	40	41	19
Food and drink	59	23	18
Engineering	45	29	26
Electrical engineering	61	23	16

the history of technical change outlined in the previous section. This may in part be explicable by the fact that in about half these cases – and about three-quarters among the non-manual samples – the changes are currently in the process of being implemented; in a number of cases, particularly in the public sector, there are also trials taking place with new types of equipment. However, what is striking is that market factors are an explanation for non-implementation of planned technical change in a substantial number of cases; the lack of demand for the company's products accounts for two-thirds of the cases of non-implementation in engineering and about two-fifths of cases in the chemicals and food and drink samples. Cost factors also figure significantly in many cases. In all, cost or market factors account for a third of the cases of non-implementation in the private sector. In other words, it would appear that in many cases the recession, far from stimulating technical innovation, has obstructed it. Where market-related factors have been less significant – notably among the public-sector and non-manual samples – an important reason for non-

Table 4.4 Percentage of establishments in which technical change was proposed and reasons for non-implementation

	Percentage of establishments in which change proposed	Reasons change not implemented (percentage of establishments where change proposed)					
		Trials	Market	Ongoing	Technical	Union	Cost
(a) Non-manual/public-sector group							
Finance	55	14	5	72	45	9	13
CPSA civil service	72	34	2	76	34	38	13
SCPS civil service	48	19	—	70	23	21	17
CPSA Telecom	58	35	59	70	65	60	25
POEU Telecom	80	46	13	52	41	43	17
(b) Production group							
Print	61	8	28	43	13	38	17
Chemicals	58	22	47	41	19	22	17
Food and drink	51	28	40	48	8	16	8
Engineering	49	6	56	31	15	6	10
(c) Maintenance group							
Chemicals	36	22	35	44	17	30	26
Food and drink	30	24	29	48	14	—	38
Engineering	43	8	60	32	24	16	16
Electrical engineering	35	29	24	47	24	6	29

implementation has been technical problems. This is particularly true of telecommunications and finance. Finally, union opposition has prevented or delayed the implementation of planned technical change in a number of cases. This is particularly so in telecommunications, and to a somewhat lesser degree in the civil service, printing and chemicals. With the exception of the last of these, what is striking is that these samples are of single-industry unions, indicating the extent to which the strategies of these unions at a national level may – for whatever reason – be an important factor in checking management freedom of action in relation to technological innovation. (This is not, of course, to suggest that all workplace organizations will need, be able or wish to engage in such action. Nor does it follow that delays are necessarily anything other than temporary.)

The Nature of Technical Change

Manual Samples from the Private Sector

Having outlined in very general terms the history of technical change found in our survey, we now turn to a consideration of the nature of that change in the last five years. However, in order to understand the pattern of technical change, we also need some idea of the more basic nature of the activities undertaken by the establishments covered by the survey. To this end we employed the conventional, if less than ideal, classification of technology for our manual private-sector samples. That is, we asked respondents whether the main products of their establishments were made as one-offs, small batches, large batches, were mass produced or manufactured by means of a continuous process. Table 4.5 shows that the general pattern is relatively clear and simple. One-offs and small batches are common in all of our engineering samples and to a lesser extent in the printing sample. There are relatively few major variations between the samples in the extent to which large-batch and mass-production techniques are used, but continuous production is concentrated in chemicals and food and drink. However, what is also clear from the table is that in a substantial number of cases more than one of these production methods is employed. In fact, in about a fifth of the establishments some combination of the three main types of production – unit and small batch, large batch and mass, and continuous process – is employed. There is no relationship between the nature of the 'base' technology and the history of technical change, nor the date at which the recent spate of technical change began.

Table 4.5 The nature of the 'base' technology (percentage of establishments)

	Routine adminis- tration	Non- routine adminis- tration	Policy- making	Mixed
(a) Non-manual/public-sector group				
Finance	78	9	9	4
CPSA civil service	76	12	4	8
SCPS civil service	56	27	11	6
CPSA Telecom	79	18	3	—
POEU Telecom	21[a]	11[b]	68[c]	—

	One- off/small batch	Large batch/ mass production	Contin- uous process	Other
(b) Production group				
Print	58	54	18	7
Chemicals	35	39	75	3
Food and drink	10	67	55	6
Engineering	63	52	18	6
(c) Maintenance group				
Chemicals	42	52	70	5
Food and drink	9	44	61	6
Engineering	97	39	19	10
Electrical engineering	80	42	20	10

[a] Internal branch.
[b] External branch.
[c] Composite branch.

The second question concerns the types of technical change that have been introduced. Here, again, there are difficulties in developing an adequate, but relatively simple classification. We finally decided to ask our manual private-sector respondents whether changes in the following areas had occurred: the control of individual machine processes, integrated central control systems, automated handling and storage, and testing and quality control. Table 4.6 shows that there was relatively little variation in the extent to which there had been changes in individual machine processes; this had occurred in some-

Table 4.6 Types of technical change that have been introduced (percentage of establishments in which technical change has been introduced)

	Inform- ation storage	Trans- action clearing	Manage- ment inform- ation	Word pro- cessing	Queries	Other
(a) Non-manual/public-sector group						
Finance	83	80	52	56	43	13
CPSA civil service	75	38	31	49	15	17
SCPS civil service	87	40	58	45	13	10
CPSA Telecom	91	82	91	91	44	9
POEU Telecom	89[a]	70[b]	78[c]	84[d]	—	40

	Individ- ual machines	Inte- grated control	Hand- ling/ storage	Quality control		Other
(b) Production group						
Print	47	14	20	8		47
Chemicals	51	48	60	36		17
Food and drink	56	39	56	23		13
Engineering	56	30	32	46		18
(c) Maintenance group						
Chemicals	54	66	54	12		16
Food and drink	67	70	53	42		17
Engineering	63	42	27	49		22
Electrical engineering	59	53	53	47		18

[a] Switching.
[b] Transmission.
[c] Installation.
[d] Customer apparatus.

where in the region of half the establishments where some form of technical change had occurred in the last five years. The introduction of integrated control systems was rare in printing, and was found in a minority of engineering establishments. Changes of this sort were more common in electrical engineering and in chemicals and food and drink (again, there are variations between the maintenance and production samples, which appear to be largely attributable to the larger establishment size in the former). Changes in handling and storage are more common in those samples where integrated control systems have been introduced (although in this case the variation between production and maintenance samples largely disappears). On the other hand, it is in all types of engineering that changes in quality control and testing have been most common. Where there is a past history of technical change, there is a slightly greater probability that recent changes have included integrated control systems. However, in the recent period of technical change it is those associated with individual machines that have been the first to be introduced. All the types of change distinguished, with the exception of handling and storage, are more common in larger establishments.

In order to develop a more useful picture of the nature of technical change, we need to see how far the different types of technical change are related to each other and to the 'base' technology. Where changes have been made to the control of individual machine processes, there is a slight tendency for there to have also been changes in testing a quality-control methods. Integrated central control systems are associated with both changes in quality control and in methods of handling and storage. There is a tendency for changes in testing and quality control, on the one hand, and storage and handling changes, on the other, to be found together. The different types of technical change are also related to the base technologies, with the exception of changes in individual machines. Integrated control systems are to be found in about half of the large-batch and continuous-process systems, but in only a third of those cases where production is by means of one-offs or small batches. Changes in handling methods and storage are found in just over half the process production establishments, but in rather fewer mass-production cases, and in only a third of the establishments employing unit and small-batch production methods. Finally, changes in testing and quality control are least common in unit and small-batch production (a quarter of cases) and most common in mass production (two fifths of cases; proportions are based on those cases where technical change has occurred). In sum, then, in unit and small-batch production technical change has largely remained at the level of the individual machine; in process production changes in both integrated control systems and in handling and storage are common, whereas in large-batch and mass production integrated control systems are quite common, as also are changes in quality control and handling systems.

The Non-manual Samples

In the case of non-manual samples, we tried to obtain a picture of the nature of the 'base' technology by asking respondents whether the 'bulk of the work in this office is: routine administration, non-routine administration or oriented to policy-making'. About three-quarters of the respondents in the finance and CPSA samples said that their work was primarily routine administration; in the SCPS sample, only slightly more than half of the respondents described the work of their offices in this way. About a quarter of the SCPS respondents said that their work could best be characterized as non-routine administration, and nearly a fifth of those in the CPSA telecommunications sample said the same. Only about one in ten of the other non-manual respondents described their work in this way. The least common type of work was that oriented towards policy-making: about one in ten of the SCPS and finance samples said their work was of this nature, but virtually none of the respondents in the other samples did so. Finally, a small number, particularly within the civil service, described their work as being a mixed nature. For the non-manual samples as a whole, there is no relationship between the nature of the 'base' technology or work process and the history or start of technical change.

We tried to characterize the technical changes that had occurred in non-manual areas, as in the case of the manual samles, in terms of functional areas and activities. We therefore asked our respondents whether changes had occurred in the following areas: information storage and transmission; word or text processing; transaction clearing, calculations, etc.; handling enquiries; and management information. Changes in information storage were found in at least three-quarters of all samples; in finance and in the telecommunications clerical sample, where much of the work involves dealing with a large number of transactions, changes in methods of handling these transactions were found in four-fifths of cases. In the civil service, changes of this kind were only half as common. In nearly half of the finance and telecommunications cases there had also been changes in the way in which queries were handled, again no doubt reflecting the importance of dealing with a large number of transactions. In telecommunications, the two other types of change identified were also particularly common, namely changes in management information systems and word processing. All the types of technical change distinguished tend to be more common in large establishments.

If we look at the relationships between these different types of technical change, the first point which is worthy of note is that the relationships are a good deal stronger than those found between different types of technical change among the private-sector manual samples. This suggests that technical change amongst non-manual groups tends to be of a more thoroughgoing nature. Moreover, central to this clustering of innovation are changes in the system of management information. Finally, we can note that changes in management information systems, word processing and information storage are more common in areas that are described as being engaged in non-routine work. At first sight this seems rather surprising. However, it should be remembered that the question concerns changes that have occurred within the last five years: in other words, it is possible that new systems of information storage had already been introduced in many areas of routine clerical work before the period covered by the question. Changes in transaction clearing and in management information systems are the two types of new technology introduced in the last five years that are most strongly related to a past history of considerable technical change. These two characteristics, along with the way in which queries are handled, are associated with an earlier start to the most recent phase of technical change. These features are again suggestive of a more thoroughgoing pattern of technical change.

Telecom Engineering

In the case of the POEU sample, we again had to develop an additional classification system of both the base technology and of recent technical changes. Our sample of telecommunications engineers covered groups of workers who were engaged in a common national network. However, the coverage of union branches varies within the POEU and so we investigated this as an indication of the relationship between groups of workers and the core technology. Hence we asked respondents whether their branch was an internal, external or composite one. An internal branch covers only engineers working within telephone exchanges; an external branch those who work outside the exchanges. A composite branch covers both types of worker. Two-thirds of our respondents came from composite branches, a fifth from internal branches and only one in ten from external branches.

Pursuing the logic relating technical change to areas of activity, we asked our POEU respondents whether, in their areas, changes had occurred in the last five years in the following: switching systems (i.e. telephone exchanges); transmission systems (i.e. the way in which messages are transferred from one point to another); installation methods; and in the types of equipment used by customers. All four types of change were said to have occurred in at least seven out of ten cases. The most common type of change was in switching systems, the least common was change in the transmission system. Changes in installation methods tend to be more common in larger areas. With this scale of change, it is not surprising that the different types of technical change were even more strongly associated with each other than was the case in the non-manual samples. Hence, technical change is even more thoroughgoing in telecommunications than in non-manual areas. Changes in switching systems are most strongly related to a history of considerable technical change; and changes of this kind, along with changes in transmission systems, are associated most strongly with an earlier start to the latest phase of technical change.

General Patterns of Change

So far we have been considering new technology without any specific reference to 'new technology', that is the incorporation of micro-electronics. We did not feel able in a postal survey to ask in great detail about the exact nature or significance of microelectronic features in any technical innovations that may have occurred. We therefore simply asked respondents: 'Did any of this new equipment incorporate "new technology", that is microelectronics?' In the vast majority of cases it did (table 4.7), and this was particularly true in larger establishments. However, within this general picture there was a slight tendency for microelectronics to be found where there was a history of considerable technical change, although it was not related to the

Table 4.7 Inclusion of new technology where technical change had occurred

	New technology (percentage of establishments where change had occurred)
(a) Non-manual/public-sector group	
Finance	97
CPSA civil service	88
SCPS civil service	87
CPSA Telecom	100
POEU Telecom	96
(b) Production group	
Print	82
Chemicals	87
Food and drink	79
Engineering	84
(c) Maintenance group	
Chemicals	96
Food and drink	99
Engineering	98
Electrical engineering	91

date at which the last phase of technical change began. In the manual private-sector samples, incorporation of microelectronics was most commonly found in integrated central control systems, and least often in new quality-control methods. In the case of the non-manual samples, microelectronics was most strongly associated with word and text processing. Among the telecommunications engineers, the use of microelectronics was most common in changes in customer apparatus and transmission systems. It was found that the inclusion of microelectronics in technical innovations had no distinctive or significant effects on bargaining, job content or union organization.

It is also useful to look at the number of different types of technical change that have occurred in the various samples. Table 4.8 shows that the range of technical change has been greatest in Telecom and in finance. At the other extreme, the smallest range of change is found in printing.

Changes in Capacity and Products

We have argued that technical change is frequently part of a broader strategy on the part of management. Moreover, the nature of that

Table 4.8 Number of types of technical change introduced (percentage of establishments where technical change has occurred)

	Number of types of technical change				
	1	2	3	4	5/6
(a) Non-manual/public-sector group					
Finance	8	23	33	10	26
CPSA civil service	38	25	14	18	5
SCPS civil service	32	13	34	13	8
CPSA Telecom	3	3	18	41	35
POEU Telecom	10	12	16	30	32
(b) Production group					
Print	73	16	11	—	—
Chemicals	36	33	19	7	5
Food and drink	45	30	15	5	5
Engineering	44	39	10	7	1
(c) Maintenance group					
Chemicals	44	24	20	10	2
Food and drink	29	21	26	20	5
Engineering	42	27	20	12	—
Electrical engineering	27	32	24	15	3

broader strategy is important, if we are to understand the reactions of trade unions and the effects of technical change on employment and work experience. Here we consider two key features associated with technical change. The first of these is the extent to which plant capacity has been changed with new technology. Most obviously, if capacity has been increased, then generally speaking any adverse effects of the new technology upon the level of employment will be alleviated, if only in part. The second aspect we consider is the extent to which the product or service has changed with the new technology. Such changes may serve to exacerbate or alleviate the employment implications of a particular technology.

Table 4.9 shows that in very few cases has new technology been associated with a fall in the capacity of the establishment. In the civil service samples, and to a lesser degree in finance, technical change has been associated with no change in capacity. Generally speaking, increases in capacity are associated with technical change. Particularly large increases are found in telecommunications and in the manu-facturing samples, with the exception of the AUEW sample. Increases in capacity are particularly common in continuous process production. In the manufacturing samples, increases in capacity are also associated with changes in handling and storage, and testing and quality-control

Table 4.9 Change in capacity associated with technical change (percentage of establishments in which technical change has occurred)

	Large rise	Small rise	No change	Fall
(a) Non-manual/public-sector group				
Finance	19	33	39	9
CPSA civil service	22	23	48	8
SCPS civil service	12	33	56	—
CPSA Telecom	52	42	6	—
POEU Telecom	55	31	9	5
(b) Production group				
Print	52	33	8	6
Chemicals	49	29	15	6
Food and drink	55	34	8	3
Engineering	29	42	26	3
(c) Maintenance group				
Chemicals	46	35	17	2
Food and drink	52	26	20	2
Engineering	42	29	24	5
Electrical engineering	44	25	22	9

methods. Among the clerical samples, changes in transaction clearing generally mean increased capacity, whereas in the POEU changes in switching and transmission are the main areas where there have been an increase in capacity. Increases in the capacity of an establishment are also associated with a history of considerable technical change and with the recent phase of technical change starting earlier.

New technology is also generally associated with some change in the product or service provided by the organization (table 4.10). This is least true in the case of the civil service and craft manufacturing areas. But even in these cases, the majority of respondents say that some change of product or service has occurred. Major changes in product/service are particularly common in telecommunications. Although they are not associated with size of establishment, such changes are more common in multi- than in single-establishment organizations. This may indicate that the technical change is often associated with a rationalization of activity across plants. Major changes in products are least common in large-batch and mass production and more routine clerical activities.

Changes in product/service are closely associated with changes in capacity: where there have been major changes in the product or service, then it is likely that there has also been a substantial increase

Table 4.10 Change in products associated with technical change (percentage of establishments in which technical change has occured)

	Major	Minor	None
(a) Non-manual/public-sector group			
Finance	50	39	11
CPSA civil service	24	53	23
SCPS civil service	31	52	18
CPSA Telecom	64	30	6
POEU Telecom	76	22	2
(b) Production group			
Print	36	31	33
Chemicals	48	31	22
Food and drink	47	42	11
Engineering	37	34	29
(c) Maintenance group			
Chemicals	53	26	21
Food and drink	40	39	22
Engineering	48	30	23
Electrical engineering	52	36	13

in capacity. Not surprisingly, therefore, these two features of technical change are also associated with substantial increases in output over the last five years. As with changes in capacity, changes in product or service are found where there is a history of technical change and an earlier start to the present phase of technical change. Among manufacturing samples, changes in products tend to be slightly more common where there have been changes in quality-control methods; among non-manual groups, they are common with most types of technical change, with the exception of information storage and word processing. In the POEU sample, changes in products are most common where there have been changes in transmission systems. It is worthy of note that the inclusion of microelectronics in technical change is associated neither with changes in capacity nor product/service.

Employment Effects of New Technology

One of the key topics of discussion in relation to new technology has been its effects on employment. In the main, it has been argued that there will be substantial job losses associated with the widespread use of new technology, although this view has in part been countered by the argument that falls in employment would be even greater if new technology were not adopted, since competitors who do use it would have substantial market advantages. Much of this debate has engaged in a form of futurology which is inevitably little more than sophisticated guesswork. In this section, therefore, we confine the discussion to the effects that technical change has so far had upon employment levels, rather than the effects that it is likely to have in the future.

However, even here we confront serious difficulties. It has already been shown that technical change rarely occurs in isolation: it is typically associated with changes in capacity and in products, for example. It follows that it is extremely difficult to distinguish between the effects of the technology *per se* and the effects of associated changes. This problem was found in an acute form in a number of our case studies. For example, as was noted earlier in this chapter, in the insurance company we studied, the introduction of new technology was associated with changes in the nature of the insurance policies offered and in the way in which policies and premiums were handled. In principle, these changes could have occurred without the introduction of new technology; but in practice they were. As a result of these changes a number of jobs were lost. But this job loss can be attributed to the new technology or to the broader changes, and it is extremely difficult to isolate the exact impact of these two sets of factors. In the same way, in our brewing case study the new lager plant differed from the older plant not only in terms of the incorporation of new technology, but also in capacity. In this instance, even the technical specialists could not strictly attribute the differences in manning between new and old plants to the technology as distinct from the differences in capacity.

It was clearly impossible in a postal survey to ask questions that would permit a fuller pursuit of these complex issues; in many cases, it is probably impossible to reach an accurate assessment as to the effect of the new technology *per se*, controlling for all other variables. Accordingly, we simply asked our respondents how many jobs had been gained and how many lost as a result of technical change over the last five years. It is fairly evident from the pattern of responses (table 4.11) that many replied in terms of the total package of changes associated with the introduction of new technology (cf. Northcott and Rogers, 1984).

In every sample, there are more respondents who say that new technology has led to a loss of jobs than say it has led to an increase; the difference is substantial in every case except electrical engineering. At the same time, however, about half the respondents in the public-sector samples and in engineering say that new technology has had a negligible or no effect on employment. Major job losses are most marked in chemicals and food and drink, that is, the two industries characterized by process production. Overall, about a quarter of all respondents say that technical change was associated with a reduction of jobs of 10 per cent or more. New technology has had a greater impact upon employment in establishments that were larger in employment terms in 1979.

None of the other characteristics of technical change discussed above are related to the proportionate change in employment associated with new technology. This finding is of considerable significance, for – at least as far as experience to date is concerned – it casts doubt upon many of the arguments that have been put forward in relation to new technology. In the first place, we find no support from the survey for the view that technical change has a more dramatic impact – at least as far as employment is concerned – the longer the time that the change has been in place: this is indicated by the lack of association between a history of technical change and the start of the recent phase of technical change, on the one hand, and employment effects on the other. Second, the findings suggest that there is no distinctive pattern of changes in employment associated with particular types of technical change or with microelectronics. We have already suggested that this

Table 4.11 Employment effects of new technology (percentage of establishments in which technical change has occurred)

	25%+ fall	10-24% fall	1-9% fall	-1-+1% change	1-10% rise	11-25% rise	25%+ rise
(a) Non-manual/public-sector group							
Finance	4	29	14	39	7	4	4
CPSA civil service	3	12	24	58	—	—	3
SCPS civil service	4	15	11	64	4	—	2
CPSA Telecom	9	22	4	48	17	—	—
POEU Telecom	—	8	27	55	5	3	3
(b) Production group							
Print	6	8	33	35	12	2	4
Chemicals	19	6	23	32	6	8	5
Food and drink	11	22	19	27	16	5	—
Engineering	9	10	16	60	2	2	2
(c) Maintenance group							
Chemicals	17	15	10	51	5	—	2
Food and drink	25	18	18	31	5	2	2
Engineering	7	18	14	47	6	3	6
Electrical engineering	7	15	15	33	19	7	4

seems quite plausible, given the variety of other changes in markets, etc., which might be occurring simultaneously with the change in technology. It may, of course, be that a more refined measure of technical change with more careful controlling of other factors might lead to a rather different picture. More detailed statistical analyses do indeed suggest, for example, that changes in handling methods account for about a tenth of the variation in the employment effects of new technology in engineering; but such relationships are found in only two of the samples, and in neither case is the explanatory power of technology as such very great.

A number of factors are more important than the nature of technology in affecting the change in employment associated with new technology. The most important of these are changes in output and capacity, management strategy and the role of the union. As might be expected, where output or capacity has increased, then the extent to which employment has been reduced is less. The impact of strong union organization and a more wide-ranging role on the part of the union in relation to change varies between the samples. In a number of cases, job loss tends to be greater where union organization is stronger and where the union bargains over a wider range of issues. This is consistent with the finding from other recent studies that job loss tends to be greater in more strongly organized plants; however, in a number of cases this relationship is not found – for example, in engineering, some maintenance groups and the finance sector.

The question then arises as to whether the relationship between job loss and strong and active unions is a causal one; one possible interpretation is that management is using new technology to reduce the power and influence of strong union organizations. But the fact that indications of management's labour relations policy do not appear in any of the best models explaining changes in employment casts doubt upon this thesis. An alternative account is that this relationship reflects the fact that strong and active unions tend to be found in those establishments that are most central to a company's operations, and hence in those locations where management is most keen to use new technology to improve competitiveness and efficiency. This seems a more plausible account, generally speaking, than a conspiracy theory of this relationship.

Finally, in the public sector, there are a number of cases where the degree of management or supervisory discretion is associated with the scale of job loss; that is, the greater the power of local management, the greater the job loss. This suggests the possibility that a policy of decentralization within the public sector is both aimed at, and is to some degree successful in, reorganizing work, with the consequence that manning levels are reduced.

It can quite rightly be objected that these figures on the employment effects of new technology are misleading, since they fail to take into account the impact of technical change upon other plants where no investment has occurred. Such 'other-plant' effects, however, can be of two kinds. The first is where the company has shifted activity away from one plant in order to load up another where new technology has been introduced. The second kind occurs where the new technology is associated with, and possibly may have given, one plant a competitive edge over another, with the consequence that the management of the latter reduces employment. Our survey data do not permit us to differentiate between these two kinds of 'other plant' effect. Nevertheless, there are a number of cases where respondents indicate that the former has happened, although the number is small. In other cases it would often be difficult to know whether the technical change followed from the rationalization of capacity or vice versa.

We can, however, see how employment has changed in the last five years in those establishments where there has been no technical change, as compared with those where such change has occurred. In fact, there is relatively little variation in changes in employment over the last five years as between establishments where technical change has occurred and where it has not. In a number of the samples, the CPSA in the civil service, chemicals, the production sample in food and drink, and the maintenance sample in engineering, slightly greater employment loss has occurred in those establishments where technical change has occurred. In other cases – the maintenance sample in food and drink, printing and electrical engineering – the reverse is the case, and in still others no variation at all is found. Nor is it evident why these patterns should exist. Again, therefore, we come back to the suggestion that the variety of factors leading to job loss and their different combinations preclude any simple conclusions concerning the employment effects of new technology.

This point is further supportd by another finding. This concerns the proportion of changes in employment over the last five years that respondents attribute to technical change. Where technical change has occurred, a substantial proportion of the total change in employment is seen to be due to the new technology. In other words, little of the change can be attributed solely to other factors which, it would seem, account for all of the job loss in cases where there has been no technical change. This seems somewhat implausible. We are led to the conclusion, therefore, that in their estimates of employment change associated with new technology respondents are generally referring to a wider package of changes rather than the technology per se. In short, this again points to the way in which technical change is intimately bound up with the operation of market forces and management's reactions to those contingencies.

A second aspect of the employment effects of new technology concerns the proportion of remaining workers whose jobs are affected by technical change. There is no *a priori* reason to assume that there is any close relationship between the job loss attributed to new technology and the proportion of workers working on the new equipment. For example, if half the equipment in an establishment was replaced by new technology that was of a highly labour-saving nature, it is quite possible that there would be a very large employment effect, but very few of the remaining workers would be working with the new equipment. Moroever, it might be expected that the effects of technical change on jobs would vary between different occupational groups. In particular, it might be the case that a change that involved relatively few production workers might affect the jobs of a much larger proportion of maintenance workers – unless specialist crews for the repair of the new equipment were set up. We therefore asked respondents: 'What proportion of workers covered by your union here currently work on the new equipment?'

Table 4.12 shows that the proportion of workers directly affected by the new equipment varies considerably between the samples. In the civil service samples and production groups in engineering and

Table 4.12 Percentage of union members directly affected by technical change (percentage of establishments in which technical change has occurred)

	<10%	*10–24%*	*25–49%*	*50–74%*	*75%+*
(a) Non-manual/public-sector group					
Finance	14	21	21	24	21
CPSA civil service	55	14	10	5	16
SCPS civil service	52	18	15	5	11
CPSA Telecom	—	6	12	32	50
POEU Telecom	11	32	20	27	10
(b) Production group					
Print	19	18	11	21	31
Chemicals	17	29	16	19	19
Food and drink	24	26	16	11	24
Engineering	55	19	11	7	8
(c) Maintenance group					
Chemicals	6	10	15	14	56
Food and drink	5	8	3	12	73
Engineering	20	7	15	7	51
Electrical engineering	50	13	6	—	31

electrical engineering, about half the respondents say that less than 10 per cent of their members work with the new technology. At the other extreme, three-quarters or more of workers covered by the respondents' union work on the new equipment in the clerical tele-communications sample and in the maintenance groups. Hence, the suggestion put forward in the preceding paragraph – that maintenance groups are more affected than production groups – receives support from the data. A number of other points are also worthy of note. The first is the relatively high proportion of workers affected in the print sample, where the main changes have concerned individual machines. Second, a relatively low proportion of workers are affected by the new technology in the two samples that represent activities that are central to the new 'technological revolution', i.e. telecommunications engineers and workers in electrical engineering (a sample which includes electronics). There is no relationship between the proportion of workers directly working on the new equipment and size of establishment.

The proportion of respondents' members directly affected by the new equipment tends to be greater in the manual samples, where integrated central control systems have been introduced and, to a lesser extent, where changes in handling and storage have been introduced. In the non-manual samples, the greatest effect on jobs is found where changes in transaction clearing, the handling of queries or management information have been introduced. Changes in installation methods have had the greatest effect on workers in the POEU sample.

We can also see how far the arguments discussed in relation to the employment effects of new technology apply when we turn to the 'job effects' of technical change. In general terms, they receive rather greater support. The first thesis concerns whether or not technical change has a greater effect on jobs as time passes. This is indeed the case; the proportion of workers affected by the new technology is greater where there is a history of technical change and where the recent phase of technical change started earlier. However, as was noted above, there are a variety of ways in which this relationship might be interpreted. The first is that this is a direct reflection of management strategy: that is, employers initially introduce technical change gradually and do not fully exploit it, in order to build up the confidence of workers. Once the equipment is installed, the argument runs, then management will begin to exploit its potential more fully, with the result that a much larger proportion of jobs is affected. A second argument would claim that there are particular types of activity that are inherently more susceptible to technical innovation so that change will start earlier and have a more widespread effect upon jobs.

Along with this, there might be a learning curve in relation to new technology: as time passes, management builds up an expertise in the new technology and is thereby able both to use existing equipment more effectively and to see the possibilities of further technical change. The third 'option' is indicated in a number of our case studies. In the chemicals study, for example, it has been noted above that management had been steadily introducing technical changes over many years and had paid considerable attention to the way in which particular problems might be overcome by introducing new control methods. Similarly, in our machine-tool case study there was a lengthy period of experimentation in which management – or more strictly supervisors – tried a variety of different kinds of jobs upon the numerically controlled machines. They would walk through the shop to see which jobs had to be done and select certain jobs to be undertaken on the new equipment. In this way, they gradually built up an expertise in the way in which the machinery could be used most effectively. As this learning process occurred, efficiency increased and this acted as a further incentive to introduce more and newer equipment. In addition, in this instance, some workers on the new equipment also developed a very high level of skill with computerized equipment and were able to expand its potential, sometimes beyond that outlined by the manufacturers. Not dissimilar processes of learning and modification could be seen in our insurance case study: management were gradually learning which functions could most effectively be performed at local level and which. tasks – typically those of a more routine nature – might be most efficiently undertaken in a more centralized and specialist manner.

There is, however, a further argument, noted previously: that the job effects of new technology have less to do with management strategy or the nature of the new technology as such or associated learning curves. More important than these, it might be argued, are market forces. From this perspective, the greater job effects of technical change over a longer time period would reflect changes in the market situation. At the most simple level, it might be suggested that where technical change occurred earlier, then companies avoided the worst effects of the recession and hence could engage in more widespread technical change. Those who introduced changes more recently confronted market and financial constraints upon the scale of technical change. A subsidiary argument might be that where technical change was introduced earlier, then companies were more competitive; as a consequence, they could better ride the recession and were therefore able to introduce further technical change.

Although our data are not of a kind to permit a full evaluation of these different possibilities, we can throw some light upon the relative importance of these hypotheses. We can evaluate the management conspiracy theory by looking at the extent to which a history of technical change is associated with a variety of adverse effects upon jobs in terms of effort, skill and control. Here we find that there is no relationship between a history of technical change (or the date at which the recent phase of technical change began) and changes in skill, control or effort of those working on the new equipment. There is, however, a slight tendency for improvements in health and safety standards to be associated with a history of technical change and an earlier start to recent technical change. This suggests that there is little overall evidence in support of the conspiracy theory, at least in terms of the degradation of work.

The second hypothesis concerned the nature of technology and the learning cruve. Here we can employ two types of indicator from our data. The first concerns whether or not earlier changes are associated with different types of 'core' production system. The second is the extent to which non-implementation of planned changes is attributable to technical problems. The learning-curve thesis would lead one to expect that this kind of problem would be more common where there was little technical change in the past and where technical change had started more recently. On the first point, there is a relationship between the 'base' technology and both a history of technical change and an earlier start to the recent spate of technical change (see above). On the second point, there is no relationship between the non-implementation of planned changes due to technical problems and our two indicators of past technical changes (it may be the case, however, that those with a history of technical change are more ambitious in their plans and thereby confront problems on a scale comparable with more cautious companies with more modest plans). In short, the available evidence supports the view that particular types of technology are more susceptible to change, but does not support a simple learning-curve thesis.

We turn finally to the questions of the impact of the recession and competitive advantage. There is a strong relationship between the proportion of workers working on the new technology and changes in capacity; in addition, greater change in the past and an earlier intro-duction of new technology are both associated with increased capacity. The market-forces thesis, however, is not really applicable to the civil service, or possibly to telecommunications (in the sense that there is only limited competition). If we confine our attention to the private-sector samples, then we find that our two indicators of a history of technical change are both associated not only with increased capacity, but also increased output. In addition, those who started on the recent phase of technical change later and who have little history of technical change are more likely to confront market and cost constraints upon plans for technical change.

We should emphasize once more that the 'tests' we have been able to conduct to explain the relationship between the 'job effects' of technical change and the history of technical change are extremely crude. But they give no support at all for the conspiracy theory nor for a simple learning-curve view. There is, however, some support for the contention that particular types of 'base' technology are more susceptible to widespread and continuing change than others. But perhaps the most important explanation of greater job effects over time concerns market factors and competitive edge: that is, those who embarked upon technical change earlier were able to introduce it more widely because they achieved an advantage in the the market place and, relatedly, because they embarked upon change prior to the recession. We therefore return to a point made earlier: namely, that the exacerbation of market forces in the recession appears to have checked rather than promoted the extent to which companies have taken up new techology.

Conclusions

In this chapter, we have attempted to provide a broad outline of the nature of the technical change found in the survey largely as a background to our discussion of the way in which unions affected, and were affected by, technical change. But in characterizing new technology along a number of dimensions, we have considered two key aspects of technical change for workers and unions. The first of these was the job loss associated with new technology. Here we found that job loss was considerably more common than job gain; this was particularly true in the two samples where process production was common – chemicals and food and drink. Morover, strong union organizations often appeared to be unable to prevent any job loss (although it is possible that they were able to affect the precise number of jobs lost). However, it was clear that respondents often felt unable to differentiate between the employment effects of the new technology per se and the effects of other factors included in the broader package of change introduced by management. Our detailed case studies also indicated the very real difficulties of accurately assessing the impact of new technology upon employment.

We also looked at the argument that new technology had progressive effects upon employment levels; that is, as time passed, the job loss attributable to new technology would increase. We found no support for this view. However, there did appear to be considerable 'job effects' as time passed: that is, the greater the history of technical change and the older the recent phase of technical change, the larger the proportion of workers working on the new equipment. But it appeared that this could not be explained in terms of a management conspiracy of gradually exploiting the new technology in order to win worker consent to changes that would subsequently 'degrade' their work. Two other factors appeared to be of greater significance. First, particular 'core' production systems were more susceptible or amenable to widespread technical change than others; second, the role of market forces and the competitive advantage of new technology affected the scale of technical change. An important implication of these findings is that, at least as far as the adoption of new technology is concerned, the deflationary policies of the government militate against the improved competitiveness of many firms.

5 Trade Unions and the Process of Technical Change

The previous chapter has outlined the general pattern of technical change found in the survey. Given this background, we now go on to look at the role the unions played in the introduction of new technology. In doing so, we pay particular attention to a number of hypotheses, which were outlined in chapter 1. It is, however, useful to consider these more fully before we turn to the actual findings.

The primary thrust of our argument has been that different types of union organization are likely to pursue different priorities both generally and in relation to technical change. We have suggested, for example, that, other things being equal, unions that deal with one employer or industry will seek to negotiate over a wider range of issues than will unions that cover a variety of employers and industries. This argument relates to the national structure of the union. But we have also argued that this tendency may be cross-cut by a number of other factors. The first of these concerns the nature of union organization within the establishment. Hence, where a variety of unions exist within a plant, then, we have suggested, the issues over which they bargain will be affected by the extent to which they co-operate; that is, the greater the degree of unity, the more they are able to go beyond sectional interests and seek to influence issues that structure and shape more detailed negotiations. A similar point applies in relation to the union's own organization within the plant; that is, the more 'sophisticated' its organization, or the more internally united it is, the greater the role it can play. Other factors of relevance in this context include the size of the union within the workplace and its relative importance. The larger it is, and the greater the proportion of union members in the establishment it has, the greater the role it can play. Finally, and related to the arguments concerning the nature of the larger union, we have suggested that the union within the plant is also likely to play a greater role, the stronger its connections with the larger union. In short, in addition to factors relating to the size and relative importance of the union within the establishment, we have suggested the importance of three different types of unity or integration; these relate to the individual union within the plant, the various unions within the plant, and the links between the in-plant and the larger trade union. Moreover, we have suggested that these three features will be related to the nature of the larger union. Hence, in the case of the single-employer union, and to a lesser degree the single-industry union, the links with the larger union – external integration – will be stronger. The degree of integration of the individual union within the plant is likely to be affected by the size of its membership, but also by the degree of external integration and the degree of unity across unions. The extent to which the various unions within the establishment are integrated will tend to be greater where the major union is multi-industry and multi-occupational in character, and covers a substantial number of union members.

These arguments have been broadly confirmed in part 1 as far as the general pattern of bargaining activity is concerned. We are arguing that the same pattern will be found in relation to new technology. A further hypothesis therefore suggests itself, namely, that the pattern of union activity in relation to new technology will be broadly comparable with that found more generally.

The role the union plays is also likely to be affected by the level at which bargaining takes place. This is closely related to the nature of union organization, and it is often difficult to disentangle the effects of bargaining, on the one hand, and union structure, on the other. However, it is worth noting the way in which bargaining structure is likely to affect the union's role in relation to new technology. Given any particular level of sophistication, the more centralized bargaining is, the greater the role that the union is likely to play in terms of the range of issues over which it negotiates. This is so not only because the degree of union unity is likely to be greater both in relation to other unions and the larger union under these conditions, but also because the unions are thereby induced to take a broader perspective. The opposite situation perhaps makes the argument more obvious: where unions negotiate over new technology solely at shop-floor level, then it is less likely that they will be able to play any significant role on more strategic issues. Moreover, there are often limitations on the extent to which all issues can be negotiated at any one level; we would therefore further suggest that the greater the number of levels at which bargaining occurs, the greater is likely to be the range and degree of union influence.

These institutional and organizational features cannot totally encapsulate the factors that shape the role the union plays. We need also to take into account the precise nature of the occupations covered by the union, as noted in chapter 1, and the traditions of negotiation and consultation within different establishments and companies. In particular, we would point to the importance of three features found in our survey. The first is the tradition of widespread negotiation and consultation within the public sector, and particularly in telecommunications (which at the time of the survey was still in the public sector). In other words, the traditions here have been of a kind that has encouraged a widespread role for the unions (see, e.g., Batstone *et al.*, 1984). Despite changes in the 'political contingency' over the last few years, we would expect this tradition still to be evident. Second, we need to take into account the fact that the NGA, although much of its membership is concentrated in relatively small establishments, has traditionally achieved a very high level of influence through its pursuit of traditional craft strategies; this is reflected in a high level of external integration and the frequency of multi-employer bargaining. Third, in much of the finance sector, the role of the union – in terms of union density, organizational sophistication and the range of bargaining – has gradually been developing over the last decade or so. Particularly given its widespread effects in the finance sector, technical change might be associated with the further strengthening and development of union organization. This certainly appeared to be so in our insurance case study. There the changes associated with new technology had seen the strengthening of the union in terms of all three aspects just outlined. This was not attributable solely to new technology, but to a range of changes of which technical factors were only a part. These changes affected member and management attitudes and provided a vehicle on which the union could ride into some areas that had traditionally been the preserve of management.

This case also highlights another point of relevance. The role that the union plays might be expected to vary according to its perception of the technical-change package proposed by management. For example, if the change involves no job loss, then one might not expect unions to bargain over job security. In other words, the arguments outlined above concerning the way in which union structure affects bargaining are likely to be modified by the union's interpretation of the proposed technical change itself. However, a more sophisticated union organization may seek to establish certain principles concerning technical change, even if these do not immediately arise. In other words, the range of union activity may not be shaped significantly by the nature of management's proposals.

This raises the question of so-called new technology agreements. A number of unions have recommended their members to seek agreements with management concerning procedures and conditions for introducing new technology. The precise nature of these agreements varies: some tend to be of a primarily procedural nature, others focus on substantive issues. Most obviously, we would expect to find such agreements where the union has stressed their significance. But they are probably more common where the plant is closely involved with the larger union. However, it might also be expected that more sophisticated organizations would be more ready to seek such agreements in order to establish and protect the future interests of their members. On the other hand, well-organized groups may prefer not to separate out new technology from the more general run of bargaining: that is, they may believe it is preferable to ensure that all issues are covered by the normal pattern of bargaining.

Whether new technology agreements exist will also depend on management. In fact, only one or two respondents reported that the question of a new technology agreement was a matter of serious disagreement. But our case studies indicate the extent to which new technology agreements are dependent upon management views. In our machine-tool study, both management and union were ready to make such an agreement, and negotiations were therefore entered into with relative ease. In our insurance case study, the union was also quite keen to have a new technology agreement, but management was opposed to this on the grounds that the very existence of an agreement might encourage a form of new technology phobia among employees. No agreement was made, but management agreed to negotiate many issues that would have been included in a new technology agreement. In the other two cases, there was no union pressure for a special agreement.

At several points in the preceding discussion we have raised the question of the approach adopted by management. We have been at pains throughout this study to stress that technology in and of itself has few clear effects; it is the broader strategy within which new technology is encapsulated that is more important. That is, the nature of technical change has to be seen as an aspect of management strategy. To the extent, therefore, that one can talk of a coherent management strategy, it might be expected that technical changes that brought serious adverse effects for unions and their members might reflect a more general company policy of effort intensification, and reducing the power and role of both unions and workers. However, the effects of such tactics on the part of management are likely to vary. For example, to the extent that management did weaken the unions, then the range of bargaining might be reduced and the union might have less influence over the pattern of change. On the other hand, if the union had not been seriously weakened, then it might be spurred to greater opposition to management goals.

Finally, market forces may affect the pattern of bargaining over new technology. Strictly, we cannot trace market pressures, but simply the way in which management reacted to changes in its market position. This is particularly true in multi-plant companies, where decisions arise as to where to concentrate production in the face of reduced demand. This will be reflected in changes in output and in employment in individual establishments. We have already seen that there is a relationship between the state of the market and the policies adopted by management. But it might also be expected that adverse market trends will both shift the balance of power and possibly change the attitudes of the union and its members. The conventional argument would lead one to expect that large falls in employment and in output would lead to a lower range of bargaining and a moderation of demands on the part of the union.

In sum, this chapter will be guided by a number of hypotheses. The first of these concerns the effects of the structure of union organization and the general pattern of bargaining upon the role of the union in the process of technical change. The second focuses on the nature of the technical change itself. The third theme relates to the more general labour relations strategies pursued by management, and the fourth to the impact of market forces upon union activity. In pursuing these themes, we will consider a number of dimensions of the union's role. Most obviously, we will look at the areas of negotiation over new technology. We also consider the pattern of major disagreements and union proposals concerning new technology. Third, we consider how far management conceded to these proposals and the extent to which the union imposed sanctions upon management in pursuit of its goals and demands. First, however, we discuss the level of bargaining over technical change and patterns of union decision-making.

The Structure of Bargaining and Union Decision-making over New Technology

Bargaining Levels

We consider first the level at which bargaining over new technology occurred. Briefly, it was expected that this would be a reflection of the more general pattern of bargaining. Table 5.1 shows the pattern

Table 5.1 Percentage of establishments negotiating technical change at various levels

	Company level	Establish- ment level	Shop-floor level
(a) Non-manual/public-sector group			
Finance	88	48	18
CPSA civil service	86	62	22
SCPS civil service	83	44	14
CPSA Telecom	94	71	31
POEU Telecom	96	60	11
(b) Production group			
Print	59	64	42
Chemicals	19	68	44
Food and drink	26	60	51
Engineering	16	64	56
(c) Maintenance group			
Chemicals	16	50	36
Food and drink	21	51	36
Engineering	—	67	36
Electrical engineering	23	81	23

of responses to the question: 'Were issues relating to the new equipment the subject of negotiation at any of the following levels: above the establishment, at the establishment, on the shop-floor?' Respondents were asked to tick as many as applied. The vast majority of public-sector and non-manual respondents said that bargaining occurred at company level. In addition, roughly half of them also said that bargaining occurred at the level of the establishment; and in the case of the CPSA samples, in particular, some bargaining also occurred at shop-floor level. The NGA sample is characterized by a rather distinct pattern in which bargaining was relatively common at all three levels distinguished. In the remainder of the manufacturing samples, establishment-level bargaining was the most common, although generally with additional bargaining at shop-floor level, particularly in the case of the production group.

The pattern found, then is strikingly similar to that found more generally as far as bargaining is concerned. Indeed, there is a strong relationship between the level at which negotiation occurred over new technology and the level of general bargaining activity. This is the case both when we consider the formal level of bargaining over pay and the number of issues actually bargained at different levels. This relationship is marked in the case of company-level bargaining, particularly for the public and non-manual samples. Hence 90 per cent of those groups who normally bargained at company level also did so in relation to new technology; 58 per cent negotiated at establishment level, and only 19 per cent at shop-floor level.

The pattern is rather less strong in the case of the production samples. In this case bargaining over technical change generally occurred at establishment level, even when bargaining on pay typically took place at company or multi-employer levels. Indeed, company-level bargaining on new technology was rather more common where the general level of bargaining was multi-employer than where it was at company level. Moreover, no matter what the general level of bargaining, shop-floor negotiation over technical change was also relatively common.

The pattern of bargaining over new technology is different again in the case of the maintenance samples. Although establishment-level bargaining is once more the most common in relation to new technology, the maintenance samples differ in two respects from the production samples. First, company-level bargaining is less common, except where this is the normal level of bargaining; second, particularly where bargaining generally takes place within the company, shop-floor negotiation over technical change is somewhat less common than in the production samples.

About two-thirds of respondents in the manual manufacturing samples say that bargaining over new technology occurred at only one level (table 5.2); just under a quarter negotiated at two levels, and about 10 per cent bargained at all three levels distinguished. Multi-level bargaining is especially common in printing. Among maintenance samples bargaining typically occurs at only one level, and few negotiated at all three levels distinguished. Multi-level bargaining is most common among the non-manual and public-sector samples: here nearly half the respondents say that they bargained at more than one level; a third at two levels; and one in seven at all three levels. The frequency of multi-level bargaining in printing and the public sector suggests the importance of company or multi-employer bargaining, if negotiations over new technology are to occur at several levels.

In all three groups of samples, multi-level bargaining is more common where union organization is more sophisticated. Closer integration with the larger union and a more active involvement of the larger union in the process of technical change are also associated with multi-level bargaining in the maintenance samples and, to a lesser degree, in the non-manual/public-sector group; no such relationship exists in

Table 5.2 Number of levels at which technical change was bargained over (percentage of establishments)

	1	2	3
(a) Non-manual/public-sector group			
Finance	66	17	17
CPSA civil service	47	35	18
SCPS civil service	65	25	10
CPSA Telecom	34	34	31
POEU Telecom	43	46	11
(b) Production group			
Print	57	17	25
Chemicals	62	31	7
Food and drink	67	21	12
Engineering	66	26	8
(c) Maintenance group			
Chemicals	84	11	5
Food and drink	74	16	10
Engineering	80	20	—
Electrical engineering	73	23	4

the case of the production samples. Indications of management adopting a 'hard-line' towards the unions and large-scale job loss are associated with less multi-level bargaining only in the case of the maintenance samples. Finally, in all groups, the greater the range of changes in technology, the more likely that bargaining will occur at a number of levels.

Union Decision-making

The pattern of union decision-making on new technology is closely related to the level at which bargaining occurred (table 5.3). Again, this reflects the pattern found more generally. We investigated two aspects of union decision-making. The first concerned who ratified 'major agreements relating to the new equipment', the second the role that the larger union played. On the first point, we asked respondents about the role of the same groups as we had asked about in relation to ratification generally. In overall terms, there was a 'match' in 79 per cent of cases; that is, in these cases the normal practice of some or no ratification was followed in the case of new technology issues. The main exception to this 'matching' was that a fifth of respondents

Table 5.3 Ratification of agreements on technical change (percentage of establishments)

	Any ratifica-tion	Ratification by:				
		Branch	Mass meeting	Ballot	Shop stewards	Large union
(a) Non-manual/ public-sector group						
Finance	91	18	9	24	57	33
CPSA civil service	85	22	6	3	47	65
SCPS civil service	75	12	2	—	33	57
CPSA Telecom	97	29	12	21	53	62
POEU Telecom	100	43	—	—	21	71
(b) Production group						
Print	86	37	28	15	20	48
Chemicals	86	57	19	9	44	4
Food and drink	84	41	22	13	69	9
Engineering	77	—	25	8	73	17
(c) Maintenance group						
Chemicals	45	—	30	9	57	17
Food and drink	49	9	38	9	50	9
Engineering	56	4	25	13	65	9
Electrical engineering	76	—	19	8	85	8

who said that agreements were generally ratified in some way said this was not the case with new technology. The matching of particular kinds of ratification was on a similar scale. Shop stewards ratified more agreements concerning new technology than they did normally; hence in 42 per cent of the cases where stewards did not normally ratify major agreements, they did so in relation to new technology. Shop stewards played a greater role in this respect at the expense of the larger union and, to a lesser degree, mass meetings. It seems that the less frequent resort to ratification procedures and the enlarged role of the shop stewards reflected the relatively moderate changes involved in, or associated with, new technology; stewards accordingly assumed the functions generally undertaken by the membership or the larger union.

As was the case more generally, the pattern of ratification is related to the level of bargaining. The larger union ratified agreements more frequently where bargaining over new technology occurred at company level; in this case, steward ratification was relatively rare. Where negotiation took place at the establishment, then those within the workplace were more likely to ratify agreements on new technology; the same pattern is found with shop-floor bargaining.

The second aspect of union decision-making that we investigated specifically in relation to new technology was the role of the larger union. We asked respondents whether the larger union played a direct role in negotiations; whether it offered specific advice; whether it gave general information; or whether it played no role at all. The larger union was most active in telecommunications, where it was said to have played a direct role in negotiations in well over half the cases (table 5.4). The larger union also often negotiated over new technology in the other non-manual samples and in printing – these findings again suggest the importance of bargaining level and union structure. In these samples, the union was also more frequently said to have given specific advice. In the remainder of the samples, about half the respondents said that the union played no role at all in relation to new technology, and, where it had, rarely did this go beyond the provision of general information. With the exception of engineering, the larger union was typically less involved in the case of maintenance than production samples: this again reflects the small numbers of electricians

Table 5.4 Role of the larger union in technical change (percentage of establishments)

	Negotia-tion	Advice	Infor-mation	No role
(a) Non-manual/public-sector group				
Finance	47	24	53	18
CPSA civil service	56	31	40	7
SCPS civil service	45	30	37	5
CPSA Telecom	74	35	32	6
POEU Telecom	61	27	33	5
(b) Production group				
Print	44	28	31	13
Chemicals	12	12	31	49
Food and drink	21	13	26	49
Engineering	8	7	29	60
(c) Maintenance group				
Chemicals	8	8	36	55
Food and drink	12	7	22	59
Engineering	10	8	31	51
Electrical engineering	12	6	36	49

found within any individual plant. Where the union is more strongly represented – as in electrical engineering and to some degree in engineering more generally – then it plays a greater role; and, for any given size of membership, the EETPU tends, if anything, to play a marginally more active role than many other unions.

In all the groups of samples, the role of the larger union was greater when technical change was the subject of negotiation at company level; in the non-manual and public-sector samples, the larger union actually played a role in negotiations in 62 per cent of cases where technical change was negotiated at company level, whereas it did so in only a fifth of other cases. In the production samples, 41 per cent of the respondents said that the union played a direct role in negotiations where bargaining was at company level, whereas this was so in only 12 per cent of other cases. Finally, in the maintenance samples, the larger union was involved in a quarter of the cases where technical change was negotiated at company level, but in only 8 per cent of other cases. In addition, where the establishment was more strongly integrated with the larger union generally, there was a greater probability that the latter played a more active role in relation to new technology. In the case of the production and maintenance samples, the greater the degree of sophistication of the respondents' own union organization within the plant, the greater was the role of the larger union in relation to new technology.

Areas and Issues in Bargaining over New Technology

Bargaining Range

We asked respondents the following question in order to find out about the range of bargaining: 'Which of the following issues relating to the new equipment were the subject of negotiation by your union at some level?' The issues listed were: investment strategy, the precise equipment used, manning levels and working practices, job grading and pay levels, the selection and training of workers, and working conditions and health and safety. Table 5.5 shows that negotiations tended to be confined to traditional industrial relations issues. Matters concerning investment strategy, for example, were rarely the subject of negotiation, except in the case of the POEU, a union that has a long tradition of discussing both management strategy and new technology (see Batstone et al., 1984). Within the manufacturing samples, the negotiation of investment was rather more common among production than maintenance samples. Bargaining over equipment was rather more common; this was often the case in the POEU, but it

Table 5.5 Areas of negotiation over technical change (percentage)

	Invest-ment	Equip-ment	Manning	Pay	Training	Health
(a) Non-manual/public-sector group						
Finance	—	30	70	70	27	84
CPSA civil service	5	51	88	67	67	90
SCPS civil service	7	23	87	54	57	89
CPSA Telecom	17	77	100	80	71	97
POEU Telecom	40	52	75	82	34	59
(b) Production group						
Print	16	31	80	75	58	63
Chemicals	17	21	83	64	41	79
Food and drink	23	33	82	92	54	77
Engineering	16	16	75	68	52	57
(c) Maintenance group						
Chemicals	12	5	51	45	41	60
Food and drink	10	8	57	44	53	51
Engineering	7	7	51	42	56	51
Electrical engineering	6	16	63	63	44	63

was also a frequent occurrence in both the CPSA samples. Again, maintenance groups were less likely to negotiate over this issue than production (or non-manual) groups.

In contrast to the rarity of negotiation over investment strategy and equipment, the vast majority of respondents said that bargaining did take place over manning and pay, issues that can be seen as central to the traditional bargaining pattern. Three-quarters or so of the non-maintenance respondents said manning was a matter of negotiation; among the maintenance samples such bargaining was less common. Maintenance groups negotiated over pay even less often than over manning. In telecommunications, print and the production food and drink sample, negotiations over pay were particularly common.

Training and health come between the two extremes of management strategy and the wage-effort bargain as traditional issues for bargaining. In fact both issues were frequently negotiated in relation to new technology. Training was most commonly negotiated by non-manual public-sector groups; the contrast between these, on the one hand, and the POEU and finance samples, on the other, is particularly striking. In addition, the maintenance groups were, relative to their bargaining on other new technology issues, much more likely to negotiate over training: this, along with the frequency of negotiation over training in the printing sample, is consistent with a craft strategy of maintaining and promoting the qualifications of its members. The EETPU has been particularly keen to ensure that its members are trained in microelectronics. Negotiation of health and safety is virtually universal in the non-manual samples; production groups, particularly where continuous process production is common, are more likely than maintenance groups to bargain over health and safety.

The pattern of bargaining over new technology can best be summarized by looking at the number of issues that respondents say were negotiated. Table 5.6 shows that the smallest number of issues were negotiated by the maintenance samples, whereas, at the other extreme, the greatest range of bargaining occurred in the public sector. Simple cross-tabulations indicate that, within the groups of samples, there is a tendency for a greater scale of technical change – as indicated by the number of different types of change occurring and, in the case of the maintenance and non-manual/public-sector groups, the proportion of workers working on the new technology – to be associated with a wider range of negotiation. Neither management's labour relations policy nor the scale of job loss have much effect upon the range of bargaining.

Most important in explaining the range of bargaining are two factors. The first is the number of levels at which bargaining occurs. The

Table 5.6 Number of issues negotiated (percentage of establishments)

		1/2	3	4	5+
(a)	Non-manual/public-sector group				
	Finance	46	26	21	8
	CPSA civil service	31	18	25	27
	SCPS civil service	30	25	30	14
	CPSA Telecom	11	14	14	60
	POEU Telecom	22	31	21	26
(b)	Production group				
	Print	35	25	22	19
	Chemicals	34	24	28	14
	Food and drink	25	25	18	33
	Engineering	44	21	24	11
(c)	Maintenance group				
	Chemicals	65	21	12	2
	Food and drink	67	7	21	4
	Engineering	62	19	19	—
	Electrical engineering	51	24	19	5

second is the role that union organization plays (although a fairly high level of union sophistication is a pre-condition of multi-level bargaining). Where the larger union plays a role, there is a tendency for there to be a greater range of bargaining; moreover, where internal union organization is more developed, we find that more issues are bargained over. Crucial in the non-manual/public sector and production groups is the degree of 'own union' sophistication; in the case of the maintenance samples, it is the sophistication of union organization more generally which is more important. More detailed statistical analyses confirm that the number of levels of bargaining is the crucial factor, whereas features of union organization play a secondary role. In these more sophisticated analyses, the scale of technical change along with other characterizations of the new technology fail to play any significant role; the scale of job loss and management strategy are also unrelated to the range of bargaining over new technology.

Related to these findings is the hypothesis suggested above: that the pattern of bargaining over new technology would largely reflect the pattern of bargaining found more generally. This is indeed the case; however, so few of the respondents said that they did not negotiate the four issues investigated generally (see table 3.7) that a more detailed analysis of this theme is of limited value. However, the thrust of the argument concerns the union maintaining its frontier of control with management. We can therefore usefully look at how far respondents' assessments of the degree of union power and influence are related to the range of bargaining over new technology. We find that the greater the control the union exercises over management, the more likely it is to bargain over issues relating to new technology.

Disagreements and Union Initiatives

As was noted above, a further question which we need to address is the extent to which unions took initiatives in relation to new technology. Two types of initiative can be distinguished: the first concerns the extent to which they challenged management proposals, with the result that significant disagreements arose; the second concerns the extent to which the unions put forward their own proposals.

On the first point, we asked respondents: 'Were there any major disagreements between management and your union on matters relating to the new equipment?' Table 5.7 shows that in a significant number of cases respondents say that there were such disagreements. This was particularly true in the telecommunications samples, where over three-quarters said that this was the case. With the exception of the printing and chemicals production samples, disagreements were less common among the manual manufacturing and maintenance samples than the non-manual group. We also asked about the issues over which these disagreements arose. Disputes over management strategy and equipment account for a quarter of the finance disagreements, but for few of the disagreements in the other samples. In these, more conventional industrial relations issues were the subject of dispute. With the exception of disagreements over strategic issues and equipment, the finance sample tends to follow the pattern of the other non-manual samples; that is, relatively frequent disagreement over manning and health issues. In the SCPS sample, however, job security was relatively more important than the question of health and safety. With the exception of engineering, manning was a frequent topic of disagreement among the manual production samples, although AUEW respondents said they often had disagreements on the related issue of demarcation. Among the printers and electricians, pay (or grading) were common sources of disagreement, and the latter often argued with management over the question of training. Respondents rarely mention more than two issues of disagreement.

The existence and scale of disagreements between management and unions might be expected to be related to the nature of management's proposals. We did not feel able to investigate the details of the process of negotiation in the survey and hence our subsequent discussion is somewhat partial. Nevertheless, our general hypotheses are of relevance here. We might expect, for example, that disagreements would be more frequent where management adopted a tougher approach to the unions. Where there had been substantial job losses, the unions might be less able to challenge management. We might also expect that where the scale of technical change was greater, the unions would be more likely to disagree with management's proposals. Finally, the stronger the union organization and the more centralized the pattern of bargaining, one might hypothesize, the greater will be the frequency of disagreements.

Although bargaining level is not related to the number of disagreements, the number of levels at which bargaining takes place is. In all three groups, the greater the number of levels of bargaining, the greater is the likelihood that there has been a serious disagreement with management over the question of technical change. Related to this is the finding that the more sophisticated the union organization, the greater is the likelihood of disagreement. However, there are a number of interesting variations in the role that different aspects of union organization play. In the case of the non-manual/public-sector samples and the production samples, it is the sophistication of the

Table 5.7 Disagreements over new technology: (a) any disagreement; (b) percentage of those who disagree on specific issues; (c) number of disagreements

	Any disagreement (%)	Percentage of those who disagreed re:						
		Management strategy	Equipment	Health	Training	Grading	Manning	Work organization
(a) Non-manual/public-sector group								
Finance	47	27	27	27	—	7	27	14
CPSA civil service	53	9	11	24	4	20	33	9
SCPS civil service	59	9	12	15	9	15	53	12
CPSA Telecom	77	4	12	32	8	8	48	20
POEU Telecom	82	11	3	—	8	15	61	11
(b) Production group								
Print	59	6	8	8	3	7	44	3
Chemicals	50	5	10	12	10	21	52	21
Food and drink	40	7	7	27	7	7	60	20
Engineering	30	—	16	16	11	—	16	—
(c) Maintenance group								
Chemicals	38	7	7	—	33	13	27	7
Food and drink	23	—	—	7	14	14	14	7
Engineering	42	7	13	7	33	27	7	7
Electrical engineering	44	—	—	14	7	7	—	21

Table 5.7 (*continued*)

	Percentage of those who disagreed re:						Number of disagreements (%)	
	Job security	Pay	Hours	Demarcation	Procedure	Other	1	2+
(a) Non-manual/public-sector group								
Finance	33	7	—	7	—	—	21	16
CPSA civil service	13	9	2	2	9	7	36	17
SCPS civil service	38	12	—	9	3	6	28	33
CPSA Telecom	12	4	—	—	—	16	42	33
POEU Telecom	2	5	2	11	2	15	54	27
(b) Production group								
Print	8	42	8	6	6	3	40	20
Chemicals	5	10	5	5	—	7	29	17
Food and drink	13	13	13	7	—	—	24	16
Engineering	11	16	5	37	—	—	24	6
(c) Maintenance group								
Chemicals	7	20	—	13	—	7	19	10
Food and drink	—	36	—	29	—	—	15	4
Engineering	13	20	—	13	—	20	17	19
Electrical engineering	14	29	—	14	—	7	38	6

respondents' own union organization that plays the greatest role; but for the maintenance samples, it is the degree of sophistication of the unions collectively within the establishment that is crucial. This again reflects the fact that the number of electricians in establishments is typically small; they therefore need to be integrated with the other unions in order to achieve the resources required for strong bargaining stances. In the case of the private-sector samples, a greater role for the larger union is also associated with a greater level of disagreement; it may be that where disagreements occur, shop stewards turn to the larger union for advice and support. However, the general pattern of the data – as, for example, in the case of union proposals – suggests the importance of the wider awareness of the nature of technical change and union interests which full-time officials bring into negotiations.

Also relevant to the scale of disagreements is the policy adopted by management. Where management pursues a tougher approach, then disagreements are more likely. But shifts in the balance of power, as indicated by the scale of job loss, appear to be relatively unimportant in their effect upon the amount of disagreement over new technology.

Finally, we can look at the extent to which features of the technical change itself affect the level of disagreement. With the exception of the production samples, the number of different types of change taking place is related to the number of disagreements. In the case of the private-sector manual samples, we also find that the greater the proportion of workers affected by the technical change, the greater are the number of disagreements.

More detailed statistical analyses indicate that organizational variables play the major role in all the samples, although in the case of the non-manual and public-sector group the scale of technical change – as indicated by the number of different types of technical change occurring – plays a secondary role.

The second aspect of union initiative concerns the extent to which the union developed its own proposals. Part (a) of table 5.8 shows that in a substantial number of cases the unions did develop their own ideas in relation to technical change and presented them to management. Moreover, the more likely the union was to put forward any proposals, the more likely it was to put forward a number of them. Union proposals were particularly common in the non-manual and public-sector samples, and least common among the maintenance samples.

Part (b) of table 5.8 shows the areas in which the unions put forward proposals. The POEU is distinctive in that a quarter of the respondents say that their union made proposals relating to management strategy, whereas this was very rare in other samples. The frequency of proposals on equipment was greatest among the clerical telecommunications respondents and in the food and drink production sample. Maintenance groups and the POEU were less likely to concentrate their proposals in this area. Non-manual unions often made proposals on health and safety matters, as did those in the food and drink production sample. Training, on the other hand, was very much a concern of the maintenance unions. Reflecting more bureaucratic labour-management patterns, perhaps, non-manual and public-sector groups were the most likely to put forward proposals on the regrading of jobs, and the public-sector groups were generally also the most prone to developing their own ideas on work organization. These groups, together with the production samples, also frequently put forward proposals concerning manning levels. Craft groups were more likely to take initiatives relating to demarcation questions. Finally, pay was an area where production groups were likely to put forward suggestions.

Union proposals tended to cluster around a group of issues: health, grading, manning, pay and, to a lesser degree, training and work organization. The pattern of union proposals is closely related to the pattern of disagreements over new technology. We cannot tell from the survey, however, whether unions developed their own proposals as a result of disagreements with management or whether disagreements arose as a result of union initiatives.

The greater the number of different types of technical change that have occurred, the more likely unions are to have put forward their own proposals in the non-manual/public-sector and the maintenance groups; this relationship is not found in the production samples. The number of workers affected by technical change is not related at all to the degree to which the union took initiatives. The nature of management's approach towards the unions and the labour force appears to be relevant only in the case of the maintenance samples, where a tougher management approach is associated with a greater tendency for the union to take initiatives. The scale of job loss is not related to union proposals.

The most important factors explaining the extent to which unions put forward their own ideas, however, are the number of levels of bargaining and the sophistication of union organization. In all three groups, the greater the number of levels at which bargaining occurred, the greater is the tendency for the union to put forward its own proposals. A greater role for the larger union is also associated with a higher initiative rate; as far as internal union organization is concerned, we find the same pattern as in the case of disagreements: that is, the union's own degree of sophistication is most important for the non-manual/public-sector and production groups, whereas the

Table 5.8 Union proposals regarding new technology: (a) percentage of establishments where there were any proposals; (b) percentage of those establishments where there were union proposals with proposals on specific issues

	Any proposals (%)				Percentage of those with proposals regarding:				
	None	1	2	3+	Strategy	Equipment	Health	Training	Grading
(a) Non-manual/public-sector group									
Finance	26	29	21	24	4	11	71	10	22
CPSA civil service	21	29	26	24	7	20	71	23	33
SCPS civil service	33	21	11	35	8	8	60	22	40
CPSA Telecom	18	30	18	34	—	44	78	19	30
POEU Telecom	17	41	32	10	27	12	18	9	25
(b) Production group									
Print	19	32	17	32	2	21	25	19	8
Chemicals	42	23	18	17	8	22	31	28	24
Food and drink	43	18	18	21	9	32	64	18	9
Engineering	61	23	5	11	8	21	25	25	17
(c) Maintenance group									
Chemicals	63	23	8	6	—	11	16	47	16
Food and drink	59	31	9	1	4	4	18	50	11
Engineering	57	26	10	7	—	6	19	71	29
Electrical engineering	54	28	9	9	—	7	20	33	20

Percentage of those with proposals regarding:

	Manning	Work organization	Job security	Pay	Hours	Demarcation	Procedure	Other
(a) Non-manual/public-sector group								
Finance	19	11	41	14	4	—	11	5
CPSA civil service	38	23	12	15	6	1	—	1
SCPS civil service	57	19	30	19	5	11	5	11
CPSA Telecom	44	19	4	4	4	—	—	7
POEU Telecom	43	21	3	9	—	5	—	15
(b) Production group								
Print	38	13	2	46	15	15	8	10
Chemicals	53	14	6	16	6	6	2	12
Food and drink	36	27	9	41	5	9	5	9
Engineering	25	8	8	25	—	17	—	4
(c) Maintenance group								
Chemicals	21	11	—	26	—	11	—	—
Food and drink	18	—	4	7	4	11	—	—
Engineering	6	12	11	18	—	—	—	12
Electrical engineering	7	13	13	33	—	20	—	—

general level of union sophistication is the key factor in the case of the maintenance samples. More detailed analyses confirm the centrality of bargaining levels for the level of union initiatives.

In sum, then, broadly the same pattern is found in the case of the range of bargaining, the degree of disagreement and the extent to which unions put forward their own proposals. What is crucial is the pattern of bargaining and the degree of union sophistication. These two sets of factors are related: it is only with more sophisticated union organization that bargaining is likely to occur at a number of levels; in addition, it seems likely that the opportunity for multi-level bargaining is greater when the formal structure of bargaining is more centralized (on the grounds that it is easier for a union to bargain informally at levels below the formal bargaining structure than it is for it to do so at higher levels). Relative to the importance to these institutional and organizational features, the evidence suggests that the state of the labour market, management strategy and the nature of the technical change itself play a relatively marginal role.

Sanctions and Concessions

The survey also permits us to look at what happened when unions took initiatives. First, we can see whether the unions threatened or imposed sanctions in the course of technical change; second, we can investigate how far management agreed to union proposals. Table 5.9 shows, first, the proportion of the various samples that threatened to impose sanctions upon management in relation to new technology, and, second, the proportion that actually did so. It can be seen that both the threat and use of sanctions was particularly high in telecommunications; in the civil service, printing and the chemicals production sample sanctions were also relatively common. However, only about a quarter of the other private-sector samples threatened action and only about one in ten actually put the threat into practice. The threat and use of sanctions were most strongly related to disagreements over management strategy and, to a lesser degree, work organization, manning and job security. Relatedly, they were more common the wider the range of bargaining, the greater the role that the larger union played, and the more sophisticated establishment-level union organization was. Finally, where management adopted a tougher approach, there was a greater likelihood that the unions would resort to the use of sanctions.

The question, then, arises of the extent to which the threat or use of sanctions induced management to make concessions to union proposals. Management was more ready to agree to union proposals

Table 5.9 Percentage of establishments in which sanctions are (a) threatened and (b) used

	Sanctions threatened	Sanctions used
(a) Non-manual/public-sector group		
Finance	16	9
CPSA civil service	34	20
SCPS civil service	30	18
CPSA Telecom	59	38
POEU Telecom	72	26
(b) Production group		
Print	31	22
Chemicals	29	20
Food and drink	28	10
Engineering	20	7
(c) Maintenance group		
Chemicals	25	7
Food and drink	28	9
Engineering	20	5
Electrical engineering	21	9

when these were backed up by the threat or use of sanctions. More generally, table 5.10 shows that management often did accept union proposals to a fairly substantial extent. This was so in the majority of cases where the unions put forward proposals, except in the case of the maintenance samples and the higher civil servants. In addition, we find that management was more ready to agree to union proposals on some issues than on others; for example, it was more ready to do so on health and safety and, to a lesser degree, manning. Management was least ready to accept proposals on job security. More generally, the greater the range of bargaining and union initiative, the more ready management was to make significant concessions (although, not surprisingly, the greater the number of disagreements, the less likely management was to concede to union demands). Therefore, it is not surprising to find that management made concessions where the larger union was more active and where establishment-level union organization was more sophisticated. Management's labour relations policy was only weakly related to its readiness to make concessions, and employment trends were only relevant in the maintenance samples.

These findings, then, provide additional support for the contention that what is crucial to an understanding of the role of the union in

Table 5.10 Extent to which management agreed to union proposals (percentage)

	Great deal	Fair amount	Not much	Not at all	No proposals
(a) Non-manual/public-sector group					
Finance	17	33	19	5	26
CPSA civil service	17	36	18	8	21
SCPS civil service	11	15	23	19	33
CPSA Telecom	6	59	11	6	18
POEU Telecom	9	41	29	4	17
(b) Production group					
Print	31	33	11	6	19
Chemicals	14	20	11	13	42
Food and drink	16	19	10	10	44
Engineering	12	15	5	7	61
(c) Maintenance group					
Chemicals	2	10	14	12	63
Food and drink	10	9	12	11	59
Engineering	—	10	18	15	57
Electrical engineering	—	31	9	6	54

relation to new technology is the structure of union organization. In particular, we have pointed to the importance of the degree of sophistication of the respondents' own union in the case of the non-manual, public-sector and production samples. These samples are characterized by relatively large concentrations of members and a relatively high proportion of total establishment union membership being accounted for by the respondents' own union. In the case of the maintenance samples, the respondents' union typically has a small number of members, which are only a small proportion of the total union membership in the plant. As a result, the extent to which it can independently build up its own organization is limited. At the same time, the fact that in maintenance areas the EETPU's membership is widely dispersed across a very large number of employers means that it is difficult for it to maintain close relations with many of its members. Consequently the general sophistication of the union organization within plants plays a more significant role for the maintenance groups than it does for comparable production groups.

However, in all cases, the role of the larger union is also relevant to understanding the scope of bargaining and the range of union initiative. Generally, when we find both full-time official involvement and a high level of union sophistication in organizational terms, we also find that bargaining occurs at a variety of levels. This was found to be important in explaining the scope of union action in relation to new technology; where there are three levels of bargaining, for example, it means that, at one extreme, there is greater opportunity to negotiate general issues relating to management strategy at company level, and to bargain about detailed aspects of change on the shop-floor, at the other (possibly within a framework of agreements made at higher levels). Indeed, such multi-level bargaining appears, overall, to be the most important factor in explaining the range of union activity in relation to technical change. Relative to the importance of union organization and multi-level bargaining, indicators of the nature of technical change, changes in the labour market and management's more general labour relations policies appear to be of limited significance. They are relevant in some cases, but their direct impact upon the range of bargaining and union activity is small, relative to the indicators of bargaining structure and union sophistication.

Finally, it is useful to spell out what is implicit in much of the preceding discussion – namely, the relationship between broader union structure and the pattern of bargaining. If we average across the relevant samples, we find that the range of bargaining over technical change is highest in single-employer/industry unions (over half of respondents claim that they negotiate over four or more issues), whereas in multi-industry, multi-occupation unions less than two in five and under one in four from multi-industry, single-occupation unions negotiate over this number. The same pattern is found for union proposals; these are twice as common in single-employer/ industry unions as in single-occupation, multi-industry; multi-industry, multi-occupation unions come between these two extremes. Moreover, similar variations in bargaining and union initiatives are found on strategic issues, relating to investment and equipment. On the other hand, on issues relating to the protection of the occupation – notably training – the single-occupation respondents play a much more active role. These findings, then, give considerable support to the arguments outlined in chapter 1.

Our case studies provide a useful illustration of many of the preceding arguments. In the brewery and the engineering company, the unions had – relatively speaking – a good deal of influence over the way in which technical change was introduced. In the former, in particular, they were given the opportunity to discuss management's plans, but, more importantly, they negotiated on many issues: these ranged from manning levels and job gradings, through to safety, training and selection methods. In addition, they put forward proposals concerning single-grade manning which were accepted (although this can be attributed to union pressure only in part): this meant upgrading of jobs and hence increases in pay. Similarly, in the engineering company the union was involved in a wide range of issues; three key points of union strategy in this case are worthy of note. First, the union used the introduction of new technology as a basis upon which to put forward a wide range of claims relating to pay and the payment system, hours of work and related issues. Second, they negotiated a new technology agreement (see below); and, third, they argued for operator programming of the new CNC machines (as in the brewery study, their success in this respect cannot be solely attributed to union pressure). At the other extreme, in the chemicals plant the union had virtually no influence over the way in which automated plant was introduced. They were merely informed of management plans and no negotiations occurred over matters relating to manning and work organization. Between these extremes was the insurance case: here the range of bargaining at company level over the move to on-line processing of personal lines insurance was significant. It covered matters relating to health and safety, manning levels and issues relating to redundancy and transfers. However, these extensions to the traditionally limited range of bargaining were attributable to the fact that the introduction of new technology was part of a wider process of rationalization, which raised many of these issues in a more acute form than did new technology alone. These patterns of bargaining over new technology, then, broadly reflect the more general pattern of bargaining in the various plants: even in the insurance company, it can be argued that the range of negotiation over new technology reflected the more general extension of bargaining range. In addition, therefore, we find that the range of bargaining over new technology is related to the degree of union sophistication (see chapter 3).

However, what is also striking in the case studies was the lack of trauma over the introduction of new technology. This is related to the link between general patterns of bargaining and that relating to new technology. One of the reasons for this link is that, unless management wishes to use new technology as an opportunity to transform the pattern of industrial relations (and in none of our case studies was this the case), many 'new technology' issues are already covered by existing agreements, or else those agreements indicate the direction in which issues should be resolved. For example, in the brewery, the union extended its influence somewhat over the matter of training and into the selection of workers to work on the new plant. The union had always been involved in training workers – and important in this was the fact that more experienced workers trained junior workers. On the new plant there were clearly no experienced workers: the union insisted that one worker should be formally trained initially and he would then train the other workers. In the same way, the traditional patterns of selection could not be applied to the new plant; the union insisted that traditional practices should be conformed to as far as was possible and, in addition, discussed the criteria by which workers should be chosen. Similarly, and particularly in the engineering case study, we see the way in which 'new' demands flow from traditional interests and strategies. Here a largely craft workforce had traditionally been concerned to ensure that less skilled manual workers did not begin to man machines. The introduction of CNC machines introduced a new source of challenge to their position – that non-manual groups would invade their traditional job territory. Accordingly, the union sought to preserve that territory and the claims to craft status by pushing for operator programming.

A Note on New Technology Agreements

So far in this chapter we have said nothing about new technology agreements, and yet a good deal of the literature has focused upon their potential significance for protecting member and union interests when technical change occurs. Hence a number of unions have encouraged shop stewards to seek to establish new technology agreements with their employers. In our survey, we found that such agreements were particularly common among the public-sector and non-manual respondents and in printing. They tended to be least common among the maintenance samples (table 5.11). It might be expected that such agreements would be more effective where they covered a wider constituency: that is, where they covered a variety of unions and particularly where they covered both manual and non-manual groups. The second part of the table shows that where new technology agreements existed, they typically covered only the respondent's union; rarely did they cover both manual and non-manual groups. The main exceptions to this pattern were the civil service samples. New technology agreements were more common in all the groups of samples where bargaining occurred at company level, and where the union played a more active role in negotiating technical change. In the private-sector manual samples, the existence of new technology agreements was also associated with a greater degree of union sophistication.

The third part of table 5.11 shows respondents' answers to the question of how useful such new technology agreements were. In the main, respondents say that they found such agreements were very or fairly useful, but there were particular noteworthy exceptions to this pattern. They appear to have been least useful among the more senior

Table 5.11 New technology agreements: (a) percentage of establishments with agreement; (b) coverage of agreement; (c) usefulness of agreement

	Coverage of agreement				Usefulness of agreement			
	Percentage with agreement	Own union only	Comparable unions	Manual and non-manual unions	Very	Fairly	Not very	None
(a) Non-manual/public-sector group								
Finance	58	80	—	20	58	21	21	—
CPSA civil service	63	40	45	15	27	45	23	5
SCPS civil service	45	11	72	17	6	37	49	8
CPSA Telecom	97	93	—	7	26	26	39	10
POEU Telecom	57	95	2	3	20	51	18	11
(b) Production group								
Print	59	81	14	5	49	32	14	5
Chemicals	22	48	8	44	29	51	20	—
Food and drink	28	45	28	28	28	62	10	—
Engineering	15	33	54	13	33	40	14	13
(c) Maintenance group								
Chemicals	8	(50)	(50)	—	25	25	25	25
Food and drink	22	(83)	(8)	(8)	21	50	21	8
Engineering	13	(50)	(50)	—	19	19	31	31
Electrical engineering	21	14	43	43	—	84	16	—

civil service groups and among clerical workers in telecommunications; in addition, maintenance groups seems to be less impressed by their utility than production groups. When we seek to understand why assessments of the usefulness of agreements vary, we do not find any variation by the coverage of the agreements. The main factors that explain favourable assessments are both simple and obvious: they are seen in a more favourable light when management agrees to union proposals, when there are fewer disagreements, and when there is less resort to collective action. In the private-sector manual samples, new technology agreements are also seen as more useful when they are associated with strong union organization and a greater role on the part of the larger union.

If we seek to assess the significance of new technology agreements by means other than respondents' assessments, it appears that they are associated with a wider range of negotiations, a greater range of union initiatives and fewer disagreements with management. In other words, they appear to expand the range of union bargaining and initiative. However, if we control for other factors, then these relationships become much weaker: in other words, the significance of new technology agreements reflects, in the main, the characteristics of those unions that have them. These tend to be stronger and better organized groups, which would in any event be more likely to have a wide range of bargaining and to take initiatives. This is not, however, to deny the potential utility of these agreements. It has already been noted that many of those who have such agreements say they find them useful. It may also be the case that such agreements provide additional institutional security to the range of bargaining and may, in rather less strong organizations, provide some additional strength to the bargaining range and influence of the union.

There is, however, another point. We have noted that disagreements are less likely where there are new technology agreements, even though there is, if anything, a greater range of bargaining. What this suggests is that either management is more likely to accept union demands and proposals when they come within a new technology agreement, or that the sorts of managements who are prepared to accept new technology agreements are in any event likely to be more sympathetic to union proposals: that is, the existence of such an agreement may be an indication, rather than a cause, of good relationships. However, the relationship between management's approach towards unions and the existence of new technology agreements is not very strong. It may, however, be that the agreements were signed when management adopted a more supportive approach towards the unions and that this has subsequently changed. If this is the case, then it provides added support for the contention that the significance of such agreements lies in the provision of a degree of institutional security for the activities of the union in relation to new technology.

When we look at the effects of technical change upon workers, we do not find that such agreements are associated with more favourable outcomes, once we control for other variables. Nor, once other factors are controlled for, do new technology agreements appear to ensure a greater degree of union control, once the change has actually been introduced. A final possibility is suggested by the experience in our engineering case study: here a new technology agreement was negotiated as new equipment was being introduced. However, by the time this agreement on principles had been made, the details of the actual implementation of the CNC machines had already been agreed. Hence the new technology agreement had no significance for the era of technical change upon which our research focused: it may, however, be of relevance in the future. If this experience is at all common, it suggests that it is too early to assess the general utility of new technology agreements. However, we suggest that their significance will generally depend upon the factors discussed in this and preceding chapters – in particular, the degree of union sophistication.

6 The Effects of Technical Change on Job Content and Rewards

In this chapter, we turn to the question of the way in which technical change affected the nature of jobs and pay. For a number of years there has been a good deal of discussion of this topic; some have argued that new technology deskills and degrades jobs, whereas others have argued the reverse. For example, Blauner (1964) argued that although in earlier phases of industrialization technical developments had tended to reduce skill levels and demean jobs, more recent technological innovations had the reverse effect. Against this view, it has been widely argued that new technology degrades jobs and leads to a reduction in skill levels. This point of view has a very long radical tradition, and has recently been associated with theories of the labour process. Hence, for example, Braverman (1974) argues that the degradation of work, in terms of reduction of skill levels, the eradication of any degree of worker control, and the intensification of effort, is crucial to the profitability of large modern enterprises. One of the central means by which this is achieved is through technical innovation. This argument has not only been applied to manual workers, but has also seen a recent popularity in the case of clerical jobs. Crompton and Jones (1984), for example, have recently argued that new technology has marked degrading effects upon white-collar work.

These highly general arguments, as has been increasingly recognized, can be criticized on a number of grounds. In the first place, they fail to take into account the possibility of variations in the effects of technical change upon jobs. Technical change may increase the skill levels of some occupations and reduce that of others. The effects of new technology may also vary according to the precise nature of the technical change and the nature of the 'base' technology. But, more fundamentally, these general arguments either embody a form of technological determinism or a belief that all employers pursue identical strategies, which workers are unable to moderate and change. We have argued against such technological determinism at a number of points in the preceding chapters, and those criticisms apply with equal force in this instance.

The second point just raised – the unanimity of employer policies – raises once more the question of management strategy. After the initial phase of debate within the labour process school, a number of writers have begun to recognize that there are a range of quite different strategies which employers may pursue (e.g. Edwards, 1979; Friedman, 1977). In the main, the attempts to differentiate between managerial strategies have been poorly based empirically and have sought simplicity rather than any very close approximation to reality. However, they do suggest that not all managements will seek to degrade workers' jobs through technical change. Indeed, a number of recent developments in job design indicate that many employers are becoming increasingly aware of the disadvantages of a very detailed division of labour and tight controls over workers. These disadvantages can arise both from the nature of the production process itself (Kelly, 1982), and the adverse effects of degradation upon worker motivation and compliance with management goals. For our purposes, the important point is that the effects of new technology upon jobs are likely to vary according to the strategies of management.

If management's strategies affect the way in which jobs change with new technology, then it seems equally reasonable to expect that worker strategies will have a similar effect. Indeed, one of the major criticisms of the Braverman thesis of degradation is its failure to take into account the effects of worker resistance. The importance of worker behaviour and action has been demonstrated in a number of historical studies, perhaps most notably that of Lazonick (1979). Here again, however, we would expect variations in the degree to which workers can affect the way in which technical change shapes their jobs. More strongly organized workers are likely to have more influence. This is likely for at least two reasons: first, because of the resources that they are likely to have at their command; and second, because well-organized groups are better able to identify the implications of management proposals and develop strategies to countract them. In other words, well-organized groups will be more likely to achieve influence over a wider range of issues relating to new technology and to intrude further into managerial prerogative. We would expect more favourable job effects not only in strongly organized plants, but also where the range of union initiatives and proposals is greater.

These arguments, however, assume that the process of technical change is comparable in all cases. But it is possible, for example, that management seeks to use technical change to reassert control precisely in those sectors that are strongly organized. This may come about either because a primary rationale for technical change is the reduction of worker control, or indirectly because the sorts of plants in which large-scale technical change takes place happen to be those that are well organized. For example, it might be reasonable to expect that management will concentrate any large-scale change upon large plants; but large plants are more likely than smaller ones to have well-developed union organizations. Hence, we find an association between strong union organization and large-scale change, but that relationship may not be a causal one. Second, we have to take into account the possibility that the balance of power changes not only because of technical change itself, but for other reasons. Most obviously, it seems plausible to suggest that where workers have been particularly hard hit by job loss, they will be less able to check management attempts to reduce worker skills and exert tighter control over jobs.

We are back, then, to our general set of hypotheses concerning the relative impact on jobs of technical change itself, management strategy, union organization and behaviour, and market forces. However, it is also necessary to take into account three other sets of considerations. The first of these concerns the nature of work. The discussion of the effects of technical change has paid scant attention to the fact that jobs vary along a number of dimensions. There is a tendency, therefore, to assume that new technology will have similar effects upon skill, control, and so on. Relatedly, notions such as skill and control have been used in a rather cavalier fashion; they have not been clearly defined. This is an important problem, as is illustrated in a number of our case studies. Two examples will suffice.

In our insurance study, the work of underwriters was changed considerably. Prior to the introduction of new technology, they had some degree of discretion over the premiums charged to customers and they also had to employ arithmetical skills in order to calculate those premiums. With the introduction of computerized systems, the range of discretion of underwriters was reduced and at the same time the computer performed the necessary calculations. On two counts, therefore, the job of the underwriter could be seen as being deskilled. There were also a number of countervailing tendencies, however. First, the underwriter had to learn new skills in order to use the computerized system. Second, it is far from evident that the loss of arithmetical skills to the computer was undesirable from the viewpoint of the underwriters themselves. Put crudely, how many people would prefer to spend a considerable part of their working day doing the same arithmetical calculations rather than being able to key in the information to a computer, which then does the calculations? Third, although the computer (and associated changes in types of policy) undoubtedly reduced the amount of labour required, it meant that proportionately more time was spent on less routine tasks, such as answering telephone queries from clients. Moreover, the fact that such queries could not be predicted in any reliable manner meant that the computerized system could not really be used as a very effective means of control over underwriters: it was not possible to know in advance how many calls they would be required to answer, nor how long it would take to sort out the problems of different clients. Accordingly, one could not lay down rules concerning the required inputting rate of underwriters. Finally, underwriters were now required to deal with a larger range of policies so that their knowledge requirements were increased.

The second example is from our machine-tool case study. In this instance, the introduction of numerically controlled machines meant that many of the physical tasks central to the skills of the engineering craftsman were now undertaken by the machine; this suggests a reduction of skill. However, against this, the craftsmen now had to learn not only how to use the new machines, but also how to program them. In other words, their skill changed. They now had to think of their traditional functions in a more conceptual way. In some instances, with more modern machines, this was not too difficult a task – or so it seemed at first sight – since the machine asked a number of questions of the craftsman. But in a number of cases, the craftsmen, using their traditional knowledge, could conceive of more effective ways of machining parts than was permitted by the machines' internal programs, and they developed the ability to alter the parameters set by these programs. Here, then, two important points arise: first, we have the problem of evaluating the relative importance of the decline in traditional craft skills and the requirements of new conceptual ones. Second, we have to take into account the effects on skill levels of worker initiative in learning to change programs (see also Sorge *et al.*, 1983; Wilkinson, 1983).

An important limitation upon the discussion in this chapter is that we were unable in the survey to investigate these complex questions of skill in any depth. We were, however, able to ask respondents about different aspects of jobs. We considered four areas: the effects of technical change upon skill (as defined by the respondents, who in effect had themselves to resolve the complex problems just outlined); the way in which the control of the individual worker over his or her work had changed; changes in the level of effort required of workers as a result of new technology; and, finally, the effects of technical change upon health and safety standards.

The second factor that we need to take into account is the extent to which changes in job content may be affected less by the technology itself than by the extent to which, and the manner in which, management chooses to allocate the functions associated with the new technology. Changes in task allocation are likely to vary between different types and scales of technical change. New technology not only provides an opportunity to change the content of jobs, but in many cases forces management to consider job content. For the new technology may take over certain tasks previously done by workers, and therefore the question arises of whether there are enough tasks to be done if traditional job descriptions are left unchanged. Similarly, the new technology often creates new sets of tasks, and decisions have to be made as to who should do these. Third, technical change sometimes means that conventional criteria for differentiating between jobs become confused; it is therefore necessary to decide which should take predominance or to create new criteria.

This sort of problem has been particularly common in the case of craft demarcations, but it is also to be found in many other cases. Again, our case studies can be used to illustrate these points. Perhaps the most interesting example comes from our brewing case study. The new plant was installed for market reasons and the question of the gains from new technology was a relatively peripheral issue. In part because of this, little consideration was given at the planning stage to how the new plant would be manned: it was simply assumed that traditional arrangements would apply. However, as the construction of the plant progressed, it became increasingly clear to management that, since the new technology would undertake a number of tasks that were done by workers on the older plant, conventional manning patterns would mean that several workers would be seriously underemployed. As a result, it was necessary to decide how a reasonable level of manning could be achieved. The final solution, supported by the union, led to a considerable increase in the skill requirements of those working on the new plant relative to the old.

In the chemicals case study, the nature of the base technology, the type of technical change, and the scale of new plant introduced were all similar to the brewing case. This made for a particularly interesting contrast in the organization of work between the two situations. In the chemicals study, we found that the traditional grades were transposed, in so far as was possible, to the new plant. The only exception was in the creation of the new job of control-room operator. However, even this was in line with the traditional practice of rigid, formal task and job demarcation. Managers agreed that the type of organization found in the brewing case could, in theory, have been introduced in the new chemicals plant. But, in practice, they felt that to have done so would have disturbed industrial relations too much by changing the established grade structure. In addition, they were concerned to reduce plant-operator discretion (which was seen to be one cause of quality problems), and felt that the form of work organization adopted facilitated that goal. The union played no discernible role in the organization of work in the new chemical plant, and was quite satisfied with what had been established. In considering the cases of chemicals and brewing independently, it was clear that management policies, as well as the pattern of industrial relations, had influenced the form of work organization adopted quite independently of the technology. A comparison of the two cases makes this even more evident.

In the machine-tool case study, problems arose over the question of who should prepare programs for the CNC machines. Although it seems that top management were finally in favour of this task being given to the craftsmen, there was an initial period when this was a subject of disagreement. The shop-floor finally won the day and programming became the responsibility of the craftsmen.

These examples indicate the need to investigate the extent to which functions are shifted between groups when new technology is introduced. Such changes may have a considerable effect upon the various dimensions of job content outlined above. Accordingly, we asked respondents whether functions had been moved from their group to higher-level groups (e.g. from manual to non-manual), and whether any tasks had been moved in the reverse direction. We also asked whether there had been many changes in demarcation between manual (or white-collar) groups with the new technology. Again, these questions are very crude; we did not ask what functions were changed, not did we ask whether changes in demarcation had led to favourable or unfavourable changes in jobs for the respondents' members.

The third and final point that needs to be considered in this introduction concerns further limitations of our data. In a postal survey it was not possible to trace in great detail the process of negotiation, so that our picture is very crude. It is necessary to recognize, as was noted in the previous chapter, that a union may be induced to put forward proposals because management is planning changes that adversely affect members' jobs. But we do not know whether or not this was so; all we know is whether the union put forward proposals, how far management agreed to them, and how jobs changed. Hence, it is possible that a greater range of union initiatives is associated with adverse changes in job content, which would have been even worse if it was not for union pressure. However, if unions react when member interests are endangered, then our initial thesis may be seen as achieving greater support if, for example, there is a relationship between management agreeing to union proposals and favourable job effects. In short, we cannot fill out the whole picture concerning why it was that changes in job content occurred, and hence our findings can only be taken as indicative.

In this chapter, then, we consider the effects of technical change upon jobs. In the first section, we consider the extent to which changes in task allocation were associated with new technology. We then go on to look at the four aspects of job experience distinguished earlier in this introduction. Third, we look at the material rewards deriving from new technology: that is, we discuss how far technical change was associated with favourable or unfavourable effects on the pay and grading both of those working directly upon the new equipment and workers more generally. Here we again pursue the question of the relative importance of union organization and strategy, management's approach, the state of the labour market, and the nature of the technical change itself.

Changes in the Alloction of Functions

In this section, we consider three aspects of changes in task allocation: the first concerns changes across broadly comparable groups, for example, between production and maintenance grades. The second concerns the extent to which technical change is associated with the removal of tasks from the respondents' group (e.g. manual workers) to a higher group (e.g. non-manual grades); and third, we consider moves in the reverse direction.

Part (a) of table 6.1 shows that there has been a great deal of change in demarcation with technical change. It is only among the civil service, production engineering and electrical engineering samples that more than two-fifths of respondents say that no such changes have occurred. At the other extreme, in many samples a third or so say that there have been substantial changes of this kind (the codes 'great deal' and 'fair amount' of change). Such large shifts are least common in the civil service and engineering production, but they are also rare in finance. There is also a slight tendency for greater changes in demarcation to take place among maintenance rather than production groups. This may be due either to attempts by management to remove craft demarcations or to shift certain maintenance functions on to production workers; or it may simply reflect the extent to which maintenance groups are affected by technical change. Certainly other data indicate that new technology often means that the traditional skills of the various crafts have to be fused (e.g. Sleigh *et al.*, 1979).

Table 6.1 Changes in task allocation in connection with technical change: (a) extent of change in demarcation among comparable groups; (b) percentage of establishments where functions shift to higher groups; (c) percentage of establishments where functions shift from higher groups

	Extent of change in demarcation among comparable groups:				Establishments where functions shift to higher groups (%)	Establishments where functions shift from higher groups (%)
	Great deal	Fair amount	Not much	None		
(a) Non-manual/public-sector group						
Finance	8	14	44	33	13	31
CPSA civil service	—	19	30	51	2	3
SCPS civil service	8	13	34	45	3	—
CPSA Telecom	—	43	37	20	20	20
POEU Telecom	10	24	39	27	21	2
(b) Production group						
Print	13	19	37	32	19	3
Chemicals	13	23	35	30	21	21
Food and drink	21	11	32	37	6	10
Engineering	5	19	31	45	21	8
(c) Maintenance group						
Chemicals	16	26	41	18	31	6
Food and drink	14	23	32	32	15	12
Engineering	7	31	31	31	32	8
Electrical engineering	9	21	27	42	31	9

The extent to which changes have occurred in demarcation is not related to the extent of job loss. However, there is a slight tendency in the case of the non-manual/public-sector and maintenance groups for the nature of management's labour relations policy to be associated with the degree of change in task allocation. In these two groups, the less supportive the approach of management, the greater the extent to which changes have occurred. The fact that this relationship is not found in the production groups suggests that one important aspect of management attempts to reassert control is to shift work away from maintenance groups and to production workers. Such changes may appear very significant to the maintenance groups, but be relatively marginal for the production workers. However, an even stronger relationship is found between the scale of changes in demarcation and the range of technical change that has occurred. The greater the number of changes, the greater the changes in demarcation (there is no relationship between changes in demarcation and the date at which technical change began). In short, then, the scale of technical change and, to a lesser degree, the nature of management's approach towards labour account for a substantial part of the variation in the extent to which there have been changes in task allocation between comparable groups.

It was noted in the introduction to this chapter that there were limitations upon the extent to which we could assess the significance and meaning of changes in task allocation and the success of union strategies in relation to these matters. We can note, however, that changes in demarcation have been greater where union organization is more developed, in the case of the non-manual/public-sector and maintenance groups; no such relationship, however, is found in the production samples. Moreover, we find that greater changes in demarcation are associated with a wider range of bargaining and a greater number of disagreements. The latter suggests that frequently the unions have been opposed to the nature of the changes (conceivably even demanding that they be greater) or the precise terms on which they have been made. However, there is no relationship – except in the case of the maintenance samples – between the scale of change and the extent to which management has agreed to proposals put forward by the union. In other words, it is not the case that strong unions or unions that took greater initiatives were able to prevent changes in demarcation. We do not, however, know that they wished to do so (as will be seen in subsequent sections, changes in task allocation are not systematically related to adverse effects of technical change on job content).

Changes in task allocation within comparable groups have been considerably more common than shifts of functions from respondents' groups to higher groups. Changes of the latter kind have been extremely rare in the civil service; they are more common among the maintenance groups (see parts (b) and (c) of table 6.1). Again, it is difficult to know to what extent such moves have been favoured by the unions. The EETPU has often supported a move of its more skilled members from hourly to staff status, and such moves could be classified as a shift of functions to white-collar grades.

These changes in task allocation are not associated with the scale of change in employment, although in the private-sector samples they are more common where management has adopted a tougher policy towards labour. However, widespread changes in demarcation have occurred more often where the range of technical change is greater (although this relationship is relatively weak in the case of the maintenance samples). Once more, changes of this kind are more common, the stronger the union's organization within the workplace and the greater its tendency to take initiatives in relation to technical change.

The respondents' own grade has less often received additional tasks than it has lost them to higher grades. The one notable exception to this pattern is the finance sector. This sample and the clerical group in telecommunications are the most likely to have received additional functions as a result of technical change, along with the production chemicals sample. Changes of this kind are least common in the civil service, the POEU and the printing samples. Again, we find that the scale of employment change is not associated with shifts of tasks to the respondents' group; nor are they related to management's labour relations policy. Only among the non-manual grades are task changes of this kind associated with the range of technical change. The scale of union bargaining and initiative appears to be significant only for production groups, where the number of disagreements tends to be greater where such shifts have occurred.

In summary, the data indicate that there have been substantial changes in the allocation of tasks as a result of technical change. The most common changes have been within broad categories of labour. The loss of functions to higher-grade groups is, however, rather more common – except in finance – than is an accumulation of additional functions by the respondents' own group. In the main, changes in task allocation are more common the greater the scale of technical change and, to a lesser degree, the more aggressive management's stance towards the unions and the workforce. Moreover, many changes of this kind are to be found in the more strongly organized establishments, where unions have played an active role in relation to technical change. But, with the available data, we cannot assess whether the changes have been of a kind favoured by the unions, and hence whether the relationship between union initiative and shifts in tasks reflects the success of union endeavours or attempts to change management plans which have failed. The reality is probably that both elements are to be found. However, the next section shows that changes in task allocation are not related to adverse changes in job content.

The Impact of Technical Change on Job Experience

A survey is always dependent upon the knowledge and perspectives of its respondents. It is particularly important to keep this in mind when we turn to issues that are complex or when the experience of respondents may provide them with a partial or distinctive perception. Hence, for example, it is possible that some respondents were unaware of the full range of new tasks associated with technical change, because many of them were assumed by management without any discussion with the union. But this problem may also be particularly acute when we turn to questions of job content, and particularly to issues relating to 'skill'. This notion is a difficult one to define in any clear and objective manner; indeed, we argue in our case-study volume that it is not a useful concept in any detailed analysis. However, we felt that in the survey it was an area which we had to investigate, no matter how crudely. Here, then, the crucial questions concern what respondents meant by skill and how they implicitly measured it. Clearly, this is likely to vary between respondents. In addition, the very experience of having to learn new skills, even if they are less demanding than 'traditional skills', might lead respondents to identify an increase in skills, where an outsider might claim that deskilling had occurred. These problems mean that our findings on job experience have to be treated with a good deal of caution. However, some confidence can be placed in them, since the general picture they provide is consistent with the findings of both our own and other case studies (e.g. Wilkinson, 1983).

In our brewing case study, for example, there was a loss of many of the old manual and tactile 'skills'. Operators no longer needed to know just how much force to apply to a particular valve, nor did they have to move raw materials around by hand. Some manual tasks remained that were broadly comparable with those in the old plant, but control of the production process no longer depended on them to the same extent. Process control on the new plant was effected from a control room; information was given by a display, and then operators adjusted parts of the process using a VDU keyboard. Job rotation (at the discretion of the workers themselves) ensured that all the operators took part in this work. Thus, instead of being tied to one part of the plant, and using mainly manual competences, all the brewery operators knew about all process-control tasks. If any job had been 'deskilled', it was that of the foreman, whose role in process control had diminished – monitoring tasks had been taken over by the computerized control system. In the chemical plant, the bulk of the operators performed similar tasks to those they were used to doing on the older dedicated plants. The control-room operators' jobs were in many respects the same as the brewery operators' and hence required not only familiarity with the new control systems, but also a broader understanding of the plant. Again, the foreman had lost certain of his supervisory functions to the computerized system. Examples of the enhanced competence of the machine operators in the engineering plant have already been mentioned, as has the problem of assessing skill levels in the case of the insurance underwriters.

The following discussion of job content, then, is necessarily crude and has to be treated with caution, particularly on the question of 'skill'. Nevertheless, we believe the findings are of sufficient interest to merit discussion in some depth.

Table 6.2 shows respondents' assessments of changes in work experience as indicated by their answers to the question: 'As far as your union members working with the new equipment here are concerned, would you say that these changes in equipment have meant – overall – a rise or fall' on the four dimensions of work investigated: skill, worker control, effort, and health and safety. The overall picture suggests that skill levels have tended to increase rather than fall and that effort levels follow the same pattern. In the case of worker control and health and safety standards, the picture is more mixed. The overall pattern of the findings, however, indicates the importance of differentiating between different aspects of jobs.

Skill Levels

In every sample, except the printers and the clerical workers in telecommunications, a majority of respondents say that skill levels have increased as a result of technical change. This is particularly marked in the case of the manual samples generally, although it tends to be more true of maintenance than production workers. Relatively few respondents report a fall in skill levels, and in no sample is there a 'net' fall in skill, although the printing sample comes fairly close to this. Losses of skill are more common among non-manual and public-sector groups than among production groups, with the exception of printing. Deskilling, as well as increased skill, is marginally more common among maintenance than production groups.

Table 6.2 Percentage of establishments where new technology has brought about a change in job content, with respect to (a) skill; (b) worker control; (c) effort; (d) health and safety standards

	Skill			Worker control			Effort			Health and safety standards		
	In-crease	No change	Fall	In-crease	No change	Fall	In-crease	No change	Fall	In-crease	No change	Fall
(a) Non-manual/public-sector group												
Finance	54	26	20	33	28	39	26	54	20	18	49	33
CPSA civil service	55	34	11	16	57	27	26	63	11	12	58	30
SCPS civil service	55	36	10	23	53	25	33	61	7	3	66	31
CPSA Telecom	43	37	20	20	34	46	71	20	9	14	40	46
POEU Telecom	61	13	26	11	58	31	40	43	17	23	69	8
(b) Production group												
Print	40	27	33	42	32	26	41	44	14	44	37	19
Chemicals	74	23	4	48	32	20	51	35	14	48	40	12
Food and drink	66	34	—	30	46	24	49	22	30	56	39	5
Engineering	64	31	5	39	41	20	39	42	19	32	58	10
(c) Maintenance group												
Chemicals	77	14	10	26	64	10	47	49	4	42	54	4
Food and drink	88	11	2	39	52	9	51	44	5	37	57	6
Engineering	74	17	10	31	57	12	49	42	10	29	67	5
Electrical engineering	73	15	12	44	41	16	59	31	9	42	49	9

In the previous section, we looked at the redistribution of tasks with technical change, since it was expected that these might be related to changes in job content. In fact, the relationships which are found are relatively weak as far as skill is concerned. The strongest relationships are found in the case of the public sector: there, skills are more likely to have increased where functions have gone to higher grades, and are more likely to have fallen where tasks have been taken over from those higher grades. In other words, the patterns are the reverse of what was expected. Given this, a plausible interpretation of the findings of the previous section might be that strong union organizations and those that put forward a wide range of initiatives are less concerned with the fact of changes in tasks than in protecting member skills, and that they are relatively successful in this endeavour.

In the manual private-sector samples, there is a fairly clear tendency for skills to increase, the greater the range of technical change that has occurred; the same pattern is also found in the case of the non-manual and public-sector groups, although in the latter case there is also a tendency for skills to fall with greater technical change. Skill effects of technical change vary with the 'base' technology only in the case of maintenance groups; there, skills are more likely to have increased where mass-production techniques are employed. The state of the labour market, as indicated by the scale of job change, is not related to skill trends, although in the public sector there is a clear tendency for skills not to rise where management adopts a tougher policy towards the workforce and unions. This is not the case in the other samples.

Multi-level bargaining is associated with more favourable trends in skill levels in the public sector, and, in all the groups distinguished, establishment-level bargaining over new technology is associated with increases in skill. Again, we find that indicators of union organization and strategy are associated with changes in skill. In the production group, skills are more likely to rise the stronger the internal organization of the union; in the case of the maintenance group, the crucial factors are not the internal organization of the union, but the role of the larger union in negotiations and the extent to which the union takes initiatives. In the public and non-manual samples, the relationship between union organization and changes in skill are weaker, but point in the same direction; in addition, there is a strong relationship between the extent to which the unions challenge management and increased skills: the more disagreements with management, the more likely skills are to increase.

It is also useful to look at the extent to which workers on the new technology received training for their new jobs. Such training can be of a wide variety of kinds: often it seems to involve simply a few days of training on the job. This was the case, for example, in our insurance case study. At the other extreme, in our brewing case study, workers had a good deal of off-the-job training and were intimately involved in the lengthy process of putting the plant on-stream and testing it. In order to differentiate between different degrees of training, without entering into a great deal of detail, we simply asked respondents what proportion of workers covered by their union and working on the new technology had 'undergone special training of a week or more'. Table 6.3 shows that – as other studies have found – the amount of training is often extremely limited. In none of the samples did more than half of the workers receive training on this scale; indeed, in eight of the samples over half the respondents said that less than 10 per cent of their members had received training on this modest scale. The highest levels of training were found in telecommunications, printing, the food and drink maintenance sample, and production workers in chemicals. It is difficult to see any clear pattern here, although it is perhaps significant that single-occupational unions with substantial memberships in establishments appear to be better able to insist upon training. But other craft groups – notably the maintenance samples – are not always able to achieve the same degree of training provision.

Table 6.3 Percentage of establishments in which a proportion of members working with new technology received training of one week or more

	<10%	*10–24%*	*25–49%*	*50–74%*	*75%+*
(a) Non-manual/public-sector group					
Finance	58	21	11	3	8
CPSA civil service	67	4	5	2	21
SCPS civil service	61	7	9	3	20
CPSA Telecom	43	18	9	12	18
POEU Telecom	13	28	17	22	20
(b) Production group					
Print	39	16	10	10	25
Chemicals	40	16	12	11	21
Food and drink	51	19	14	8	8
Engineering	67	10	5	3	15
(c) Maintenance group					
Chemicals	59	12	10	6	14
Food and drink	35	8	14	8	35
Engineering	62	17	5	10	7
Electrical engineering	59	13	6	13	10

A more detailed analysis of the provision of training indicates that, in all samples, the more sophisticated the union organization and the stronger the links with the larger union, the greater the proportion of those working with the new technology who receive any substantial amount of training. There is a tendency for training to be greater where skill has increased, except in the case of production workers, although here – as in other groups – training is associated with greater worker control. In the maintenance group there is also a higher level of training, the wider the range of bargaining that occurs. Neither the state of the labour market, nor the nature of management's approach towards labour affects training provision. Finally, in all the groups, the greater the range of technical change, the higher the proportion of workers who received training of a week or more.

In the case of skill, then, we find a fairly complex pattern. Various aspects of union organization and activity appear to play a role in all the groups, as does the level of bargaining. In addition, the wider the range of technical change, the more likely it is that skills will increase. The state of the labour market appears not to be important, and the nature of management strategy is of relevance only in the case of the public sector.

Worker Control

Turning to the effects of technical change upon the degree of worker control, part (b) of table 6.2 indicates that there has been considerable change. In the manual private-sector samples, worker control has typically increased rather than fallen, although there appears to be no regular pattern in the differences between production and maintenance groups. In the white-collar and public-sector group, however, the main direction of change has been downwards, and this move towards a reduction of worker control is particularly marked in the case of telecommunications, both for clerical groups and the engineers.

The greater the changes in task allocation, the more likely it is that the degree of worker control has increased. This is particularly true, in all groups, as far as changes in demarcation among comparable groups are concerned. In this instance the labour market does appear to have more important effects. Particularly in the public-sector and non-manual group, there is a tendency for workers to lose control when there have been larger job losses; along with this, a tougher approach towards labour on the part of management is associated with reduced worker control; this pattern is least strong for the maintenance group. In the private-sector manual groups, there is also a tendency for a greater range of bargaining and a larger number of union initiatives to be associated with increases in worker control. In all the groups, a greater acceptance of union proposals on the part of management – itself related to the strength of union organization – is associated with workers achieving greater control over their work. Except for the non-manual and public-sector group, more sophisticated internal union organization, and, in the case of the maintenance group, a more active role in negotiations on the part of the larger union, are associated with workers achieving greater control. We find very different effects as a result of the scale of technical change: in the public-sector and non-manual group, a greater range of change is associated with a reduction in worker control, in the production group no pattern exists, whereas in the maintenance group greater change is associated with a rise in worker control. Finally, in the manual production group, worker control is more likely to have increased in mass-production systems; no variation by the 'base' technology exists in the case of the non-manual and public-sector group.

The overall findings, then, can best be summarized as reflecting the extent to which worker control is affected by the strength and strategies of management and unions; a tougher approach on the part of management, particularly if buttressed by large job losses, tends to lead to a reduction in worker control. On the other hand, stronger trade unions are more able to defend and even extend that control in the private sector. The fact that no such pattern is found in the public-sector samples suggests the power of the changed political environment, which impinges more directly upon public-sector workers than upon those in the private sector. In particular, the impact of the movement towards privatization in telecommunications is striking; here, strong union organization has only achieved limited success in checking management attempts to increase its control over work organization.

Effort Levels

Technical change has often had no effect upon effort levels and in some instances has even led to a reduction (part (c) of table 6.2). However, the general pattern is for effort to have increased: that is, in every sample the percentage of respondents who say that effort levels have risen is greater than the percentage saying they have fallen. This pattern is most marked for clerical workers in tele-communications; it is also relatively marked in the maintenance samples and in the case of production workers in chemicals. One of the striking features is that increases in effort are strongly related to increases in both skill levels and in worker control. In other words, it is not the case that management are extracting greater effort through deskilling or exerting tighter control over work; rather, they are using a 'strategy' – consciously or otherwise – which is the direct opposite of this. This may be part of the bargain implicitly or explicitly worked out between management and unions: that is, the content of jobs is improved, and in exchange workers achieve higher effort standards (but workers also often obtain increased pay for increased effort, as will be seen in the next section).

The interesting question then arises of how far such deals are confined to cases of technical change. Although we did not ask more generally about changes in skill and worker control, we did ask about trends in effort levels: the general pattern was an increase, often to what respondents saw as unreasonably high levels. We therefore need to look at whether such trends were more marked where technical change had occurred than where it had not. If we compare changes in effort levels between establishments where technical change has occurred and where it has not, significant variations occur only in the production samples. There it is found that effort levels are more likely to have risen to high levels where technical change has occurred; there is a very weak pattern of a similar kind in the maintenance group, but no variation at all in the public-sector and non-manual group.

Increases in effort (where technical change has occurred) are more common, in the public-sector and non-manual group, where the scale of technical change is greater; this pattern is not found, however, in the manual manufacturing groups (in addition, it is only in the case of the maintenance group that we find a relationship between trends in effort and the nature of the 'base' technology: effort levels are more likely to have increased in mass-production systems). Nor is there any systematic relationship between the scale of job loss and trends in effort levels in any of the groups. A tougher approach on the part of management towards the labour force is associated with greater effort levels in the production group, but the pattern is, if anything, reversed in the case of the public-sector and maintenance groups.

Greater effort, then, may be the *quid pro quo* for increases in skill and worker control. That is, at least in the private sector, it is difficult for management to weaken the strength and control of workers on all fronts: they can either increase effort or reduce worker controls, but it is difficult to do both. However, this pattern is not found in the case of the public sector. Conversely, it also suggests that if unions protect the level of skill of their members and the degree of worker control over work, they may have to make concessions on effort levels. This would help to explain the finding that, with the exception of the production group, there is a slight tendency for effort levels to have increased, the more sophisticated union organization is. In sum, the data indicate that there may be trade-offs concerning job content; and, given this, it is not surprising that the relationship between effort and the strength of union organization is stronger in the case of maintenance than production groups: for, given the choice, the maintenance samples, which are mainly single-occupational craft groups in our samples, will seek to preserve and even extend their job territory, even if this means higher levels of effort. But it should also be remembered that increases in effort do not generally go unrewarded financially.

Health and Safety

The fourth aspect of job content we investigated concerned health and safety standards. This has been a considerable topic of debate, particularly among non-manual groups. Very crudely, the data suggest that technical change is associated with improved health and safety among manual groups, and the reverse for non-manual workers (see part (d) of table 6.2). This finding is scarcely surprising. New technology will often mean that clerical workers are, for the first time, becoming closely involved with large-scale capital equipment; in contrast, for some manual workers new technology means that they become rather more divorced from many aspects of the production process, as functions are taken over by machinery.

Health and safety standards do not vary significantly according to the scale of technical change in the case of the non-manual and public-sector group; but among manual private-sector workers there is a strong tendency for safety and health to improve, the greater the range of technical change occurring. However, it is again evident that the process of bargaining and the balance of power are important. Hence we find that the greater the scale of job loss and the tougher management's approach towards the labour force, the less health and safety standards have improved. Conversely, the more sophisticated the union organization, and, in the private sector, the greater the extent to which the union takes initiatives, the more safety standards have risen. In this instance, then, we find that widespread technical change provides opportunities for improvements in health and safety. But in all cases, the structure and strategy of management and unions, and the balance of power, shape the degree to which health and safety have improved.

In this section, we have looked at the effects of technical change upon jobs. It has been found important to differentiate between various aspects of work experience, since they vary in different ways as a result of technical change. Second, it was found that technical change has been associated with an overall, or net, increase in skill for all groups and with greater worker control for manual private-sector groups. Manual groups have also seen health and safety standards rise, whereas the reverse has happened in the case of non-manual workers. However, together with these favourable trends (at least for manual workers), there is an intensification of effort in many cases. It therefore appears that among private-sector manual groups there has been a trade-off of a greater intensity of effort in order to maintain and improve skill levels and the degree of worker control. Such trade-offs are shaped to some extent by the scale of technical change. But the structure and strategy of the unions and the policies adopted by management are also relevant. Hence it is striking that workers in the public sector, even in the case of the POEU, have done less well out of technical change than private-sector workers. This appears to be largely attributable to the tough approach towards labour fostered by the government. It is more able to apply this philosophy to its own employees than to those in the private sector, despite the much greater scale of job loss in the latter.

Technical Change and Financial Reward

Much of the discussion of new technology has focused on its presumed effects upon employment and skill levels. However, the primary rationale of work in our society is to obtain an income, and therefore it is necessary to see how technical change has affected pay either directly, or indirectly by affecting the grading of jobs. For many radical writers, the implication of management strategy in technical change – namely, reducing the control and skill of workers – is that workers would suffer pay reductions and downgrading. On the other hand, if technical change leads to increases in skill and control, then it seems reasonable to expect that pay levels will increase.

It has also been common over the past two decades for management to 'buy in' change and 'buy out' traditional working practices. It might therefore be expected that even when skills fell, pay might increase. However, if the balance of power between employer and unions has shifted as a result of substantial job loss, or if management has adopted a tougher approach towards labour, then management may have tried to break with such traditions and may even have attempted to avoid giving any additional payments or upgrading when skills and effort levels have increased. Against this, it seems likely that unions that have a more sophisticated form of organization, either within the workplace or in the form of closer ties to the larger union, and that take more initiatives in relation to technical change, may gain more favourable changes in pay and grading.

The main relationship between technology and changes in pay and grading is likely to come through either the effects of technical change upon skill and effort levels, or through its effects on the balance of power, (for example, by employment effects), or as a reflection of management's more general approach to labour. However, in order to ensure that the change is implemented swiftly and efficiently, management may be willing to pay increases and upgrade jobs in order to win worker support: where the change affects a significant number of workers, or where the changes are in other respects on a large scale (for example, as indicated by the number of changes occurring), this may be especially likely.

Another important aspect of the relationship between technical change and pay and grading concerns the extent to which any gains or losses are confined to those immediately involved in the change, or whether they are spread more widely. Where management seeks to win support for technical change, where it adopts a less tough approach to labour, and where union organization is more developed, then one would expect that any gains from technical change would be spread more widely. In addition, where a larger proportion of the workforce has been affected by change, it seems reasonable to expect that any gains will be spread to other workers.

Table 6.4 shows the effects of technical change upon the pay and grading of those directly working on the new equipment and workers more generally. In the majority of cases, technical change has had no effect upon pay or grading. The exceptions to this pattern are manual production groups: most notably, it is a craft group that has a significant number of members within any workplace – the NGA – that is least likely to see no change in the pay or grading of its members as a result of technical change. In addition, the production groups in food and drink and chemicals also tend to see rather more change in pay and grading than the other samples. But the overall direction of change varies between the samples. In the private-sector manual samples, changes are generally favourable, whereas the reverse is the case in the non-manual and public-sector samples (with the partial exception of the pay of those directly involved with the new technology).

Changes in pay and grading are most strongly related to changes in job content. In all the groups, pay and grading both for those working on new equipment and more generally are considerably more likely to have improved where jobs have become more skilled and give the

Table 6.4 Effects of technical change on pay and grading: (a) grading of new technology jobs; (b) grading of jobs generally; (c) pay of new technology jobs; (d) pay of jobs generally

	Grading of new technology jobs (%)			Grading of jobs (%)			Pay of new technology jobs (%)			Pay of jobs (%)		
	A	B	C	A	B	C	A	B	C	A	B	C
(a) Non-manual/public-sector group												
Finance	18	53	29	5	53	42	11	71	18	8	71	21
CPSA civil service	21	65	14	9	79	12	18	79	3	1	85	14
SCPS civil service	15	66	20	9	70	21	7	90	3	—	93	7
CPSA Telecom	6	79	15	9	79	12	18	79	3	21	76	3
POEU Telecom	9	67	24	4	74	21	1	89	10	—	88	12
(b) Production group												
Print	63	23	15	42	29	29	71	24	5	35	53	12
Chemicals	46	41	13	28	60	12	39	57	4	33	58	8
Food and drink	53	39	8	34	57	9	53	27	21	46	34	20
Engineering	33	62	5	16	79	5	32	65	4	28	68	4
(c) Maintenance group												
Chemicals	14	74	12	8	79	13	17	60	23	20	65	15
Food and drink	26	71	3	22	77	2	26	73	2	23	69	8
Engineering	31	62	8	10	82	8	28	62	10	16	79	5
Electrical engineering	27	57	17	19	73	8	41	48	11	36	50	14

A Favourable effect.
B No change.
C Unfavourable effect.

worker greater control. In addition, in the private sector, although not in the public, there is a strong relationship between increases in effort and widespread changes in demarcation, on the one hand, and improved pay and grading on the other. In the public sector, changes in demarcation tend to be associated with deteriorations in pay nd grading. Relatedly, where more workers have been trained, pay and grading are more likely to have improved. However, it is worth stressing that – with the notable exception of the public-sector and non-manual group – the increases in effort noted in the previous section are typically compensated for by improved pay and grading.

It is also useful briefly to consider the relationship between payment systems and changes in pay and grading. In the public-sector and non-manual group, there is a weak tendency for various types of incentive payment to be associated with less favourable trends in pay and grading, while work study limits changes in grading to those directly involved with new technology. Work study has a similar effect in the case of the manual production samples. However, the use of job evaluation appears to have no effects except in the case of the main-tenance samples. Here it is associated with favourable moves in pay and grading for those directly working on new equipment, and elec-tricians more generally.

The same factors explain variations in changes in pay and grading, both for those directly involved with new technology and, more gen-erally, in all three groups. The more sophisticated the union organ-ization internally, and the more active the role of the larger union, the more favourable are changes in pay and grading; this is particularly true in the private sector. Relatedly, the wider the range of bargaining, the more favourable are the changes. Not surprisingly perhaps, the more management agrees to union proposals, the more pay and grading have improved; and, as was noted above, management is more likely to agree where the union organization is more sophisticated.

The state of the labour market, as indicated by the extent of job change over the last five years, does not affect the way in which pay and grading have changed as a result of new technology. However, where management adopts a tougher approach towards labour, then generally there is less likely to have been any improvement in pay and grading, even for those directly involved with the new equipment. The scale of technical change, as indicated by the number of changes that have occurred and the proportion of workers working on the new technology, only has any role in explaining changes in pay and grading in the case of the public-sector and non-manual samples: but the two indicators work in different directions. The larger the proportion of workers employed on the new technology, the more likely it is that pay and grading have increased. On the other hand, pay and grading are likely to have deteriorated where there has been a greater variety of technical changes.

Conclusions

In this chapter, we have been concerned with the effects of technical change upon job content and rewards. The general pattern, we discovered, was generally favourable as far as skill levels were concerned and, in the case of private-sector manual workers, there was also a tendency for worker control over work to increase and for health and safety standards to improve. But for non-manual and public-sector workers, the effects of technical change upon worker control and health and safety were less favourable. At the same time, however, technical change was often associated with greater effort levels, particularly where skill and worker control had increased. Moreover, it was found that there had been widespread shifts in the allocation of tasks between groups both vertically and horizontally: however, it did not appear that such changes worked in any systematic manner as far as job content was concerned.

In seeking to explain these patterns, it was found once more that although in some cases particular features of the technical change itself appeared to be important, the crucial factors were invariably related to the nature of management strategy, and the structure and strategy of the unions. The more sophisticated the union organization and the broader its strategy in relation to technical change, the more favourable the effects upon workers. However, it did seem that in order to preserve skills and worker controls, and at the same time obtain improvements in pay and grading, the unions were often forced to accept an intensification of effort. But only in the production samples was it found that increases in effort levels were markedly greater where there had been technical change than where there had not. Given these findings, it is not surprising that in all the samples, and particularly among the manual production groups, stewards said that their members tended to be in favour of technical change; very few said that they were mainly against change (table 6.5).

Table 6.5 Members' attitudes to technical change

		Strongly favourable	Favour-able	Uncertain or neutral	Opposed	Strongly opposed
(a)	Non-manual/public-sector group					
	Finance	5	26	63	6	—
	CPSA civil service	2	24	66	4	3
	SCPS civil service	10	26	57	3	3
	CPSA Telecom	6	18	74	3	—
	POEU Telecom	2	34	58	2	3
(b)	Production group					
	Print	22	40	35	3	—
	Chemicals	16	29	49	5	1
	Food and drink	18	26	47	5	3
	Engineering	15	33	46	7	—
(c)	Maintenance group					
	Chemicals	14	44	42	—	—
	Food and drink	27	40	34	—	—
	Engineering	24	29	44	2	—
	Electrical engineering	15	21	59	6	—

7 The Impact of Technical Change on Trade Union Organization

In the preceding chapters, we have placed considerable emphasis upon the extent to which trade union structure and strategy has affected the process of technical change and its impact upon workers. But of equal importance is the question of how the process of technical change affects trade unions in the workplace. This forms the theme of this chapter.

For a number of commentators, new technology poses a considerable threat to the role of the union within the workplace. If technical change is informed by a management strategy of shifting power from workers to employers, it is argued, then trade union organization will be seriously weakened by new technology. The power base of the union – members' readiness and ability to impose sanctions upon the employer – will be seriously challenged. At the same time, management may use technical change as an opportunity to remove the institutional supports for workplace union organization and seek to establish a regime in which joint regulation plays little, if any, part.

The findings of the previous chapters suggest that this view is grossly exaggerated as far as the general experience of technical change is concerned. The survey has continually indicated that factors other than any inherent characteristics of new technology or management conspiracy affect the course of technical change. Moreover, the same point is evident in other recent studies of new technology (e.g Wilkinson, 1983) and in the experience of technical change in the more distant past (e.g. Lazonick, 1979; Turner, 1962). What is evident is that in some cases technical change has favourable effects upon workers and unions. This may be due to management initiatives, or to union endeavours to prevent management reducing manning or deskilling work; in other cases, unions have been able to ensure that their members learn new skills so that the strength and identity of the union is maintained. There are, of course, also cases where trade unions have been seriously weakened as a result of technological innovation. But it is perhaps worth remembering that over the history of industrialization and increasingly rapid technical change, trade unions in this country have become stronger and increased their overall influence. The question is whether they will continue to do so.

It is beyond the scope of this study to engage in any prophetic endeavour. But what the debate on the effects on union organization of new technology does require is a more careful consideration of recent experience. The preceding chapters have shown that the more sophisticated union organizations have, at the minimum, been better able than the less sophisticated to impose a greater control over the process of technical change and thereby obtain certain advantages, or at least reduce the disadvantages, for their members in terms of job content and financial rewards. These findings would lead one to expect that the impact of technical change upon union organization itself will often be limited: if strong unions shape the effects of technical change to any significant degree, then they will tend to be as strong after the change as they were before it, other things being equal. Indeed, the logic of this argument is that the process of technical change will tend to strengthen strong unions and further weaken the less strong.

There are, of course, many qualifications that need to be attached to such a general statement. One exception to this pattern is found in our insurance case study. Here, the former staff association had merged with BIFU around the time that the new technology was introduced and, in addition, a wide range of other changes were occurring. These factors encouraged a rather more 'unionate' approach on the part of members, while key members of management were aware of the need to change the pattern of industrial relations, given the involvement of BIFU. The broad pattern of rationalization, of which technical change was a part, therefore became the means by which formal union involvement in issues increased.

Similarly, one might expect that, if there is a clear tendency for new technology to endanger the power base of unions (in terms of the strategic position of members in the production process or the union's role in job regulation), and if union organization is particularly strong, then the effects of technical change on union organization will be very different to that outlined in the previous paragraph. But the point still holds that strong unions will be better able to protect their members where changes of this kind occur than will weaker unions.

The basic qualifications to this argument concerning the relative stability of union strength and organization, then, are similar to those outlined in previous chapters. Reference has already been made to the nature of technical change itself. In addition, we also need to take into account the labour relations policy of management, which may be reflected both in the technology it chooses and the way in which it introduces new equipment. Other things being equal, the less supportive of trade unions that management is, the more adverse the effects of technical change upon trade unions are likely to be. Third, changes in the balance of power, either due to new technology or to other factors, are also likely to affect the impact of technical change upon union organization. More specifically, where there has been large-scale job loss, many commentators would argue that the ability of unions to maintain their organization will be seriously weakened.

In addition to the hypotheses that have been proposed throughout the preceding chapters – concerning the nature of the technical change itself, management's approach towards labour and trade unions, the role of labour-market forces, and union structure and strategy – a further argument is relevant in the present context. This concerns the way in which union organization is likely to be affected by the changes in jobs and rewards associated with new technology. More specifically, it can be hypothesized that where skill levels and worker autonomy have increased (and the union was involved in negotiating technical change – so that the union can claim, rightly or not, that it played a role in bringing these changes about), and where workers have received some additional monetary reward as a result of technical change, then the role of the union is likely to be greater. This argument rests upon two bases: the first of these concerns the effect of changes upon member attitudes. Put at its crudest, members are likely to be more committed to the union when it appears that it can bring them substantial and real benefits (see, e.g., Batstone et al., 1977). Second, where the technical change has increased the skill and control of workers, then the power base of the union is materially strengthened and augmented with the result that it is potentially able to play a significant role in the future. There is, however, a counter-argument: namely where technical change has led to job insecurity for members, they may turn increasingly to the union in an attempt to rectify the situation.

The preceding comments have been of a fairly general nature. But it is possible that technical change will be associated with different effects upon various aspects of union organization. For example, it is possible that union organization within the workplace is weakened, but as a result its ties with the larger union grow as it seeks greater external support. Similarly, workers in new technology areas may adopt a highly sectional, but effective approach, although as a result union unity declines. In short, it is necessary to distinguish between various aspects or dimensions of union organization.

In the questionnaire, we made a basic distinction between union organization in new technology areas and more generally. In the former, we asked about four aspects of union activity and organization. The first of these concerns the pattern of representation for new technology workers. Such representation might foster a sectional identity on the part of new technology workers, with the result that overall unity declines. On the other hand, of course, it could mean that the special problems of these workers were more adequately dealt with by the union and were integrated into broader union thinking. The second aspect we asked about, therefore, was whether workers on the new equipment tended to see themselves as having special interests, which separated them from other workers. Third, we decided to see whether new technology workers tended to be more or less active union members than those in other parts of the establishment. Fourth, and perhaps most basically, we asked how the role of the union in the new technology areas compared with its role more generally.

We also investigated the more general effects of technical change upon union organization. Throughout preceding chapters, we have placed considerable emphasis upon the degree of sophistication of workplace organization and its links with the larger union; we have seen that these are important factors in shaping the role that the union plays within the workplace. In order to assess the impact of new technology upon workplace unionism, therefore, it is sensible to try to assess how sophistication and external integration have changed. Ideally, we would have asked for details of the various dimensions of sophistication and external integration not only in the present, but also five years ago. We were unable to do this because the pilot studies indicated that many stewards could not readily and accurately provide this information (although, as chapter 2 showed, the crude measures of union sophistication were very stable). We therefore asked a series of more general questions that related to these measures. In the case of the sophistication of the respondents' own union organizations within the workplace, we investigated three features. The first of these concerned the way in which member activism had changed as a result of new technology; member commitment to the union is clearly a precondition of union strength. Second, union sophistication requires that the various sections and groups within the union co-operate together; hence we asked how technical change had affected the degree of unity. Third, the measures of sophistication place considerable emphasis upon senior stewards; they are crucial to the maintenance of unity.

Hence we asked whether the authority of senior stewards had increased or fallen as a result of technical change.

In addition to the sophistication of the respondents' own unions, we have also stressed the importance of the overall sophistication of workplace union organization. An important component of this measure is the extent to which the various unions within the workplace co-operate with each other. In order to tap this aspect, we asked respondents whether relations between the various unions were better or worse as a result of changes associated with the new equipment. In order to assess any changes in the degree of external integration – that is, links with the larger union – we posed the question: 'As a result of changes associated with the new equipment, would you say the relationship between the workplace and the wider union has become stronger or weaker?'

However, the central issue for trade union organization concerns the protection and promotion of members' interests. An important aspect of the role of the union is therefore the extent to which it can shape the day-to-day experience of workers, that is, work organization. We therefore asked respondents whether changes associated with new technology had led to a situation where 'unions have more or less control over work organization'. Finally, we asked respondents whether the experience of technical change had made the unions in the workplace more or less concerned about general management policies. Although this question does not relate directly to union organization and strength, we felt it was a useful theme to investigate. The argument has often been put forward that British unions have only a limited impact upon the process of technical change because they focus their attention upon the wage–effort bargain rather than the factors, such as wider aspects of management strategy, that shape that bargain. As we have seen, the survey findings also indicate the importance of a wide range of bargaining, if unions are to influence the pattern of technical change. It therefore seemed interesting to see if the experience of new technology had made unions more aware of the need to develop a broader definition of their role.

In the remainder of this chapter, we look first at the effects of technical change upon union organization in new technology areas. We then go on to consider the effects of new technology upon workplace union organization more generally.

Trade Union Organization in New Technology Areas

We turn first to the role that the union plays in new technology areas. One factor which we suggested might be important here was whether those working on new equipment had their own shop stewards. Where this was so, then two things were likely to happen: first, the particular interests and problems of those workers would be better represented; but, second, such representation might encourage workers to develop their own special interests. In other words, the existence of special steward constituencies in new technology areas highlights the tension found in all trade unions: that between the full representation of diverse interests and the maintenance of unity. In fact, this tension might be less great than one would suppose. For strong union organizations, able to ensure special stewards, are also generally better able – by definition – to check any tendency towards excessive sectionalism. More generally, it might be expected that the role that the union played in new technology areas would depend upon the degree of success it achieved in protecting and promoting workers' interests at the time that the change was introduced. This will be so for two reasons. First, where the union successfully negotiated over a wider range of issues, then it is likely that it will have established procedures and patterns of work organization that facilitate a continuing role for the union. Second, where the union has clearly achieved gains for members, then member commitment to the union is likely to have been reaffirmed.

It follows from this that, given a certain degree of success, the greater the role that the union played in the implementation of the technical change, the greater is likely to be its role once the change is in place. Hence, related to the role of the union, such factors as the strategy of management and the more general balance of power are of relevance. These, then, form the themes of this section.

New Technology Stewards

Part (a) of table 7.1 shows that, in the majority of cases of technical change, those working on the new technology do not have their own shop stewards. Such special representation is particularly rare in finance and printing, possibly reflecting the fact that in these cases those involved with the new technology are working alongside other workers engaged in more traditional tasks. With these exceptions, new technology workers have their own stewards in about a fifth to a quarter of cases. Special representation is most common in the food and drink production sample, possibly reflecting the fact that new technology often involves the construction of separate production facilities or lines, as in our brewing case study.

We did not ask respondents whether areas of technical change involved distinctive workgroups, although this is likely to be important in explaining whether or not new technology workers have their own

Table 7.1 New technology areas: (a) percentage of establishments with own shop steward; (b) activism of members working with new technology compared with other members; (c) extent to which members working with new technology have special interests; (d) relative role of union in new technology areas; (e) reasons for change in union role

	Percentage with own shop steward	Activism of new technology members compared with others (%)			Extent to which new technology members have special interests (%)			
		Greater	Same	Lower	Great deal	Fair amount	Not much	Not at all
(a) Non-manual/public-sector group								
Finance	3	18	82	—	5	18	28	49
CPSA civil service	21	12	80	8	9	21	31	39
SCPS civil service	17	15	82	3	5	26	34	36
CPSA Telecom	17	6	85	9	9	29	41	21
POEU Telecom	11	8	83	9	6	43	40	11
(b) Production group								
Print	3	13	76	11	9	25	28	38
Chemicals	17	9	83	8	2	25	32	41
Food and drink	34	8	83	10	3	23	45	30
Engineering	15	3	93	3	2	10	40	48
(c) Maintenance group								
Chemicals	23	8	87	4	13	15	38	34
Food and drink	25	9	91	—	11	26	25	39
Engineering	18	8	88	4	5	32	37	26
Electrical engineering	24	9	85	6	9	18	32	41

Table 7.1 (*continued*)

	Relative role of union in new technology areas (%)			Reasons (where change) (%)					
				Number of issues		Problems to management		Management concern	
	Greater role	No change	Smaller role	Greater role	Smaller role	Greater role	Smaller role	Greater role	Smaller role
(a) Non-manual/public-sector group									
Finance	18	66	16	67	22	11	55	25	50
CPSA civil service	23	76	1	82	—	41	5	32	—
SCPS civil service	21	79	—	77	—	15	—	23	—
CPSA Telecom	29	71	—	90	—	22	—	40	—
POEU Telecom	10	84	6	57	14	50	7	50	7
(b) Production group									
Print	22	72	6	78	11	39	6	28	6
Chemicals	12	83	5	60	33	40	27	27	13
Food and drink	15	83	3	29	—	29	14	43	14
Engineering	7	90	3	20	60	20	—	20	—
(c) Maintenance group									
Chemicals	7	91	2	75	25	—	33	—	—
Food and drink	12	83	5	55	—	27	18	55	9
Engineering	13	83	4	57	14	29	43	43	14
Electrical engineering	18	77	5	75	—	38	—	38	—

stewards (since this is generally a significant factor in the pattern of steward constituencies). The only other general factor relevant to explaining separate representation across all the sample groups in the survey is the level of sophistication of respondents' own union organization within the plant. There is a slight tendency for such representation to be more common in instances where the union organization is more sophisticated. In the case of the public-sector and non-manual group, special representation is more often found where there is a smaller proportion of union members working with the new technology. In the production group, new technology workers are more likely to have their own shop steward where the union has been more involved in negotiating technical change. In the maintenance samples, greater external integration is associated with more frequent special representation of those working on the new technology.

Member Activism in New Technology Areas

The second theme that we investigated in new technology areas was whether 'members directly affected by the new equipment are more or less active in the union than other members'. The clear overall pattern is that they are no different to other members (see part (b) of table 7.1): this is so in at least four-fifths of cases. Where differences in activism do exist, the net pattern is one of greater activism, except in the case of the clerical telecommunications sample and production workers in food and drink. Increases are particularly notable in two non-manual groups, where member activism has probably been less common in the past – finance and the higher-grade civil servants.

Greater activism on the part of new technology workers is more common where, as was suggested above, technical change has been associated with improvements in pay and grading. In the production group, members are also more active where their control over work has increased. In addition, features of the negotiation process are associated with member activism. With the exception of the production group, new technology workers are more likely to be active where bargaining over new technology took place at establishment level. The employment effects of new technology are also relevant: in the non-manual and public-sector group and among the maintenance samples, the smaller the job loss (or the greater the job gain), the greater tends to be the level of activism; but the reverse is the case among production groups.

Greater activism is also associated with a greater role on the part of the union in negotiating technical change. However, the effect of a more aggressive management approach towards labour and the unions differs among the three groups. In the non-manual/public-sector and the maintenance groups, a tougher approach on the part of management is associated with greater member activism in new technology areas, but the reverse is the case among production workers. Finally, member activism is associated with new technology stewards only in the case of the non-manual and public-sector group.

Sectionalism in New Technology Areas

The third feature of union organization in new technology areas that we asked about was how far 'members working with the new equipment have problems or interests which mean they see themselves apart from other workers'. Part (c) of table 7.1 shows that this was generally not the case, at least to any significant degree. It was most common in the public sector and among several of the craft groups – printers and two of the maintenance samples. Such special interests were more common where they had some means of institutional expression: that is, where the new technology workers had their own steward. But there was no relationship between the level of activism of new technology workers and their having special interests.

A number of factors are important in explaining the existence of special interests on the part of those working with new equipment. The first of these is changes in pay and grading associated with technical change. Where these had changed, either favourably or unfavourably, it was more likely that new technology workers were seen to have special interests. Second, favourable changes in job content, particularly in skill levels, encouraged the development of special interests. The third factor was the level of union activity and initiative in relation to new technology; where this was higher, then there is a greater probability that the new technology workers perceive themselves as having special interests. Fourth, as we suggested above, special interests are more likely to be found where the respondents' union has a more sophisticated organization within the workplace and where new technology workers had their own steward. A tougher approach towards labour on the part of management is associated with a greater probability that new technology workers will see themselves as in some way distinctive in the non-manual/public-sector and maintenance groups, but not in the case of the production group. In the latter case, a separate identity is more likely where links with the larger union are stronger. Relatedly, in the manual manufacturing groups – both production and maintenance – new technology workers are more likely to see themselves as having special interests where the larger union played a more active role in negotiations.

The Union's Role in New Technology Areas

The three themes we have just discussed are likely to affect the role of the union in new technology areas. We asked respondents: 'In areas where new equipment has been introduced, does your union play a greater or smaller role in day-to-day issues which affect members than it does elsewhere in this establishment?' Where they said the union's role was distinctive, we asked them whether this was due to more problems arising in new technology areas; or to workers in these areas being more or less likely to take problems direct to management; or to management being more or less concerned with worker problems than they were elsewhere; or if it was due to some other reason, which they were asked to specify. Part (d) of table 7.1 shows, once more, that technical change does not generally affect the role that the union plays; in about three-quarters or more of the samples, respondents say that the union's role in new technology areas is no different to its role elsewhere. Where any change has occurred, it has invariably, in net terms, involved a greater role for the union. This is least true in the case of the finance sample, where almost as many respondents say that the union's role has been reduced as say that it has risen. Increases in union activity are particularly marked among non-manual groups in the public sector. The union was more likely to play a greater role where new technology members were more active, and where they had their own shop steward.

In every sample except production engineering, the most common reason given for greater union activity was that there are more problems in new technology areas (see part (e) of table 7.1). In production engineering, fewer problems mean that the union is less involved. However, in some of the samples, other factors, according to respondents, are also relatively important. In two of the maintenance samples and in finance, a lower level of union involvement is attributed to the fact that members in the new technology areas are more likely to go straight to management with any problems; in most samples, however, the reverse is the case. Finally, in a considerable number of cases, a greater union role is attributed to the fact that management demonstrates less concern for workers' problems; only in the finance sample do we find that greater attention on the part of management to the problems workers have led to reduced union activity in new technology areas.

A more detailed analysis of the findings also suggests the relevance of a number of other factors in accounting for changes in the part that the union plays in new technology areas. We again find that changes in conditions and rewards are relevant. Among the non-manual/private-sector and maintenance groups, improvements in pay are associated with greater union involvement; in the production group, any change in pay, favourable or unfavourable, appears to lead to greater union activity. The union also tends to become more involved where health and safety standards have deteriorated; other changes in job content appear to affect the role of the union only in the case of the maintenance group.

The greater the range of bargaining activity and union initiative during the implementation of technical change, the fuller subsequent union involvement is likely to be. Relatedly, the more sophisticated union organizations tend to extend their role where technical change occurs; and, in the case of the private-sector groups, involvement in negotiations over technical change by the larger union also provides a basis for the union within the workplace to play a more active part. Management's approach towards labour affected union activity only in the maintenance group, and in no case was the scale of employment change relevant. However, it was also found that the union was likely to play a greater role where the number of types of technical change that had occurred was greater.

The overall picture, then, as far as new technology areas are concerned is one of few dramatic changes. Where changes have taken place, these tend to be in the direction of greater union strength. Such changes are primarily attributable to improvements in job content and rewards, and to the factors that led to those changes: the range of bargaining during the course of technical change, and the degree of sophistication of union organization. In a number of cases, special representation of workers involved with the new technology has fostered the importance of the union.

Reported Effects of Technical Change upon Union Organization

We now turn to the question of whether, and how, the process of technical change affected union organization more generally within the establishments covered by the survey. Given the findings outlined in the previous section, one would expect that the introduction of new technology would generally have little effect upon unions. This is in fact the case. Furthermore, such changes as did occur might be expected generally to be similar to those occurring within the new technology areas. The data support this view: there are close relationships, for example, between changes in member activism in new technology areas and more generally.

General Member Activism

Part (a) of table 7.2 shows that the experience of technical change has not affected the general level of member activity in the vast majority of cases. Only in the POEU and in printing are there marginal net declines, whereas among certain non-manual and maintenance groups there are – relatively speaking – quite marked increases in member activism. The explanation of changes in member involvement and commitment to the union generally is broadly similar to that for new technology areas. With the exception of the production group, improvements in pay and grading foster union activity; greater worker control also encourages workers to be more active. In the non-manual/public-sector and maintenance groups, workers are more likely to show greater commitment to the union where there have been widespread changes in job demarcation. In the public-sector and non-manual group, a tougher approach on the part of management towards the unions serves to reduce member commitment, whereas a greater range of disagreements over technical change encourages it; but this pattern is not found in the manual production groups. In the latter, a wider range of bargaining over new technology, particularly where this includes shop-floor negotiation, fosters a stronger identification of members with their unions.

Unity within Individual Unions

Here, a central issue is one that has been touched upon in the previous section: namely, the extent to which the development of special interests among new technology workers endangers the broader unity of the union organization. This is indeed the case, although the relationship is relatively weak. On the other hand, the existence of new technology stewards does not appear to weaken the unity of the trade union: it seems, then, that the more sophisticated unions, where such stewards tend to be found, are able both to permit the recognition of special interests and maintain the larger unity of the union.

However, it is important to maintain some perspective upon these patterns. In the majority of cases, respondents say that their union is no more or less united as a result of technical change (part (b) of table 7.2). Where changes are identified, they are typically in the direction of greater unity; however, there are weak trends in the reverse direction in the case of the two telecommunications samples and three of the manufacturing groups. The key factor affecting the degree of unity is nothing directly to do with technical change; it is the nature of management's approach towards the unions. The 'tougher' management's approach is, the more union unity has declined in all three groups. In addition, in the non-manual and public-sector group, wide-scale changes in demarcation foster unity; in the other groups, financial gains from technical change and favourable changes in job content discourage factionalism. Relatedly, greater union sophistication (except in maintenance) and a wider range of bargaining (except in the non-manual/public-sector group) are both associated with greater internal unity. Changes in employment, whether attributable to technical change or not, do not appear to affect union unity.

The Authority of Senior Shop Stewards

The degree of trade union unity is an important aspect of what we have called union sophistication. Another aspect is the authority of senior shop stewards. These two factors are closely related: where the unity of the union has increased, there is a strong tendency for the authority of senior shop stewards to have grown as well. Similarly, trends in senior steward authority are closely related to changes in the level of member activism. This indicates the importance of member commitment as a pre-condition of any central direction on the part of the union.

But, again, it has also to be remembered that (as section (c) of table 7.2 shows) in over three-quarters of the cases covered by the survey the authority of senior stewards has not been affected by technical change. Where changes have occurred, the overall trend has been towards increased influence on the part of senior stewards, except in the case of the maintenance samples. Particularly marked increases have occurred among the manual production samples.

The findings suggest that the authority of senior stewards is largely determined by their ability to achieve gains for their members. Hence, where pay and grading have improved, where worker control has increased, and where there has been no effort intensification, senior stewards have experienced an increase in their authority. Again, we also find that, in the private sector, senior steward authority is more likely to have increased where union organization is sophisticated and where the range of bargaining over new technology was greater. These patterns are not found in the public sector. There, the nature of management's approach towards the union and changes in employment play a more crucial role. The tougher the approach and the greater the scale of job loss, both due to new technology and other reasons, the more likely it is that senior stewards have experienced a decline in their authority.

Table 7.2 General effects of technical change: (a) member activity; (b) intra-union unity; (c) authority of senior shop stewards; (d) inter-union unity; (e) external integration; (f) union control; (g) concern regarding management policy

	Member activity			Intra-union unity			Authority of senior shop stewards		
	Rise	No change	Fall	Rise	No change	Fall	Rise	No change	Fall
(a) Non-manual/public-sector group									
Finance	26	74	—	17	83	—	5	92	3
CPSA civil service	20	79	1	19	78	3	13	77	10
SCPS civil service	16	77	7	15	77	8	10	80	10
CPSA Telecom	12	82	6	12	74	14	17	69	14
POEU Telecom	11	74	14	14	69	18	12	81	7
(b) Production group									
Print	11	75	14	28	54	19	35	52	12
Chemicals	14	75	11	20	68	12	18	76	6
Food and drink	5	93	3	10	78	12	21	74	5
Engineering	7	90	3	12	85	3	15	85	—
(c) Maintenance group									
Chemicals	8	90	2	8	78	14	6	84	10
Food and drink	14	83	3	15	78	8	11	74	15
Engineering	10	83	7	12	78	10	5	85	10
Electrical engineering	15	82	3	12	74	14	15	79	6

Table 7.2 (continued)

	Inter-union unity			External integration			Union control			Concern regarding management policy		
	Rise	No change	Fall	Rise	No change	Fall	Rise	No change	Fall	Rise	No change	Fall
(a) Non-manual/public-sector group												
Finance	4	88	8	16	81	3	8	74	18	66	34	—
CPSA civil service	25	69	7	28	69	3	12	65	23	62	37	1
SCPS civil service	18	75	7	26	67	7	3	61	36	61	37	2
CPSA Telecom	37	46	17	21	65	14	14	54	31	80	20	—
POEU Telecom	20	68	12	14	56	30	4	68	28	90	8	1
(b) Production group												
Print	11	84	5	42	42	16	26	57	17	68	29	3
Chemicals	11	82	7	18	64	18	14	69	17	60	36	4
Food and drink	3	91	6	3	87	11	21	62	18	71	29	—
Engineering	16	82	2	9	86	5	9	85	7	49	49	2
(c) Maintenance group												
Chemicals	8	82	10	10	72	18	—	82	18	53	41	6
Food and drink	19	73	8	14	65	21	4	78	18	60	31	9
Engineering	8	80	13	7	68	24	13	73	14	61	34	5
Electrical engineering	12	88	—	9	69	22	12	71	17	47	53	—

Inter-union Relations

Inter-union relations are an important feature of the overall sophistication of trade union organization within the workplace. The survey findings indicate that an important pre-condition for improved relations between trade unions at the place of work is that the individual unions should themselves be united with authoritative senior stewards.

Again, however, the main finding is that technical change has had little effect upon the relationships between unions; in most samples, about four-fifths of respondents say that this is the case (part (d) of table 7.2). But there are a number of exceptions to this pattern, notably in the public sector. There, we find a good deal of change, although generally in the direction of an improvement in relations between the various unions. Indeed, more generally, the overall trend where change has occurred is towards better inter-union relations. Minor exceptions are found in finance, two maintenance samples and the production sample in food and drink.

Changes in rewards and job content are once more associated with the pattern of change in union organization. Where pay or grading have improved, inter-union relations have done the same. In the private sector, increased skill is associated with better relations between the unions. This pattern is not found in the public sector: here, the only aspect of job content that is relevant is effort levels. Where these have increased, there is a slight tendency for inter-union relations to have improved. In the private sector, a wider range of bargaining over new technology and a greater degree of sophistication in overall union organization are also associated with stronger inter-union relations. In none of the groups do changes in employment levels affect inter-union relations, and only in the case of the maintenance group does management's approach towards the unions affect the degree of inter-union co-operation.

Relations with the Larger Union

Throughout the preceding chapters, we have been concerned with the way in which relationships between the union within the workplace and the larger union affect the process of technical change. We now turn to the converse question, namely, the way in which technical change has affected this relationship. In all but one sample, a clear majority of respondents say that relationships with the larger union have not changed (see part (e) of table 7.2). The exception is the printing industry, where two-fifths of respondents say that relationships have become stronger. This is consistent with the craft nature of the

NGA, and the fact that it accounts for a relatively large proportion of total union membership in establishments. In the other craft samples, there has often been a small net decline in relations with the larger union. In the case of the POEU this reflects the decentralization policies of management, whereas in the case of the electricians this finding reflects the small numbers of members typically found in any one establishment – so that they often depend upon the broader union organization within the workplace. In all the white-collar samples, the net trend is towards closer relationships between the workplace and the larger union. There is no clear pattern in the case of the non-craft production groups.

Generally speaking, the various aspects of unity and sophistication are fairly closely related: that is, increases in member activism, internal unity, the authority of senior stewards, and improved inter-union relations are all strongly associated with improved relations with the larger union. Except in the case of the production group, more sophisticated organizations are likely to have stronger ties with the larger union as a result of technical change. In the private sector, greater involvement in technical change on the part of the union further cements workplace–larger union links, whereas a tougher approach on the part of management towards unions serves to weaken links with the larger union. Finally, the scale of job loss only appears relevant in the case of the production group, where ties with the larger union tend to be weakened as a result of large-scale reductions in employment.

Union Control over Work Organization

A central question for trade unions, however, concerns the way in which technical change affects the control they are able to exert over work organization. Overall, the majority of respondents say that new technology has had no effect in this respect (see part (f) of table 7.2). However, where changes have occurred, the overall direction of change is downwards. This is particularly true in the case of the non-manual and public-sector samples; it is also the case in both chemical samples and in the maintenance groups. The strongest net increase in union control is in the printing industry.

A decline in union control is associated quite strongly with falls in intra- and inter-union unity and in the authority of senior shop stewards, along with declines in member activism. It is attributable to the failure of unions to win financial gains for their members from technical change, and to reductions in skill levels and worker control. Related to these is the importance of management's approach towards the unions. Where management adopts a tougher approach, then union control decreases, although interestingly this relationship is less strong in the public than in the private sector. Union control is also weakened by job loss as a result of technical change. In the case of the private, but not the public sector, more sophisticated unions, those with greater involvement with the larger union, and those who bargained over a wider range of issues are more likely to preserve and possibly increase their control over work organization.

Union Concern over General Management Policies

One of the themes in our discussion of new technology has been the range of bargaining and union initiative. This was important in affecting both the impact of technical change upon jobs and union organization. But we also saw that unions had typically confined their bargaining activities to relatively conventional industrial relations issues; few demonstrated much active concern with the broader structure of management strategy. Many would see this as a fundamental weakness. The question therefore arises of whether unions have become more aware of the need to understand general management policies as a result of their experience of technical change. Part (g) of table 7.2 shows that there has been a considerable change in union concern over such policies; with the exception of electrical engineering, there is a clear majority who say that this has happened. Very few respondents say that there has been a fall in interest in what management is doing. The most marked increase in concern is found in telecommunications, the least in the maintenance samples. The former reflects the decentralization of management, together, no doubt, with the question of the way in which privatization was likely to affect the future pattern of technical change and industrial relations. The relatively smaller increase in concern among maintenance samples reflects, once more, their small numbers in most establishments.

Greater concern with management policies is associated with increased intra- and inter-union unity and with greater authority on the part of senior stewards. In other words, it appears that there are organizational pre-conditions for such an awareness to develop. This is consistent with our finding that more sophisticated union organizations were more likely to intrude further into traditional areas of management prerogative. Similarly, we find that those organizations that are more sophisticated, that have closer links with the larger union, and that bargained over a wider range of issues in relation to new technology are more likely to demonstrate a growing concern about general management policies. A tougher approach on the part of management is related to an extension of union horizons only in the case of the production group; here, the tougher the approach, the more likely it is that union horizons will have expanded. The scale of job loss does not appear to be relevant in any of the groups, and it is only in the non-manual/public-sector group that the scale of technical change leads to greater awareness. However, large-scale changes in task allocation and changes – in either direction – in effort levels and financial reward also encourage a greater concern on the part of the union about general management policies.

More General Effects upon Trade Union Organization

From the survey data, it is also possible to assess the impact of technical change upon union organization in two other ways. The first is to see whether the occurrence of technical change affects the sophistication of trade union organization and the role that it plays: that is, in the survey as a whole, does the fact that technical changes have occurred in the last five years contribute to the explanation of variations in union organization and influence? Second, we can investigate the extent to which various aspects of new technology and associated changes contribute to variations in organization and influence among those unions in establishments where technical change has occurred. In pursuing these themes, the discussion focuses upon the following issues: the degree of intra- and inter-union sophistication; the range of bargaining; the degree of union control over management and trends in that influence; and effort levels.

  The experience of technical change over the last five years does not appear to have had much effect upon union organization or influence. Once key variables are controlled for, technical change is associated with a marginally greater degree of intra-union sophistication in all three groups of samples; it is found to be significant – and then only very marginally – in relation to inter-union sophistication only in the production samples. Similarly, we find that the experience of technical change is associated with a fractionally greater range of bargaining, but in none of the groups of samples is it associated with the level of union control. In the non-manual/public-sector group, however, union influence is somewhat less likely to have increased over the last five years where technical change has occurred: but closer inspection reveals this to be due to the fact that technical change and reductions in union influence tend to be concentrated in particular samples. Finally, only in the production group does the experience of technical change appear to play a role in explaining trends in effort levels – these tend to be higher where new technology has been introduced. In sum, the effects of technical change appear to be very limited, once other variables are taken into account. Moreover, such significance as technical change appears to have may in fact be due to other factors, which are not covered by the survey.

The second approach suggested above is confined to those cases where technical change has occurred. Here, we consider the same features of union organization and influence as were discussed in the preceding paragraph. The features of technical and associated change which we look at are the following: the range of types of technical change that have occurred; the employment effects of new technology; the proportion of workers employed on the new technology; and the overall effect of technical change upon job content and upon pay and grading.

In all three groups of samples, intra- and inter-union sophistication tend to be greater, the larger the range of technical changes that have occurred, even after we have controlled for more influential factors. The characteristics of the technology as such, however, contribute little to the overall explanation; in all three groups of samples, changes associated with new technology, such as changes in job content and pay, play a somewhat greater – although still fairly limited – role. But, it should be remembered, these features are typically negotiated and are most strongly influenced by more sophisticated union organizations. In other words, these findings support the argument put forward in this and earlier chapters: stronger organizations are more likely to bargain over issues and thereby achieve more favourable outcomes; in this way they tend to become stronger.

When we turn to indicators of union influence then the importance of changes associated with new technology, rather than the characteristics of the technology itself, become even more evident. The range of technical change appears to be significant only as far as effort trends among production workers are concerned – and even here changes in job content and pay are two or three times as important. Overall, the pattern is relatively clear and simple: favourable changes in pay and job content are associated with greater levels of union influence, a lower probability that union control has declined over the last five years, and less likelihood that effort levels have increased. In some cases, it also appears that the employment effects of new technology and the proportion of workers working on the new equipment are relevant: but the relationships are very weak and point in no systematic direction across the different aspects of control or across the different groups of samples. However, the basic point is the same as has been made throughout this chapter: although these relationships exist, they are very small compared with the role of other variables. In short, the impact of new technology and associated changes upon union organization and influence appears to be very limited, once other factors are taken into account.

Finally, our case studies provide general support to this picture of the limited impact of new technology as such upon workplace union organization. Certainly there were some small signs of change: for example, in the brewery where single-grade working was introduced, workers enjoyed a much higher degree of autonomy and freedom from supervision than they did in the rest of the plant. As a consequence, they were often able to resolve problems amongst themselves; hence they rarely had disagreements with the foreman, with the consequence that the steward was rather less active than his counterparts in the rest of the plant. In addition, instead of union-based departmental consultation, as in the rest of the brewery, on the new plant all workers could attend consultative meetings – but this reflected the fact that only a small number of workers were employed on the new plant. More generally, the introduction of new technology had no effect upon union organization.

In the engineering plant, there was a possibility that those working on the CNC machines would form a distinct interest group and seek to gain special rewards. The union was keen to ensure that this did not happen: it insisted that the new machines were integrated into existing departments, and that the CNC operators were included in existing steward constituencies. More generally, the main effect of the introduction of new technology was to make the stewards collectively more aware of the need to understand and try to influence the general nature of management strategy. In the chemicals case study, there was no discernible effect upon union organization of introducing automated plant. In the insurance company, there were significant changes in the role of the union; but in this case, as we have noted in preceding chapters, the changes were largely attributable to the more general changes, of which on-line processing constituted only a part.

Conclusions

In this chapter, we have discussed the effects of technical change upon trade union organization, both within new technology areas and more generally within the workplace. In general terms, the findings can be briefly and accurately summarized by saying that technical change has generally had little effect upon trade unions. The one exception to this is that the experience of new technology has made many workplace union organizations more aware of the need to understand the broader nature of management policy.

Such changes as have occurred have generally been in the direction of a strengthening of union organization; member activism has tended to grow; individual unions have generally become more united in the workplace; the authority of senior stewards has in the main increased; inter-union relations have improved; and ties between the workplace and the larger union have been strengthened. There are, of course, exceptions, but the overall pattern is of the kind described. The role of the union in new technology areas tends to be greater than in other parts of the establishment, although technical change has led to a reduction in the overall control of work organization by trade unions, rather than an increase. It should, however, once more be stressed that these patterns are relatively marginal compared with the basic picture of no change.

In seeking to account for variations in trends in union organization, a number of themes stand out in the preceding discussion. In the main, the more favourable the effects of technical change upon job content and financial rewards, the more likely it is that union organization has become stronger. Moreover, those factors that affected the way in which new technology influenced jobs and rewards were also found to affect the way in which union organization was changed. In brief, the more sophisticated the union organization and the wider the range of bargaining activity, the stronger that union organization was likely to be after the change. In addition, the nature of management's approach to the unions was also found to be relevant in many cases. What these points add up to is basically this: the process of technical change tends to augment those characteristics of workplace union organizations that were apparent before technical change took place. Stronger organizations tend to become stronger, weaker organizations weaker.

8 Conclusions

This book has examined the pattern of workplace trade unionism in the recession; a large part of it has been devoted to a 'test case', namely, new technology. Although the bulk of the volume has depended upon a large postal survey of shop stewards, we have also made use of four case studies, which we report more fully elsewhere (Batstone *et al.*, 1986). Both of the methods employed have a number of weaknesses. A survey, particularly one that is self-administered, is a blunt instrument, but, given limited resources, permits a large coverage. The case study has exactly the opposite strengths and weaknesses: it provides the opportunity for very detailed analysis, but has a limited coverage. However, the combination of two less than ideal techniques, we believe, has been useful and valuable. In particular, these two very different approaches have both suggested the utility of the basic framework we have adopted: therefore, although we would be the first to argue that there is plenty of room for further, more refined work in the area, we would equally claim that this study provides a useful basis for further research.

In this final chapter, we briefly summarize some of the main points from the study and discuss a number of more general points which derive from the findings. In doing so, we also introduce a discussion of international variations in the role of trade unions both in relation to unemployment and in the process of technical change.

Some General Considerations on Trends in Labour Relations

In chapter 1, we discussed different views concerning the impact of the recession upon trade unions. We argued that the extent to which weak product markets and high levels of unemployment, together with legislation aimed at weakening the monopoly power of trade unions, did decimate trade union organization could easily be exaggerated. Our survey data provided considerable support for this view: the high level of unemployment, of course, provided all employers with a greater opportunity for recruiting alternative labour. In addition, there had been substantial job loss in many establishments in the five years prior to the survey, although the level of business activity had often increased (in the manufacturing samples this probably reflected the fact that particular plants had been 'loaded up' and others – which could not, of course, be included in the survey – had been shut down).

Despite these adverse circumstances, union density remained high and the formal structures of workplace union organization appeared generally to be intact. Although some companies had adopted a tougher approach to trade unions over the last few years, the scale and scope of such a policy appeared to be fairly limited. This was particularly true as far as the institutional underpinnings of trade union organization were concerned. Rather more employers were described by respondents as adopting a 'tougher' approach towards the labour force more generally, and in a sizeable minority of companies, it was claimed, effort levels had increased significantly since the late 1970s. However, these characteristics were not strongly associated with either a reduction in management support for trade unions, nor with other aspect of management's labour relations strategy. It was not where the establishment was suffering in market terms, but where it was doing relatively well, that an intensification of work had occurred. It may, of course, be that the larger company was experiencing serious difficulties in the product market, and the intensification of work was part of an explicit or implicit bargain for the maintenance of the establishment and employment. But generally such bargains have not involved a fundamental challenge to trade union organization. Indeed, in many cases, respondents claimed that union influence had actually increased where effort levels had risen.

This appears somewhat contradictory at first sight. How can it be that union influence has increased, when the union appears to have failed in some of its major aims – the protection of workers from unemployment and from unreasonably high levels of effort? A number of explanations appear possible. In some cases, trade unions have been prepared to trade jobs and effort for gains such as higher pay and greater worker autonomy; hence we have found that where technical change has occurred, increases in pay, skill and autonomy are often associated with lower manning and increased effort levels. Some of our case studies, in particular, also suggest that the range of union influence has increased where effort intensification and job loss have occurred. In other words, until this point in time, the unions had only played a small role in shaping work organization: the wage-effort bargain had in the past been attributable to management 'laxity' rather than union power, for example. In such situations, the extension of the formal role of the union might be associated with a greater level of effort. This pattern may be particularly common where employers have chosen to seek changes through co-operation with the unions rather than through head-on confrontation.

This raises the question of the significance of trade union influence. Some might be inclined to the view that this is simply evidence of the incorporation of the unions – that they have 'sold out' their members in the interests of achieving a greater institutional role. Such a possibility clearly exists. But there are also other considerations to be taken into account. First, it was suggested in chapter 1 that unions may have little choice in the approach they adopt because individual members 'vote with their feet' and choose redundancy (although this may be seen, of course, as reflecting the limited control of the union over individual members). The second possibility is that, had the union adopted a different approach, adverse effects upon the labour force would have been even greater. In other words, union co-operation might be seen as a damage limitation exercise. More than this, one has to take account of the feasibility of alternative strategies: a major challenge to management might fail, with the result that union organization is decimated and the subsequent reorganization of work is even more deleterious for workers. In addition, in some cases, the union may be well aware of the plight in which the company finds itself and therefore be prepared to accept certain changes in the interests of protecting as many jobs as possible. Again, the case studies, in particular, indicate the importance of such considerations. In short, union co-operation may be both the optimum strategy for the present and for maintaining strong formal workplace organization, and its potential for the future. It would seem that, in much of the private sector, such considerations have been central to both management and union thinking. It should also be remembered, however, that in many cases the extent to which effort intensification has occurred is fairly limited: this may in part be attributable to the efficacy of the types of trade union strategy we have just outlined. (In addition, the increase in effort may often reflect extremely low levels of effort in the recession prior to 'rationalization'.)

If these conjectures are correct (and a good deal of the evidence from the survey and the case studies gives them plausibility), then one might suggest that managements – at least in much of the private sector – have had little need to launch a major challenge to the unions.

Employers may not have gained as much as they would wish (see Batstone, 1984a, pp. 283–92), but they have been prepared to accept less than 'optimal' changes in the wage–effort bargain from their point of view in order to preserve the co-operation of the workforce and the unions. In chapter 1, we outlined a number of reasons why the employer might seek to pursue this essentially accommodative approach: the state of the product market may weaken the employer as well as the union; employers are dependent upon the co-operation of the labour force and often this cannot be ensured through a punitive approach; there are limits to the interchangeability of labour and the wisdom of rapidly reversing past management styles; and – possibly most important – a heavy-handed approach on the part of the employer at this point in time may lead to corresponding strategies on the part of the union and workforce, if and when the state of the product and labour markets improves.

A further possible explanation appears to be of especial relevance to the non-manual/public-sector group. It is in the public sector that the employer has adopted the toughest approach towards the unions and the labour force, and yet at the same time it is often claimed that union influence has increased. Situations of conflict, of course, may have increased respondents' awareness of the scale of union power. But the extension of union activity at a local level may also be of relevance; that is, the nature of union influence has begun to change. Although the union's traditional influence through bureaucratic procedures and a commitment on the part of the state to being a 'good' employer has declined, there has been a compensatory change in the commitment of the membership to trade union activity, illustrated by the scale of strike action. One's assessment of the general significance of this type of change may differ from that of respondents, but such changes are by no means insignificant for the longer term. A not dissimilar pattern in terms of members' attitudes appears to have occurred in the finance sector.

The most adverse trends in union influence are to be found in those sectors where workplace union organization has traditionally been quite strong. The reasons for this vary. In the private sector, the dramatic reductions in activity and employment in industries such as engineering appear to be of relevance at a general level, although variations in the economic situation of individual establishments appear to be of lesser importance. But such an explanation cannot account for the situation in Telecom, where the market is booming. The key factor here is the nature of government policy and, in particular, the move towards privatization at the time of the survey; in addition, the structure of the union had not fully adjusted to changes in the location of management power associated with the growth of commercialism.

There are counter-trends in those sectors where workplace organization has traditionally been less strong. Here, union influence is often said to have increased over the last five years. This is particularly significant, since these tend to be the areas of employment growth (and/or less rapid decline). In other words, if we are seeking to assess the overall pattern of union influence, we should take into account not only the weakening of traditional areas of union strength in both employment and influence terms, but also the growth – in both senses – of other sectors. Moreover, even where respondents said that union influence had declined over the last five years, they also claimed that the control of the union over work organization remained substantial. Once more, we have to note the limitations of our data. Respondents from traditionally strong organizations may exaggerate the decline in their influence simply because performing their conventional role has become more awkward; those who have experienced some increased influence may exaggerate its scale and significance.

In many of the sectors where union influence is growing, trade union organization differs in a number of important respects from that in more 'traditional' areas. This has importnt implications for the nature of trade unionism in the future. The recession has accelerated the long-term trend towards an increasingly white-collar and service-based trade unionism. But, in addition, it has meant that the typical organizational characteristics of trade unions are undergoing change. Here we can most usefully turn to our notions of union sophistication, external integration and multi-level bargaining. These concepts highlight the importance of union activity and organization at a number of levels and the importance of some form of co-ordination between them. They integrate two quite different sets of considerations relating to union influence. The first of these is a 'workerist' conception, which stresses the importance of shop-floor strength and member commitment. This approach has often verged upon the romantic, and has tended to discount the important role that larger bureaucratic structures can play. The second set of considerations relate to the bureaucratic structures that formally act as mechanisms for bringing together diverse interests. Those who have focused upon this dimension in discussing union power have frequently paid insufficient attention to the importance of shop-floor activity.

Both aspects of union organization are important. The former, alone, not only leads to sectionalism, parochialism and somewhat patchy patterns of union influence, but also cannot move far beyond the most immediate aspects of the wage–effort bargain. On the other hand, centralized bureaucratic structures, in and of themselves, may permit unions to play a broader role, but union influence is likely to be limited and have little impact upon the day-to-day experience of union members. Where 'workerist' and 'bureaucratic' structures and patterns of influence co-exist and are integrated, then union organization is likely to be strong. For in such situations, meaningful general policies can be formulated; and higher levels of union organization can create conditions which are both important in themselves and facilitate action at lower levels. At the same time, particular interests and contingencies can be dealt with locally, while the realities of workplace experience can be transmitted to higher levels. Hence, where union organization is sophisticated, and where there is a high level of external integration, then there is likely to be a greater range of bargaining at all levels, and union influence is likely to be both greater and more stable. The survey and case-study findings give considerable support to this argument.

This model of trade union organization suggests that a contributory factor in the decline of union influence in some sectors may have been a lack of sophistication. Power often resided on the shop-floor and so it was dependent upon the employer still requiring the active co-operation of the workforce. It could not therefore be exercised over many matters relating to general management strategy. This long-standing weakness became particularly evident in the recession. On the other hand, union organization that was largely confined to higher levels – as was often the case in many other sectors – was invariably limited by its grass-roots weakness. Over the last few years, the 'workerist' component in such unions has often become stronger. If this trend continues without any absolute or serious weakening of the more centralized aspects of union organization, and if the two levels are co-ordinated, then in the future trade unions will achieve a greater degree of influence of a kind that is less patchy and less self-defeating. In other words, the general level of sophistication – and hence the role – of trade unionism may well increase. Such trends are not, of course, inevitable: changes in the distribution of power within trade unions can lead to major problems of the 'internal negotiation of order', thereby complicating the formulation of coherent and co-ordinated policies (see, e.g., Batstone et al., 1984; Undy et al., 1981).

These arguments are based upon less than ideal data. Our measure of union sophistication in the survey was necessarily crude. The case studies indicate areas of refinement: for example, noting the proportion of steward constituencies that remain unrepresented, and placing even greater stress upon mechanisms of co-ordination between different levels of union organization. It also focused upon formal organization: although actual patterns of union activity are likely to be related to formal structure, they are not totally determined by it. However, to move beyond formal structures requires much greater resources than were available to us on this project – and, indeed, greater resources in terms of manpower and time, and hence funding, than is generally recognized by those who plan to undertake intensive observational case studies. Despite these cautions, however, we would still maintain that our central notions are of value in that they relate to a wide range of theoretical debates and have demonstrated their utility in the analysis of the empirical data.

A further weakness of the survey is its dependence upon the subjective assessments of respondents on certain issues. The concept of influence is particularly problematical. Even in the case studies, it was at times difficult to pin down the actual degree of union power. In part, this reflected difficulties in reconstructing the past. But very often unions appeared to achieve their ends without any very lengthy process of negotiation. This was not the result of overwhelming union dominance. Rather, it reflected the way in which management and union accepted many 'facts' in common and acted accordingly. In other words, unions and management had developed a set of assumptions that were largely taken for granted; these were reflected in patterns of work organization and joint regulation. Structures embodied a 'mobilization of bias', which provided a significant, but still limited, degree of union power. In some of the case studies, it was possible to trace changes in the nature and extent of such mobilization. But in the survey this clearly was not possible. The importance of such 'structuration' serves to emphasize the complexity of the notion of power: it does not merely relate to who wins in situations of conflict, but it also concerns the determination of what constitutes an 'issue' and the more general shaping of modes of thought. To state this is not to espouse some notion of 'objective' interests: rather, it indicates the importance of detailed historical analysis – something which was also beyond the scope of our survey.

In addition to subjective assessments, other indicators of union influence were used in the survey: one such indicator was the range of bargaining. We found that this appeared to be very high – higher than other recent surveys have indicated. This raises a number of questions concerning both the significance of bargaining as a form of union influence, and the extent to which responses are affected by the precise wording of the question employed. For example, the range of bargaining found in the survey was higher than that found in a 1983 survey of personnel managers (Batstone, 1984a). It seems unlikely that the range of bargaining has expanded dramatically over the last year. Two other explanations therefore seem plausible: first, that what stewards define as bargaining, personnel managers do not. Comparisons of steward and manager responses in previous surveys (e.g. Daniel and Millward, 1983) indicate that this is the case, although to only a limited degree. Second, the precise phrasing of questions appears to be important. In the 1983 survey, the question probably biased answers towards the typical or general pattern of bargaining. In the present survey, we asked a question that may have encouraged responses in terms of whether particular issues were ever negotiated. Another difference was that the 1984 survey did not focus exclusively upon steward bargaining, whereas the 1983 survey did. Whatever the relative importance of such factors, it is clear that some caution is necessary in comparing these findings with those from other surveys.

An important theme in this volume has been the question of change. Assessing change, however, raises issues of measurement and perspective which need to be clearly specified. If they are not, even the discussion of such apparently simple questions as changes in the number of shop stewards can easily become confusing. At first sight, this seems simple enough: if the number of stewards has fallen, then union organization is weaker. But this is only part of the analysis. We know, for example, that the number of shop stewards is closely related to size of establishment or union membership. When the latter falls, we would expect a decline in the absolute number of stewards. The question therefore arises of whether the decline in steward numbers is greater than the decline in union membership or number of employees. If it is less, then one might argue that steward organization, in formal terms, is now stronger. But it should be stressed that this often means that the absolute number of stewards has actually fallen. If we are seeking to build up a general picture, we have also to take into account sectoral shifts in employment and the number of stewards. Since our survey does not cover all sectors, we are unable to do this. The general point, however, is that the significance attached to change is often attributable more to the implicit dimensions or scales selected than to differences over the 'facts'. It follows that questions of size effects and structural shifts need to be more consciously and explicitly included in future work.

Indeed, one can go further than this and suggest that in order to assess the significance of changes in the number of stewards it is necessary to know in considerable detail the precise pattern of changes in employment. For example, if a company has reduced its labour force by 10 per cent across all sections, then one might expect there to be no fall in steward numbers: if the sections required separate representation in the past, then they are likely to need it in the future. In this instance, therefore, one might be inclined to argue that any reduction in steward numbers indicates a weakening of formal union organization. On the other hand, if the same scale of job loss occurred through the closure of 20 per cent of the sections within the workplace and these had accounted for 20 per cent of shop stewards, then one would not expect those steward positions to remain, since there is nobody to represent. In this instance, then, it is possible to argue that a reduction in steward numbers that was substantially greater in percentage terms than the fall in jobs need not indicate any decline in formal union strength. Again, our survey could not deal with such complexities, but there is clearly some useful research to be done in meticulously unravelling such issues.

Despite our inability to handle many of the detailed complexities of changes in union organization, we can be reasonably confident on one basic point: namely, that within any size band (in employment or membership terms), *formal* union organization now often appears to be stronger than it did five years ago. This is consistent with our findings that few employers have seriously challenged the institutional position of the unions, preferring to find some new *modus vivendi* with them.

We have also tried to look briefly at other aspects of management's labour relations strategy. In a substantial proportion of companies, individualistic involvement techniques and the use of establishment or company-wide bonus schemes have been widely introduced. This goes along with the finding that many employers have sought to consult more with the unions. Both findings indicate an attempt to win the acquiescence of the workforce. We have already noted that in a substantial minority of cases there appears to have been a significant intensification of work; this, however, is not related systematically or significantly to the adoption of techniques to win the hearts and minds of workers or stewards. Trends vary substantially in the use of secondary labour. There appears to be trends towards the greater use of certain kinds of secondary labour in some sectors, although we were not able to assess the scale of such trends. But these were not related to other aspects of management strategy. In our case studies there were also examples of greater use of secondary labour. In the main, these moves were not part of a concerted strategy on the part of management to weaken the primary labour force. They were often acceptable to the unions as a means of maintaining job security within the primary labour force (cf. Dohse, 1984; Rubery, 1978).

There were few systematic relationships between the various aspects of labour relations strategy that we investigated. Indeed, overall, the strongest clustering was in those categories that indicated that employers were adopting none of the techniques which have recently been the subject of so much discussion and conjecture. Certainly our measures were extremely crude, and this may partly explain this finding. But, even so, our data suggest the need to look more carefully at the reality of management strategy, seeking to understand its various components and their interrelationships. A good deal of recent discussion has sought to develop categorizations of management strategy which are simple in every sense of the term. Rarely, if ever, are such models of use in understanding empirical reality (see, e.g., Deaton, 1985), for management is not a monolithic entity. Conflicting interests and approaches mean that decisions and policies are often muddy compromises both in formulation and execution (e.g. Dalton, 1959; Pettigrew, 1973). In addition, it may seem quite rational to managers to make *ad hoc* and partial changes in their approach. More throughgoing changes may appear too costly. Often managers see changes as minor or temporary and therefore refrain from any major reconsideration of their approach. The cumulation of partial policies and compromises over time serves to explain why it is often difficult to find any coherence in the overall approach of management towards labour (see, e.g., Rose and Jones, 1985).

There is a striking contrast in the nature of management's labour relations strategies between the public and private sectors. In the former, management has in recent years given much less support to the unions and has been more able to intensify effort levels. This is important in that it indicates that the 'political contingency' (Batstone *et al.*, 1984) in the public sector is a more potent pressure than market forces in the private sector. The findings also suggest that the extent to which private-sector employers have pursued the counsels of the state – at least in the industries we have considered – is remarkably limited. Within the public sector, however, there are also some marked variations between the Telecom and civil service samples. In the former, according to respondents, management has adopted a somewhat tougher approach both to the unions and to the labour force – and has succeeded in weakening the unions to a greater degree than in the latter. Telecom management has also employed a variety of individualistic techniques, which are notable for their absence in the civil service. It seems that, in preparation for the move into the private sector, Telecom management has outdone the private sector itself. This reflects, however, not market forces (which are very favourable for Telecom), but the importance of the political contingency.

The Question of Technical Change

Much of this study has been concerned with technical change. In chapter 1, it was noted that recent studies of new technology had begun to stress the weaknesses of simple models of technical (and economic) determinism, although general critiques of this kind are far from new. What is disappointing in a good deal of recent research is that this basic point had not been developed more fully; that is, research too often ends where it should have started. We have tried to look at precisely what factors shape the role and strategy of a key actor – the union – in the process of technical change.

Both our survey and case-study data clearly show that the effects of technical change cannot be attributed to the technology as such. Relatedly, we were unable to identify any distinctive effects of 'new' technology as against new technology: that is, microelectronics did not appear to have any unique effects. Nor, perhaps, is this really surprising. For the argument on the impact of new technology rests ultimately upon an economic model – the low cost of new technology means that it will be used in areas where 'macroelectronics' was less financially attractive.

We have found that new technology is often associated with job loss: but this is not invariably the case. Generally, new technology involves some notional job loss, in that labour productivity increases as machines take over what workers formerly did. That is, in order to produce a certain amount of an unchanged product, less labour is technically required (although the basic attraction of microelectronics may lie less in its labour-saving than its capital-saving qualities). But it does not follow that there will actually be fewer jobs. Manning levels may not be reduced to the technically optimum level: in the past this has not been the case, and so it is not immediately evident why things should be any different in the future. The competitive advantage achieved through the use of new technology – due to lower production costs, new or improved products and so on – may mean that, even though labour requirements per basic unit of output fall, total labour requirements increase; or, alternatively, the job loss is no greater than in firms that have become less competitive due to their failure to employ new technology. This, our survey indicates, is often the case.

We would not wish to argue that a total commitment to new technology will resolve the problems of unemployment. It is true that in the past notional job loss (that is, increased labour productivity) associated with the general process of technical change has been balanced by the employment effects of an associated growth of demand for products and services. Whether this felicitous trend will continue in the future depends upon many factors: that is, the employment effects associated with new technology are largely determined by economic, social and political, rather than purely technological, factors. Indeed these same factors also determine the pace and pattern of technological innovation. For example, our evidence suggest that, rather than new technology directly leading to mass unemployment, those factors that lead to mass unemployment have limited the adoption of new technology; this, in turn, has made companies less competitive and therefore unemployment has increased still further.

Assessing the general employment effects of new technology is also complex, because we have to take into account changes across companies and sectors. General conclusions cannot be reached from studying individual establishments or firms, since no account can be taken of 'knock-on' employment effects elsewhere. Declines in employment in one sector may be compensated for by increases in other sectors. We are not saying, of course, that such compensatory effects are inevitable: it is possible that job loss is cumulative.

The nature of our survey precluded us from assessing these general effects. What we have found, however, is that job loss is often as great where new technology has not been introduced as where it has. Moreover, the specific effects of new technology upon actual levels of employment are strongly influenced by the more general package of management strategies, of which the technical change is only a part. A survey of stewards is not a vehicle for investigating management strategy in technical change, but our case studies did show the importance of market considerations in management's decision to introduce new technology. Technical considerations were of relevance to varying degrees, as were labour questions (although they may have been more important in the minds of specialist designers of equipment). Indeed, what was striking was how small a role was played in management thinking by explicit labour considerations.

Furthermore, managements rarely considered the work organization and manning implications of new technology until fairly late in the day. Significant changes were often made only after the new technology had been introduced. In addition, it was clear that the technology did not determine patterns of work organization. Technology requires that certain tasks be performed. How those tasks are made into jobs is a matter of choice. The effects on job content are therefore also a matter of choice. Hence we have seen that, with broadly similar technology, the patterns of work organization were quite different in our chemicals and brewing case studies. It was clear from the survey that there had been considerable changes in the allocation of tasks between different occupational groups: these were not systematically related to trends towards deskilling of particular occupational groups nor to a polarization of skill.

Our findings suggest two important conclusions. First, new technology cannot simply be interpreted as a means by which management further extends its control over labour: in certain respects, it can be claimed that management often exposes itself to a greater dependence upon labour (in several of our case studies this was reflected in a reduced role for direct supervision). Second, the effects of technical change upon job content are to a large extent determined by factors other than the technology itself. They depend upon the nature of the product or service, the state of the product and labour markets, and the power and strategies of both management and workers. What was striking in the case studies was the extent to which management thought in terms of minimizing changes in work organization. Where management did consider matters rather more deeply, it often opted for maintaining or increasing the skills of routine grades. In part this may have been in order to win the co-operation of the workforce, but there were also technical and commercial reasons for adopting this approach.

It follows from this argument, however, that under certain circumstances new technology will be associated with the 'degradation' of certain occupations. We argued in chapter 1, for example, that management was likely to have considerably greater freedom of action where a new company or plant was being established; the same may be true to a lesser extent where technical innovation is of a more 'systemic' nature or is confined to a fairly discrete area within an existing plant. The latter appears to have been the case, for example, at Longbridge (e.g. Scarborough, 1984; Willman and Winch, 1985). The stimuli to management action in this case were market forces and the role of the 'political contingency' in a company that had been taken over by the state and that was seriously in debt to it. Again, therefore, we see the importance of the negotiation of new technology.

Our survey and case-study findings show that new technology can have different effects upon different aspects of work experience. This in itself seriously complicates any general statements about the overall effects of new technology. Even ignoring the important fact that skill is in large part a social construction (in which case the discussion of deskilling takes on a quite different character), in order to talk at all meaningfully about 'deskilling' or 'degradation' a number of stages of analysis are required: first, we have to differentiate dimensions of skill; second, we have to be able to measure movements along these dimensions fairly accurately; and, third, we have to be able to attribute weightings to the different dimensions so that, for example, we can state that a sizeable increase on one dimension is outweighed by a small fall in another. No one has yet developed a satisfactory means of doing this. Nevertheless such processes are implicit in many statements upon the effects of new technology.

Both through respondents' answers in the survey and through our case studies, we have indicated the way in which different types of change have occurred in different dimensions of job content. In general terms, the majority of our respondents stated that skill levels (where we passed the problem of definition to our respondents – a less than ideal tactic) had increased. Worker control is more often said to have risen than fallen in the case of private-sector manual groups, whereas the reverse is the case for non-manual and public-sector groups. Effort levels are generally seen to have increased. Health and safety standards have generally improved for manual workers, but fallen for non-manual workers. It should be stressed that these are subjective assessments by our respondents and that they are general trends – that is, there are many exceptions. To the extent that this pattern is fairly general, then it suggests that, if, for example, we attribute equal weight to each of these four aspects, the overall effect of technical change upon jobs has been more favourable for manual than non-manual workers. In many respects this should not be very surprising: the nature of new technology is typically such as to distance the manual worker further from the production process and to take over mundane tasks, while often it means that, for the first time, the non-manual worker is intimately involved with a piece of capital equipment more significant than a pen, filing cabinet or typewriter. The related question of the proleterianization of white-collar work as a result of new technology (e.g. Crompton and Jones, 1984) confronts many of the problems we have discussed in relation to the similar issue of the 'degradation' of work. We will not repeat these arguments here.

Much of the debate surrounding new technology – its effects on employment, job content and class structure – has centred upon long-term effects. Attempts at prediction have been made by extrapolating from what may turn out to be minor or temporary changes. A central problem for such predictive endeavour relates to the basic point that the effects of new technology are the result of processes of negotiation. It is therefore necessary to understand those processes and how they are shaped. In this study, a key argument has been that, other things being equal, the pattern of negotiation between management and unions over technical change will be broadly similar to the more general pattern of negotiation. Our study has focused upon the role of the union within this process of negotiation, but we would expect the same sort of argument to be relevant to an assessment of the pattern of negotiation within management, for example.

The similarity between the general pattern of bargaining and that in relation to new technology is attributable to a number of factors. First, if trade unions are able to negotiate over a particular range of issues in relation to new technology, they are likely to be already doing so more generally. In other words, there is little reason to assume that new technology in and of itself will dramatically shift the approach of either management or union. In the case studies, where there were changes in the approach of the union, they clearly followed from the basic logic of its conventional bargaining strategy. Second, particularly since managements rarely use new technology as an opportunity to introduce dramatic changes in labour relations, many aspects of technical change were covered by pre-existing agreements and systems of joint regulation. Third, we have argued that the structure of union organization will limit the sorts of strategies that unions seek to pursue and their chances of success. That is, only more sophisticated union organizations will generally be able to develop policies that intrude more deeply into traditional areas of managerial prerogative. Our data have broadly supported these points.

Arguments of this kind relate to broad tendencies. They do not deny, for example, that stewards or individuals with a broader perspective may sometimes be able to change things considerably; however, they are more likely to meet with success where union organization is more conducive to such strategies, or where they are able to create such forms of organization. Similarly, we have noted the impact that particular types of management strategy and the scale of job loss can have. Although the impact of such changes may be particularly marked in the case of new technology, they are likely to have similar effects more generally. Indeed, given that new technology is part of a more general package of changes, it is this wider policy which is likely to have greater relevance. General changes in management's labour relations strategy are more important in affecting the role of the unions than new technology as such. Hence, for example, effort intensification is about as common where there has been no technical change as where new technology has been introduced; and the unions have confronted some of the strongest challenges on the part of management where there has been very little technical change.

We are led, therefore, to the conclusion that in many respects there is little new about new technology – particularly since major technical changes have been common in many sectors for many years. If the current wave of technical innovation has any particular significance, it probably derives more from the general economic and political climate in which it is occurring than from the inherent characteristics of the technology itself.

Similar arguments apply to the question of the effects of technical change upon trade unions. In the survey, few respondents said that it had affected trade union organization on the various dimensions we investigated, and this picture of little change was supported by our more detailed statistical analyses of the survey data and by our case studies. Certainly one can identify signs of new sectional interests in some cases, for example, but their wider significance cannot yet be assessed and will in any case depend upon how they are handled by those concerned. Moreover, sectional differences are far from a new phenomenon in most trade unions.

Again, we should stress not only what we are arguing, but also what our findings do not imply. They do not imply, for example, that trade unions have exerted a great deal of control over the process of technical change. All they do is to indicate that unions generally exert about as much control on this matter as they do on others; and the extent of this is typically both variable and fairly limited. Second, it does not mean that trade unions should not be seriously considering the likely effects of changes associated with new technology. What our findings do suggest is that, when unions do consider these changes, they should not be mesmerized by the mystical qualities of high technology. Equally, our findings indicate the more general need for many trade unions to think more strategically, not only about new technology, but also about the more general nature of management strategy. For it is that strategy which is likely to shape both the impact of new technology and other changes – which may have greater effects upon union members than technical change. This lack of strategic thinking on the part of trade unions is often of long standing: it is probably no more or less important in the era of new technology than it was on many occasions in the past.

These points return us to more general questions about the nature of trade union structure and strategy, which we will discuss by moving to an international comparison of the role of trade unions in the process of technical change.

Union Structure and Strategy: A Cross-national Perspective

So far the discussion in this chapter has focused upon organization at the level of the establishment or company. However, we have also stressed both the significance of external integration and the broader structure of trade unions in earlier chapters. In particular, we have argued – and the data support this view – that, in addition to important 'size effects', the nature of the larger union affects domestic organization and the sorts of strategies it pursues. The data have shown the importance of single-employer/industry union structures and, to a lesser degree, of single- as against multi-occupational forms of union organization. In single-employer/industry unions, domestic organization tends to be more sophisticated, once size of membership and other variables are controlled for, and there tend to be stronger links with the larger union. These characteristics are also associated with a more centralized pattern of bargaining. The consequence of these structures, we have suggested, is that trade unions can more easily co-ordinate the action they take at different levels and can concentrate their limited resources upon developing a more strategic approach. This is facilitated by the way in which union scope structures its interests and definitions of problems.

The underlying logic of these arguments is that the more homo-geneous a union's membership, particularly where it monopolizes the occupation(s) or industry concerned, the better it can pursue a coherent policy. Such homogeneity appears to be particularly important in the case of single-industry and single-employer unions, since their very structure will encourage them to think in terms of more general events within the company or industry: in short, other things being equal, they will tend to think more strategically. Single-occupation unions may also think more coherently, but their focus will be upon a par-ticular swathe of the labour market which cuts across industries and employers: they may therefore attend less to the nature of the broader strategies of individual employers, except in so far as they directly impinge upon the distinctive interests of the occupation.

When we move to comparisons between countries in the role of trade unions, we need to look at the structure not only of individual unions, but also of union federations and confederations – that is, we are back to the special type of multi-industry/multi-occupation union mentioned in chapter 1. Clearly, other factors are of relevance: the nature of employers and their organization, the precise structure and state of the economy, the characteristics of the labour force and the society more generally, and so on. However, we will confine ourselves to the primary focus of this study – trade union organization.

In recent years, there has been a good deal of work undertaken from political economy and corporatist perspectives on international variations in economic performance and related issues such as strikes (see, e.g., Batstone, 1985; Goldthorpe, 1984). Much of this work has stressed the importance of trade union organization and its links with the state and political parties. Briefly, and with some over-generalization, the following tend to be the main strands of argument. Where trade unions enjoy high levels of density and are non-competing in terms of membership (including here differences of a political or religious nature), and particularly where they are industry-based and strongly centralized and united within a single powerful confederation, they represent all-encompassing organizations which are able to think in strategic or class terms. Where such unions have close relations with united social-democratic or labour parties which achieve power, then they can use political means to achieve many of their demands. In addition, their all-encompassing nature encourages them to think not only of the gains to their members, but also of the more general costs of their actions (since these also fall upon their members, who – together with their families – constitute a major proportion of the population). For both electoral and policy reasons, therefore, there is an incentive for governments, particularly of a social-democratic hue, to involve the unions in discussion of economic and social policy (see, e.g., Cameron, 1984; Korpi, 1983).

The precise nature of the arguments put forward by various writers differs. For example, whereas class analyses typically emphasize the development of union-government relationships as the result of a class or labour movement strategy (e.g. Korpi, 1983), corporatists frequently see the initiative for such developments as emanating from the state (often in terms of a functionalist argument concerning the presumed 'needs' of a modern capitalist economy; e.g. Schmitter, 1979). Moreover, whereas some writers have claimed that such 'corporatist' arrangements work against the interests of union members and endanger political democracy, others have argued that such arrangements constitute an important vehicle for the advancement of worker interests (for example, through more equitable social policies), as well as being associated with superior economic performance (e.g. Crouch, 1982; Panitch, 1981).

Many of these arguments are less than adequate. For example, there is a good deal of confusion within the literature as to what exactly is meant by the central concept of corporatism (Lehmbruch, 1982; Schmitter, 1982). Frequently, arguments relating corporatist structures and aspects of economic and social performance are less than convincing; they fail to take into account the role of other economic, social and demographic variables, and do not specify sufficiently the nature of the linkages between corporatist arrangements, on the one hand, and economic performance, on the other. Despite these serious weaknesses, the important point for our present interests is that these accounts do seek to link trade union structures and policies to a variety of economic and social issues which are of direct relevance to member interests.

This, then, is the theme which we wish to draw from these analyses, since it is a logical extension of the arguments we have developed in earlier chapters. However, we need to confront three other serious weaknesses within this literature. These concern details of national-level union organization, the links between national and local levels of trade union organization, and the tendency to assume that the gains workers achieve from corporatist arrangements emanate directly and exclusively from the political process.

If we define corporatism as meaning that there are close relationships between the state and union confederations, then it is clear that neither high union density nor a united trade union movement are necessary pre-conditions. For example, there are a number of union confederations in countries such as Sweden that are often seen as providing classic examples of corporatism. In the past, this was perhaps not too serious a weakness, since the LO was dominant and there was little competition between the various federations. But competing views over wage differentials, the shift in the occupational structure in favour of non-manual groups, and the growing confusion between what constitutes a manual as against a non-manual job – all of these have increased the tensions between the various confederations during the recession. Nevertheless, it is still the case that the central federations both wield a great deal of power and influence, and that the LO, in particular, has close relationships with the state (especially when the social democrats are in power). Similarly, close relationships between the state and the union confederations exist in countries such as the Netherlands, despite the fact that union density is low and the union federations have been divided along religious and political lines. However, the close co-operation between the confederations and the close links between individual confederations and particular political parties mean that the union movement had access to the state no matter which party was in power. In short, then, it seems that what is important is that union confederations should be fairly centralized and, if there is more than one, the various bodies should co-operate closely (following from our previous terminology, this might be called inter-federal sophistication). In these circumstances, the confederations become all-encompassing organizations (or at least aspire to such a position) and are therefore encouraged to think strategically, taking into account the wider costs and benefits of alternative courses of action.

The second weakness noted above concerned the question of the links between national and local levels of trade union organization. Although one or two writers have noted the tensions that may arise in centralized trade unions involved in corporatist arrangements (e.g. Pizzorno, 1978; Sabel, 1981), the bulk of the corporatist literature subsumes the dynamics of the internal negotiation of order under the blanket notion of centralization. It therefore fails to consider not only the question of the nature of policy formation nationally – in which local representatives may or may not play a role – but also the way in which, and the extent to which, centralized unions may shape the thinking and strategies of lower levels of union organization. Most importantly, it fails to take into account what we have suggested is particularly important: the co-ordination of multi-level bargaining. That this does occur, and is significant, in many societies where union organization is relatively centralized is indicated by a variety of factors: for example, the scale of wage drift.

Third, the political economy tradition stresses the importance of a class analysis, where class is defined in terms of the relations of production. But often these same studies focus upon direct outputs of political activity, which bear little direct relevance to the employment relationship. Hence, for example, instead of looking at the way in which wage issues are handled, emphasis is often placed upon the redistribution of income through welfare payments; even more seriously, such issues as structures of authority in the workplace are totally ignored (Batstone, 1985a).

This tendency to underplay the dynamics of the workplace is the most serious weakness as far as our present purposes are concerned, although overcoming this problem also means that we have to take into account the other problems we have just discussed. It is possible to argue that centralized and united (or co-operating) union confederations are able to structure workplace activity, and hence, for example, the way in which new technology is handled, in a number of important ways. The first of these is by establishing legislation and/or national-level agreements. These may provide structures for the conduct of labour relations at a local level, including bargaining and information rights, and principles relating to specific issues, such as the nature of work organization or the introduction of new technology.

Such legislation and agreements are likely to be more important where unions are centralized. First, it is only in such organizations (particularly where employers are organized on a similar basis, which tends generally to be the case) that power is located at a level that permits such central agreements and meaningful bargaining with the state. Second, we find that in societies with this type of union structure there is generally a long tradition of a wide range of bargaining and discussion or legislation at central levels. Questions such as those relating to new technology can accordingly be subsumed under conventional patterns of regulation and/or the distinctive features of new technology issues can be easily handled by relatively small changes to the conventional patterns of labour relations. Third, those centralized bodies with high union density typically have a relatively high degree of co-ordination between the different levels of union organization.

Local union representatives are encouraged to relate their local activities to the general policies of the union movement (for example, see Lewin, 1980, on Sweden). Fourth, where union density is high in centralized confederations, there is generally a long-standing pattern of joint regulation not only at national, but also at local level, such that management appears more readily to accept the union as a relatively equal partner on many issues.

However, although centralization and unity/co-operation are important factors, they are not the whole story. As noted above, union density is also important, since it affects the strength of workplace organization and the degree of integration between different levels of worker representation. What is particularly striking is that where union density is high, as for example in the Scandinavian countries, workplace representation is union-based. Where union density is lower, as in the Netherlands and the Federal Republic of Germany, formal structures of workplace representation tend not to be union-based. Although it is true that key works council positions are held by union activists, their primary commitment within the workplace is to the requirements placed upon them by the role of works councillor. This includes, for example, a peace obligation and also encourages them to adopt a parochial approach to many matters. Of equal importance is that the structure of works councils provides relatively fragile linkages between the company and establishment levels; relationships between works councillors and the membership are also typically weak. In contrast, in Sweden, for example, the density of union officers at establishment level is generally fairly high, they have close relationships with the membership, and they are integrated into the larger trade union structure.

National-level agreements and legislation tend to be more supportive of trade union or worker influence at local levels where centralized unions enjoy a high level of union membership. Hence, for example, in Britain, where union organization is relatively decentralized and the authority of the TUC over member unions is limited, we find that national agreements are non-existent, while legislation provides few rights for local negotiation and virtually no principles to be followed on issues such as new technology (exceptions to this are the Employment Protection Act 1975 and the Health and Safety at Work Act 1975, both of which lay down relatively vague rights to information). At the other extreme, in societies with high union density and centralized trade unions, there is a wide range of legislation, along with national agreements, which lay down not only worker and union rights within the workplace, but also principles concerning the organization of work. Among these are the codetermination law in Sweden and the legislation relating to the work environment in Norway. Societies with relatively centralized union organizations, but with low union density, as in the FRG and the Netherlands, tend to be mid-way between these extremes. Legislation exists, although it primarily provides rights to non-union-based forms of representation within the workplace. It is also less supportive of worker representation than in many of the Scandinavian countries (for a review of relevant legislation, see ILO, 1984; it is also worth noting that much of this legislation dates from the 1970s and reflects, among other things, tensions which came to the fore within centralized unions).

In sum, then, we are suggesting that the model we have developed to look at workplace and individual union organization in Britain can be extended to the level of union movements in different countries. We might therefore talk of union sophistication at national level. Where confederations are united, have a considerable degree of central control, and where union density is high, then they are likely to have a more strategic approach to the pursuit of members' interests. They are able to secure national agreements and legislation which is directly in members' interest and which provides a basis for local union activity. At the same time, the different levels of union organization are likely to be relatively well integrated, permitting co-ordinated, multi-level bargaining. As a consequence, unions locally are more likely to achieve greater influence over the strategic aspects of technical change, as well as over its more immediate and direct implications for the wage–effort bargain. Where unions are relatively centralized, but have low union density, we have suggested, the effect of their strategic thinking is constrained by their more limited ability to achieve such favourable legislation and by the fact that the key formal institutions at the workplace are not union-based. In countries such as Britain, where, at least in the private sector, the unions tend to be highly decentralized, then national-level agreements and legislation are likely to play a limited role.

We can assess the utility of the preceding arguments by looking briefly at the two key themes of this study – the impact of unemployment and the introduction of new technology – from a cross-national perspective. In the former case, we will be concerned solely with union strategy at national level. In looking at new technology, we will concentrate upon the workplace. The methods by which we are able to do this are necessarily crude and the aim of the discussion is to be merely illustrative. Moreover, the types of data we use are of quite different character: in looking at reactions to unemployment we use official and other statistical sources, whereas in looking at reactions to technical change we rely upon a small number of case studies. We consider first the question of unemployment.

Unions and Unemployment

The basic thrust of our analysis is that union movements that are centralized – so that they adopt a national perspective and are able to control workplace organizations – will be prepared to make concessions on wages in order to reduce the level of unemployment. At the other extreme, where union movements are decentralized and a significant degree of power is wielded by relatively autonomous workplace organizations, the key actors – those in domestic organizations – will be primarily concerned with those working within their establishments: consequently they will be less prepared, and indeed they will not be in a position, to make concessions over wages in an attempt to maintain the general level of unemployment. Between these two extremes we can identify a 'mixed' group: this consists first, of union movements that cannot be described as highly centralized, but have relatively weak workplace union organizations, or, second, union movements that are relatively centralized in certain respects, but have rather limited control over their workplace organizations. Such 'mixed' union movements, we can hypothesize, will 'sit' between the two extremes in terms of the trade-offs they are able and willing to make between wages and employment.

Table 8.1 shows the average rate of unemployment and the average annual rate of increase in real manufacturing earnings for thirteen European countries, classified by the structure of their union movements as outlined in the previous paragraph. Generally speaking, real earnings have fallen fractionally and unemployment remains low, where the union movement is centralized. The exception to the pattern is Austria, where, relative to the two other cases where unemployment is low in this group, adjustments have taken the form of changes in working practices (so that unit labour costs are lower). Such adjustments have also occurred in the Netherlands, where unemployment remains high.

At the other extreme, unemployment in the countries with 'decentralized' union movements has typically been much higher than in the centralized group, while the rate of growth of real earnings is a good deal higher. The rate of growth of unit labour costs has been even more dramatic.

The intermediate group in terms of union structure is also, on average, intermediate in terms of the trade-off between earnings and employment. Hence – with the exception of Belgium and Denmark – unemployment is lower than in the decentralized countries, but considerably higher than in the centralized cases (with the exception of the Netherlands). At the same time, rises in real earnings are lower

Table 8.1 Trade-offs between wages and employment

	Average standardized rate of unemployment, 1978–84	Average annual rate of increase in real manufacturing earnings, 1978–84
Centralized union movements		
Austria	2.9	+1.1
Netherlands	9.2	−0.6
Norway	2.3	−0.4
Sweden	2.6	−0.9
Mean	4.3	−0.2
'Mixed' union movements		
Belgium	10.9	+1.1
Denmark	8.8	+0.5
Finland	5.8	+0.9
Federal Republic of Germany	5.3	+0.4
Switzerland	0.5	+0.2
Mean	6.3	+0.6
Decentralized union movements		
France	7.3	+2.1
Republic of Ireland	9.9	+1.6
Italy	8.5	+2.0
United Kingdom	9.7	+2.6
Mean	8.9	+2.1

Sources: OECD; *Historical Statistics* and *Economic Outlook* (various issues); Batstone (1984b).

than in any of the decentralized cases, but are consistently positive.

Clearly, there are many other factors of significance in explaining the relationship between unemployment and earnings. In addition, the recession has led to changes in the pattern of union organization and union strategy in a number of countries: this is reflected in year-to-year changes in the relationship between unemployment and earnings. Hence, for example, in Sweden the centralized structure has come under increasing strain in recent years, whereas in Italy there are moves towards a greater centralization of union organization. The account given here has been brief (for a fuller discussion, see Batstone, 1984b), for our aim has merely been to indicate the wider utility of the framework of analysis adopted in this study.

Trade Unions and Technical Change

The international comparative project, of which our case studies were a part, permits us to assess the validity of our general argument to some degree. Case studies were undertaken in machine tools, brewing (or a similar production process), chemicals and finance in Sweden, the Federal Republic of Germany, the Netherlands and Italy, as well as the UK. Although the exact criteria of selection of case-study sites varied, as did the precise nature of the technical change investigated and the depth of the research, a common core of data was collected in each country. The findings cannot be taken as conclusive, if only because just four cases were investigated in each country. Nevertheless they do provide the best set of data currently available to investigate our theme. The arguments we put forward should therefore be seen as suggestive rather than conclusive.

It is not our intention here to discuss the findings of the various case studies in detail, but simply to compare the broad variations found between different countries. The actual range of union influence differed within countries and was affected by the detailed structure of worker representation, and the organization, ownership and control of the companies, as well as market and community factors (for a fuller discussion of the findings of the various case studies, see Levie and Moore, 1984).

The most active role played by worker representatives in relation to new technology was in Sweden. In two of the four Swedish cases, the unions were able to shape the general structure of management policy concerning new technology and related issues, and – on a simple count of the areas in which the unions played a role – all four of the Swedish cases come in the top quartile of the twenty case studies in terms of the range of union influence. This is to be explained by a number of factors. The first is the nature of legislation, and particularly the codetermination law. This provides the unions locally with rights to a relatively high degree of involvement in management planning of major changes, and from a relatively early stage. Hence, in one case the unions were able to insist that management withdraw its initial plans, because it had failed to involve the union. In most cases, joint project groups were set up in the Swedish companies to investigate aspects of the planned technical change. Indeed, in one case the initiative for the changes came from the union, and in several outside specialists were used by the union locally.

Second, union organization was relatively sophisticated: union density and 'shop-steward' density were both relatively high, and the representatives of the main union acted in a highly co-ordinated manner (although co-ordination between unions representing, for example, manual workers and supervisors was typically very limited).

Third, there was a relatively high degree of external integration, although this is not to say that full-time officials were always involved in the discussions; frequently they were not. But key local union representatives were often closely involved in the larger union, and the more general pattern of union organization ensured that close links were maintained in the thinking of the different levels of the union.

Fourth, although some local initiatives went considerably beyond the policies promulgated by the relevant industrial union – the logic of multi-level bargaining – unions both at industry and national level had been promoting ideas concerning the extended role of the union. In other words, as new technology entered upon the horizon, the unions had gradually extended their traditional interests into new forms deemed to meet the demands of the changing situation (in a way which was essentially similar to that found in some of the British case studies).

Fifth, this role was facilitated by the fact that, although the co-determination law was of recent origin, it merely served to extend what was a fairly well-established pattern of management-union relations at local level.

The Swedish case studies, then, indicate a fairly wide range of union influence. In the main, that influence was of a 'bureaucratic' and positive nature. It also has to be recognized that in some cases it involved significant trade-offs: for example, an increase in shiftworking or effort levels in return for greater job security. For some, this might indicate serious weaknesses in the role the unions played, suggesting an incorporated union organization. For others, the gains achieved – particularly in terms of job security – would appear to outweigh the costs.

It is interesting to contrast this picture of the Swedish experience with that drawn by the case studies in the Federal Republic of Germany and the Netherlands. Here, there were frequently disputes over the rights of worker representatives to involvement and information. Invariably their involvement in the planning process was a good deal less than in Sweden. Furthermore several of the German case studies highlighted problems of co-ordination between the various levels of worker representation. Works councillors often failed to collate the information that was in fact available to them. Although in one or two cases worker representatives did have a small influence over the broad nature of management strategy, their impact was largely confined to particular aspects of manning and work organization. Worker influence appeared generally to be marginally greater in the FRG than in the Netherlands, but in neither country did the overall degree of influence approximate the Swedish level. In many respects, it was not dramatically different to that found in the British studies – except, perhaps, that greater concern was demonstrated (but not necessarily with any result) over strategic issues, whereas control over work organization was more patchy. This pattern reflects the weakness of legislative support in these two countries as compared with Sweden, the fact that management often did not fully accept a joint role for the works councils, the limited degree of sophistication of worker representation, and its weak links with union organization more generally.

The Italian experience – as indicated by the case studies – provides a further contrast with the Swedish situation. In one of the Italian cases the unions achieved a relatively high degree of influence, despite the relative lack of legislative support. Other factors appeared to play an important role, and these can best be seen by considering the situation where the union played the greatest role. In this instance, union density was high, workplace organization was sophisticated, and there was a high degree of external integration with other parts of the labour movement. Moreover, at industry level the unions co-operated closely and had developed a fairly wide range of bargaining with the employers. In large part, this appeared to reflect changes in the approach of the unions which were also occurring at national level: members' interests were increasingly defined in terms of the maintenance of employment and, to this end, the unions had been increasingly prepared to co-operate with employers. Although this change was only minimally reflected in formal institutional arrangements – demonstrating its evolving nature – it did mean that the employer was not averse to union involvement in the planning of technical change. However, the transition from a zero-sum, or conflictual, to a positive and more accommodative stance created quite serious tensions within the workplace union organization. With the exception of this particular case, union influence in Italy over the process of technical change appeared to be broadly similar to – and possibly marginally greater than – that found in Britain, the Federal Republic of Germany or the Netherlands.

This has been an extremely brief discussion of union influence over the process of technical change in four other countries, and we have paid scant attention to the factors explaining variations in the role of the unions or worker representatives within the individual countries (for a fuller discussion of the findings of the Swedish project, see

Sandberg, 1984). Our aim was to suggest that the approach we have adopted in relation to variations in the British experience can be extended to an analysis at the international level. Again, it should be stressed that the findings have to be treated with caution, since they are based upon four, possibly atypical, cases in each country. However, we will be able to make more meaningful comparisons in the near future, since our survey is currently being replicated in Sweden.

The variations in the role of the union and in the effects of technical change upon workers shown in these case studies indicate that the degree of union influence over technical change in Britain is relatively limited. In addition, the experiences in these different countries provide further support to one of the basic arguments of this study: that the impact of new technology is attributable less to any inherent characteristics of the technology as such, and much more to the structures and strategies of the key actors.

This study has focused primarily upon the structure and strategy of the trade unions: there is clearly a need for comparable work on employers. In this sense, our research focus was partial. If we had been able to look with equal care at management, it is possible that our conclusions would have been somewhat different. Certainly they would have raised matters relating to the internal organization of management and how this affected corporate strategy; that is, our approach would have been broadly similar to the way we have analysed the unions.

The study has also faced other limitations, as we have stressed at a number of points thoughout this volume. Hence it should be seen as essentially exploratory in nature, giving a very broad-brushed picture. However, we see our findings as significant for a number of reasons. First, the study has demonstrated the utility of combining a variety of diverse techniques in the analysis of a single issue: we have found the combination of the detailed insights of the case studies and the wider and more superficial data from the survey to be particularly stimulating. Second, it has raised further questions – if they were needed – against theses of technological determinism. Third, it has gone beyond stating that the effects of new technology are socially determined to the creation of empirically supported models of some of the key factors within that social process. Fourth, it has made some steps towards a framework for the analysis of trade union structure and strategy, which can be applied at a wide variety of levels and, we believe, in relation to a wide range of issues.

In conclusion, however, it is useful to reiterate the basic point that comes out of the research. The ability of trade unions to handle matters relating to unemployment and new technology depends primarily upon those factors that affect its ability to handle any other issues: prime among these is good organization. Without such organization, it is unlikely that unions will be able to develop any meaningful strategy and even less likely that they will be able to apply it in practice. This is not to say that unions should not think carefully about the implications of new technology; clearly they should. But the thrust of our argument is that, where unions have not done this, it generally reflects their lack of strategic thinking more generally. This gap is as serious, if not more serious, than their failure to grapple with the problems of new technology. Nor should our discussion of the experience of other countries be interpreted as suggesting that the passing of favourable legislation or the signing of relevant national agreements will necessarily help unions. For, first, this is only likely to happen where unions have particular structures and strategies. Second, unions are only able to make much use of such laws or agreements where they are well organized. In short, the conventional wisdom of the trade union movement – that strong organization is a pre-condition of influence – applies as much to questions of new technology as to anything else. In this study, we have indicated the importance of a variety of organizational factors and, in particular, what we have termed union sophistication and integration.

Appendix: Survey and Case-Study Details

As was noted in chapter 1, the research on which this study is based was of two kinds. The first was a series of four case studies, the second a survey covering a much wider range of industrial and union situations.

The case studies were linked into a wider EEC-sponsored project looking at information disclosure and new technology in Sweden, the Federal Republic of Germany, the Netherlands and Italy as well as the United Kingdom. This wider project required that four studies should be undertaken, one in chemicals, one in food and drink, one in machine tools and one in finance. This provided a somewhat limited range of situations. The aim of the wider project was to look at what might be termed 'best practice' from a union perspective. This criterion created a number of problems: most obviously, the notion of best practice is difficult to assess, particularly before the research is undertaken. Although this vague notion of best practice played some role in our selection of case-study establishments, it was scarcely dominant. Certainly, if only with hindsight, some of the cases of technical change which we investigated could scarcely be described as embodying best practice in any sense of the term; others, however, do appear to illustrate a considerable degree of success on the part of the unions in dealing with technical change.

The importance of the case studies – as with any such intensive case-study research (see Clyde Mitchell, 1983) – lies less in questions of their typicality than in the insights they provide into processes of change. Our approach to the field research was guided by a detailed checklist of points, which were derived from previous work on union organization and debates concerning new technology. At the same time, both those original ideas and the findings from the case studies were used in the design of our questionnaire and the selection of unions and industries to be included in the survey. The survey permitted us to adopt a broader perspective upon our case studies and, in later analyses, helped to guide the writing up of our findings from those case studies. In short, the combination of the two techniques permitted a generally fruitful tension between two quite different sorts of data. It is, of course, the case that a postal survey cannot hope to cover matters in anywhere near the degree of detail that a case study can: as the discussion of the case studies indicates, there are a number of areas where intensive research leads to some caution in the interpretation of the survey findings. However, the survey points attention to themes that might be less confidently pursued in the analysis, if our work had been confined to the four case studies. This is particularly true since (as would appear often to be the case in work on new technology) there was sometimes somewhat limited evidence available concerning the detailed process of change and the rationales and strategies of the actors. Indeed, a problem for the research – but precisely because of that, an important cautionary point concerning debates on new technology – was how little importance was sometimes attached to the fact that new technology was being introduced. In seeking to answer the question of why this was the case, two factors appeared important: first, that the scale and newness of technical change was fairly limited, particularly compared with other changes that were occurring at the same time. Second, this limited concern about new technology appeared to reflect the more general pattern of union organization and activity at the workplace. The intensive case study, however, is often less than ideal for the investigation of what does not happen, rather than what does happen. Here, the survey findings have given us a good deal more confidence in putting forward our arguments. In short, the two approaches can be seen as complementary precisely because they have different strengths and weaknesses.

In this appendix, we briefly outline the details of the survey and the way in which it was analysed, and then outline some basic points concerning the case-study sites. The case studies were undertaken between March 1983 and July 1984. The surveys were undertaken between July 1984 and October of the same year.

The Survey

The first aim in the survey was to cover those industries in which case studies had been undertaken: that is, chemicals, food and drink, small-batch engineering, and finance. In the first three industries, we had focused our research upon production groups, but it was evident from data we collected during our fieldwork and from other evidence that the experience of maintenance workers was likely to be significantly different from that of direct workers. We therefore decided to include special samples of maintenance workers in these three industries: these were taken from the EETPU, since this union is of especial interest in relation to new technology and because it has a very good data base, which appeared to provide a fairly accurate and up-to-date population for drawing samples divided by different industries. In addition, in part to see the same union in the role of representing production workers, and in part to cover further large-batch and mass production, we drew a fourth EEPTU sample from electrical engineering and electronics. In fact, our responses in this sample were generally dominated by maintenance workers; we have therefore included them as a fourth maintenance group in our analyses.

We sought to include in the survey not only the same industries, but also the same unions as we had looked at in the case studies. hence, we drew our food and drink sample from the TGWU, our small-batch engineering sample (this was extended from purely machine tools, due to the small numbers of the latter that still exist in Britain) from the AUEW, and our finance sample from BIFU.

However, our chemicals case study covered USDAW. The bulk of this union's membership is not in this industry, and, at the same time, the bulk of chemical workers are not in USDAW. We therefore drew samples from both the TGWU and USDAW in chemicals. In the latter case, we were working indirectly through branch secretaries who were believed to have chemical shop stewards in their branches; this was a failure. It became evident that in a good number of cases the branches did not include chemicals establishments, with the result that we received a very small number of completed questionnaires (but several letters pointing this fact out to us). The USDAW respondents have therefore been excluded from the analysis. Hence, although our chemicals case study covered USDAW, our survey sample is from the TGWU.

In the finance sector, we wished to confine the survey to offices that employed a minimum of 75 staff. The reason for this was that otherwise there was a severe risk that we would be comparing very small units in finance with much larger ones in the other samples (where, whenever possible, we again applied a minimum-size criterion). This meant that the population that could be sampled was greatly restricted, and so we decided to draw samples from both BIFU and from ASTMS, which has substantial membership in this sector. Again, in these samples, we were working indirectly: that is, we had no means of drawing a sample directly and so we were forced to go indirectly, and indeed through two stages to reach our target groups of stewards – the national officials and the seconded representatives. We did, however, also design a separate questionnnaire for the latter. The number of responses from the seconded representatives and letters from them provide a basis for estimating the number of establishments to which the normal questionnaire was sent, and hence an estimate of the response rate. The small number of responses in these two samples have led us to combine the two for the purposes of the analysis presented here. Such differences as exist between the BIFU and ASTMS respondents appear to be largely attributable to the fact that one tends to come primarily from banking, the other from insurance.

As was argued in chapter 1, we increasingly felt that the nature of union organization was a crucial factor in understanding how unions are affected and shape the process of technical change. In particular, the range of a union's membership is likely to affect its pattern of organization nationally, the links between the workplace and the larger union, and the extent to which, with limited resources, it is able to develop a national expertise on the nature of the technical changes which are likely to affect its members. Furthermore, if one wanted to see how technical change was affecting union members, one needed to look not only at the private sector – from which all of our case studies came – but also at the public sector. We therefore included in the survey a number of other industries/unions. The first of these was the NGA in the printing industry. This was selected as an example of a single-industry union in a sector where there has been a good deal of technical change. It also meant that we supplemented the number of samples covering predominantly craft workers in a production rather than a maintenance role (this sample was drawn from lay representatives who had been on union training courses over the last year). Second, we drew samples from the public sector; these also had the advantage of all being virtually single-employer unions, thereby permitting a further test of our arguments concerning union structure. As far as we are aware, it is only in the public sector that single-employer unions are to be found, apart, that is, from staff associations. Hence we drew samples from the CPSA and SCPS from 'mainstream' government departments, notably the Department of Employment (plus the Manpower Services Commission), the Department of Health and Social Security, and the Ministry of Defence. We took both of these unions in order to see how new technology affected different grades of non-manual workers. In addition, we drew two samples from Telecom: the first of these was again from the CPSA, thereby once more giving us an opportunity to see the same union in two quite different contexts, and the POEU. The latter provided us with a skilled manual group in the public sector and one that is working at the very heart of the new technology. In all, then, we attempted to draw fifteen samples; one of these has been dropped from the analysis and another two have been combined. The analysis therefore is based upon thirteen samples.

The questionnaire was drawn up initially seeking, wherever possible, to ensure comparability of questions with earlier surveys (notably, Batstone 1984a; Daniel and Millward, 1983). In the area of technical change, there was little earlier survey work which could provide us with any guidance. It was here that pilot interviews with shop stewards attending Ruskin College's courses were particularly valuable; stewards completed the questionnaire, and then lengthy discussions were held on various aspects of the questionnaire. We would like to record our thanks to the stewards who co-operated in this pilot stage. The questionnaire is reproduced at the end of this appendix.

Co-operation from the various unions approached was considerable, and reflected the strength of long-lasting ties. These strong links meant that we were able to discuss at some length with the unions the exact ways by which the samples could best be drawn, for the method adopted varied from union to union, depending upon the nature of their records. In some cases (where the branch is based upon the place of work in single-employer unions), directories of branch secretaries were produced, giving details of the workplace and the number of members. These permitted us to draw samples from specific departments and to employ a size criterion. In other cases, names of shop stewards and branch officials were on computer; in these cases, we were able to obtain computer print-outs by industry. We then identified the most senior representative in each workplace and the sample was drawn from these. In some unions, there was no central record: reference has already been made to the way in which this problem was overcome in some cases. But in another union, there was no national source that permitted us to distinguish between industries. In this case, we approached local full-time officials in four areas and sought their co-operation. With their agreement, we sent them questionnaires and a specification of the nature of the sample we wished to draw. In all the samples, we sent questionnaires to senior stewards or to branch secretaries wherever possible. In addition, we obtained letters from national officials supporting the survey and its aims. We would like to thank the many people who co-operated in the survey: those who completed the questionnaire and those who helped us to organize it.

Wherever possible, we sent out about 200 questionnaires. We estimated that for any serious analysis we required at least fifty completed questionnaires in each sample, and we thought that the response rate might well be only about 25 per cent. In some cases, we were not able to control the number of questionnaires that actually reached stewards, because we were working through others or because there were simply too few stewards from the union in the sector in which we were interested. In the case of the union where we sampled areas, we sent out 300 questionnaires; in other cases, we sent out fewer. The number of completed questionnaires that had been returned by the time we put the data on the computer was 1,024. This represented over 40 per cent of the questionnaires sent to stewards (excluding the USDAW sample). Once allowance is made for the fact that union records are invariably somewhat out of date, due to the turnover of shop stewards and the demise of establishments, the 'real' response rate is probably well over 50 per cent. The actual numbers of completed questionnaires is given in table A.1.

For a variety of reasons, as noted above, it is difficult to give precise response rates for some of the samples; the small numbers in the finance and the CPSA Telecom samples reflect the small numbers who were in fact approached. Generally, the response rates vary from a maximum of over two-thirds (some of the white-collar and printing samples) to just over a quarter (production food and drink and electrical engineering).

The way in which the samples were drawn has both advantages and disadvantages. The advantage is that we were able to control for both union and industry, so that not only do we have a fairly large data set, but also we able to look in some detail at particular industries, etc., something which larger surveys are often unable to do. But, on the other hand, strictly speaking we cannot analyse the various samples together, nor do the total figures across the samples on any variable

Table A.1 Numbers of completed questionnaires received

Non-manual/public-sector group	No.	Production group	No.	Maintenance group	No.
Finance	41	Print	90	Chemicals	68
CPSA civil service	130	Chemicals	105	Food and drink	79
SCPS civil service	100	Food and drink	56	Engineering	63
CPSA Telecom	36	Engineering	105	Electrical	
POEU Telecom	100			engineering	51
Total	407	Total	356	Total	261

Grand total (excluding 11 USDAW): 1,024.

have much meaning. Accordingly, the analysis was undertaken in stages. The first stage involved analysing each sample separately. At this stage, a wide variety of hypotheses were tested – for example, assessing the importance of the size effect, the nature of management structure, patterns of ownership, the impact of specific types of technical change and so on. A wide variety of statistical techniques were used in this analysis: in particular, stepwise regression. This first stage of the analysis permitted us to do two things: to cluster the different samples into groups which were, in the main, broadly similar; and it enabled us to develop the various indices used in the chapters. These should be seen largely as convenient means of summarizing the data, permitting an easier discussion of the findings. If the indices are fed into regressions, the percentage of variation explained is often considerably lower than if individual variables are used; however, the indices subsume these variables and make the discussion easier. The second stage of the detailed analysis was then undertaken on the basis of the groups of samples, although at the same time a note of variations by individual samples was kept, both by reference to the first stage of the analysis and by introducing dummy variables for each of the samples into the analyses. The finer details of these statistical analyses, however, are only briefly alluded to in the text. Furthermore, tables were produced showing the relationships between the dependent variable of concern and the way in which it varied with the key independent variables.

The Case Studies

As has been noted already, the choice of case studies was determined by our involvement in the larger EEC project. A major problem was discovering which companies within the industries concerned had introduced new technology in the recent past of a kind that would be useful to analyse. A number of sources were used: these included discussions with union officials, various journals and magazines, and simply discussing the suitability of particular research sites with management. In all we approached eight companies: in two cases there was a straight refusal; in another case we discovered that another researcher was approaching the company (to look into a completely different issue) and so we did not pursue the contact. In a fourth case discussions with management made it clear that there had been little technical change involving 'new technology', and so we did not pursue the company further. The companies were approached directly by letter, explaining the purposes of our research and seeking their co-operation. In all cases, we had had prior discussions with union officials or representatives concerning the research. The co-operation of management was vital in permitting us to go on site, in providing us with documentary sources and, through these methods and interviews, helping us to build up a picture of management strategy. In all of the case studies, we employed a variety of techniques: interviews with key stewards, managers and workers; observation of work situations; and the analysis of a wide range of union and management documents; and the study of other relevant public material. In the insurance study, we also undertook a survey of local representatives attending the annual divisional conference in 1984: a response rate of over 80 per cent was achieved, representing nearly half of all the representatives.

Questionnaire: Union Structure and Strategy in the Face of Technical Change

Private Sector Manual Samples

A. Background

1. (a) What is the name of the company you work for?
   (b) Where is the establishment at which you work?
   (c) What are the main products of this establishment?

2. (a) Is this establishment:
   in the public or private sector? Private ☐ Public ☐
   foreign or British owned? Foreign ☐ British ☐
   (b) Is it the only establishment in
   the UK owned by the company? Yes ☐ No ☐

3. (a) How many people in total (full-time and part-time) are employed in this establishment?
   (b) How many of these are: skilled manual workers?
   other manual workers?
   part-time manual workers?
   female manual workers?
   (c) Roughly, how many workers (full-time and part-time) were employed here five years ago?

4. (a) Over the last five years, has the output of this establishment:
   Risen a lot ☐ Risen a little ☐ Not changed ☐
   Fallen a little ☐ Fallen a lot ☐
   (b) How are the main products of this establishment made:
   One-offs ☐ Small batches ☐ Large batches ☐ Mass produced ☐
   Continuous process ☐ Other ☐

B. Union Organization

1. (a) Which union do you belong to?
   (b) How many members does your union have in this establishment?
   (c) How many members did it have here five years ago?

(d) Altogether, how many unions (including your own) represent manual workers here?

(e) Altogether, how many manual workers are union members (including your own) here?

(f) What types of worker does *your* union here cover?

Skilled production workers ☐   Skilled maintenance/indirects ☐
Other production workers ☐   Other maintenance/indirects ☐
Supervisory grades ☐   White-collar/technicians ☐

2. (a) In practice, what proportion of the workers in the groups covered by *your* union here have to be union members to keep their jobs (i.e. are covered by a closed shop)?

(b) In practice, what proportion of *all* manual workers here are covered by a closed shop?

(c) Does management currently support the closed shop?
Yes ☐   No ☐

3. (a) In this establishment, how many shop stewards or representatives are there who are:
(i) members of *your* union?
(ii) members of any manual union (including your own)?

(b) How many senior stewards or conveners are there from:
(i) *your* union?
(ii) *all* manual unions?

(c) How many stewards work more or less full-time on workplace union affairs who are from:
(i) *your* union?
(ii) *all* manual unions?

4. Turning to stewards' meetings where no other participants are present:
(a) Do you have a committee of manual stewards which includes some representatives from your own union and some from other manual unions? How frequently does it meet?
Weekly ☐ Fortnightly ☐ Monthly ☐ Every 2–3
Less often ☐ No committee ☐ Only one union ☐ months ☐

(b) Apart from this committee, do you have meetings of stewards from your union and stewards from other unions in this establishment? How frequently do meetings of this kind occur?
Weekly ☐ Fortnightly ☐ Monthly ☐ Every 2–3
Less often ☐ No meetings ☐ Only one union ☐ months ☐

(c) Are there meetings of stewards from your own union only, apart from branch meetings? How frequently do meetings of this kind occur?
Weekly ☐ Fortnightly ☐ Monthly ☐ Every 2–3
Less often ☐ No meetings ☐   months ☐

(d) Do you have meetings between the manual stewards here and the manual stewards in other establishments of this organization (excluding branch meetings)? How frequently do meetings of this kind occur?
Weekly ☐ Fortnightly ☐ Monthly ☐ Every 2–3
Less often ☐ No meetings ☐ No other estab-   months ☐
lishments ☐

5. (a) How important a role does the wider union play in negotiations relating to this establishment?
Very important ☐ Fairly important ☐
Not very important ☐ Unimportant ☐
(b) Does your union branch cover members from:
Only this company ☐ Mainly this company ☐
Mainly other companies ☐

6. (a) Do the various manual groups in this establishment negotiate major issues jointly or separately?
All jointly ☐ Some jointly ☐ All separately ☐
(b) Do the manual union(s) here ever negotiate jointly with white-collar unions?
Often ☐ Sometimes ☐ Hardly ever ☐ Never ☐
No white-collar unions ☐

7. Which of the following best describes the way stewards/representatives operate in this establishment:
Senior stewards typically play the leading role and other stewards follow ☐
or Senior stewards do not play a leading role: all stewards collectively decide on policy which is binding on them all ☐
or Individual stewards and workgroups decide on their own course of action ☐

8. Which, if any, of the following generally ratify major agreements (e.g. on wage increases) here?
Branch meetings ☐ Mass meetings ☐ Ballots ☐
Shop stewards' meetings ☐
Wider union ☐

9. Generally speaking, how much influence would you say each of the following have in deciding union policy as far as this establishment is concerned?
Members:
Great deal ☐ Fair amount ☐ Not much ☐ None ☐
Wider union:
Great deal ☐ Fair amount ☐ Not much ☐ None ☐
Senior stewards:
Great deal ☐ Fair amount ☐ Not much ☐ None ☐
Other stewards:
Great deal ☐ Fair amount ☐ Not much ☐ None ☐

10. Which of the following best describes the behaviour of the steward organization in this establishment in relation to the membership?
It acts as the leader of the membership, stirring them to action or calming them down as the occasion requires ☐
or It simply tries to carry out the expressed wishes of members ☐

C. Industrial Relations

1. Which of the following levels of negotiation was the most important in determining the last pay settlement for the bulk of your members?
Negotiations involving more than one employer ☐
This employer only, covering more than one establishment ☐

This establishment only ☐
No negotiations/employer decides ☐
Other (please specify)

2. (a) As far as your members in this establishment are concerned, at what levels are issues relating to the following negotiated or bargained about? (Please tick *all* that apply)

	On shop-floor	At establishment	Above establishment
Manning/work-pace	☐	☐	☐
Redeployment between jobs	☐	☐	☐
Job grading	☐	☐	☐
Actual earnings	☐	☐	☐

(b) Which of the following best describes the role of formal written agreements in this establishment:

They do not play a very important role ☐
or They provide the basis for a good deal of day-to-day negotiation ☐
or They effectively restrict and limit the amount of day-to-day negotiation ☐

3. (a) How far would you say your union in this establishment affects and limits management's freedom of action over working practices and effort levels?
A great deal ☐ A fair amount ☐ Not much ☐ Hardly at all ☐

(b) Over the last five years, has union influence over working practices and effort levels in this establishment increased or decreased?
Increased ☐ No change ☐ Decreased ☐

(c) Over the last five years have effort levels here:
Increased to very high levels ☐
Increased, but still at reasonable levels ☐
Not changed much ☐
Fallen ☐

(d) Over the last five years have there been negotiations leading to major changes in working practices?
Yes ☐ No ☐

4. Over the last five years has management made more or less use of the following in this establishment:

Part-time labour	More	☐	No change	☐	Less	☐
Subcontract labour	More	☐	No change	☐	Less	☐
Casual labour	More	☐	No change	☐	Less	☐
Contracting work out	More	☐	No change	☐	Less	☐
Overtime	More	☐	No change	☐	Less	☐
Shift working	More	☐	No change	☐	Less	☐

5. (a) Do any of the following exist in relation to significant numbers of your members in this establishment?
(b) Did they exist five years ago?

	Now	Five years ago
Individual payment by results	☐	☐
Group-based payment by results	☐	☐
Plant/company bonus	☐	☐
Work study	☐	☐
Job evaluation	☐	☐

Quality circles ☐ ☐
Briefing groups ☐ ☐
Autonomous workgroups ☐ ☐
Formal consultation with union representatives (other than on health and safety) ☐ ☐
Formal consultation with non-union representatives (other than on health and safety) ☐ ☐

6. How many times during the last twelve months has action of the following kinds occurred in this establishment:
   Strikes of a day/shift or more ......
   Stoppages of less than a day/shift ......
   Other worker sanctions (e.g. overtime ban) ......
   Management sanctions (e.g. lock-out) ......

7. (a) (i) How far do management try to interfere with stewards carrying out their union responsibilities in this establishment (e.g. by refusing to let them leave their jobs)?
   Great deal ☐ Fair amount ☐ Not much ☐ Not at all ☐
   (ii) Over the last five years, has management become more or less awkward in this respect?
   More ☐ No change ☐ Less ☐
   (b) (i) How common is it for senior stewards in this establishment to have 'off the record' discussions with any senior managers?
   Very common ☐ Fairly common ☐ Not very common ☐ Very rare ☐
   (ii) Have such discussions become more or less common here over the last five years?
   More ☐ No change ☐ Less ☐

8. (a) Do specialist personnel managers exist:
   Here in the establishment Yes ☐ No ☐
   At a higher level in the Company Yes ☐ No ☐
   (b) (i) How much discretion does local management at this establishment have over industrial relations issues?
   A good deal ☐ Fair amount ☐ Not much ☐ Hardly any ☐
   (ii) Has their discretion increased or decreased over the last five years?
   Increased ☐ No change ☐ Decreased ☐
   (c) (i) How much discretion do foremen here have over the way in which they organize work and treat workers?
   A good deal ☐ Fair amount ☐ Not much ☐ Hardly any ☐
   (ii) Has their discretion increased or decreased over the last five years?
   Increased ☐ No change ☐ Decreased ☐

D. Trade Unions and Technical Change

1. Over the 1970s had there been much technical change in this establishment which affected groups covered by your union?
   Yes ☐ No ☐

2. During the last five years has management ever proposed introducing any changes in plant machinery or equipment in this establishment and not (as yet) actually done so?

Yes ☐   No ☐

If yes: For which of the following reasons did management not implement its proposals?

Invested elsewhere ☐	Technical problems ☐
Market conditions ☐	Union/worker opposition ☐
Proposals not yet finalized ☐	Not cost-effective ☐
	Other ☐

3. During the last five years have any changes in plant, machinery or equipment actually been made in this establishment which affected workers covered by your union?

Yes ☐   No ☐

If no, please go to section E, page 10   If yes, continue

4. (a) In what areas have these changes occurred?
       Control of individual machine processes ☐
       Automated handling/storage ☐
       Integrated central control systems ☐
       Testing/quality control ☐
       Other ☐
  (b) Could you briefly describe the main changes which have taken place?
  (c) When did these changes actually start?
  (d) Did these changes in equipment lead to or involve:
     (i) changes in overall capacity?
       Large rise ☐ Small rise ☐ No change ☐ Fall ☐
    (ii) changes/additions to products made?
       Yes – major☐ Yes – minor ☐ No ☐
  (e) Did any of this new equipment incorporate 'new technology', that is microelectronic monitoring or control systems?

Yes ☐   No ☐

5. (a) (i) Roughly, how many jobs have been created here as a result of introducing new equipment over the last five years?
    (ii) Roughly, how many jobs have been lost here as a result of introducing new equipment over the last five years?
  (b) Overall, would you say that these changes in equipment were associated with favourable or unfavourable changes, as far as your union members here are concerned, in the following:

	Favourable	No change overall	Unfavourable
Grading of jobs directly associated with new equipment	☐	☐	☐
Grading of jobs more generally	☐	☐	☐
Earnings of workers working on new equipment	☐	☐	☐
Earnings of workers more generally	☐	☐	☐

6. (a) (i) What proportion of workers covered by your union here currently work on the new equipment?
Less than 10% ☐   10–24% ☐   25–49% ☐   50–74% ☐
Over 75%   ☐

    (ii) What proportion of these have undergone special training of a week or more?
Less than 10% ☐   10–24% ☐   25–49% ☐   50–74% ☐
Over 75%   ☐

(b) As far as your union members working with the new equipment here are concerned, would you say that these changes in equipment have meant – overall – a rise or fall:

In skill levels   Rise ☐   No change ☐   Fall ☐
In worker control over
their work   Rise ☐   No change ☐   Fall ☐
In effort levels   Rise ☐   No change ☐   Fall ☐
In health and safety
standards   Rise ☐   No change ☐   Fall ☐

(c) How far has the introduction of new equipment over the last five years led to changes in demarcations between manual workers' jobs?
Great deal ☐ Fair amount ☐ Not much ☐ Hardly at all ☐

(d) Have changes in equipment over the last five years been associated with any transfer of tasks and functions between shop-floor and staff?
Yes – from shop-floor to staff ☐   No ☐
Yes – from staff to shop-floor ☐

7. (a) Which of the following issues relating to the new equipment were the subject of negotiation by your union at some level?
Investment strategy ☐   Job grading/pay levels ☐
Precise equipment used ☐   Selection/training of workers ☐
Manning levels/working practices ☐ Conditions, health and safety ☐

(b) Did your union put forward its own proposals on any matters associated with these changes in equipment?
Yes ☐   No ☐
If yes:
(i) On what issues?
(ii) How far were these accepted by management?
Good deal ☐ Fair amount ☐ Not much ☐ Hardly at all ☐

8. (a) Were there any major disagreements between management and your union on matters relating to the new equipment?
Yes ☐ No ☐
If yes:
On what issues?

(b) Did your union threaten or use any sanctions on management over questions relating to new equipment?
Threatened ☐ Used ☐ No ☐

(c) Were issues relating to the new equipment the subject of negotiation at the following levels (please tick as many as apply)
Above the establishment ☐   At the establishment ☐
On the shop-floor ☐

9. (a) What was the attitude of the majority of your union members to the idea of the new equipment?
   Strongly in favour ☐   In favour ☐   Uncertain/neutral ☐
   Opposed ☐   Strongly opposed ☐

(b) What role did the wider union play over issues relating to the new equipment?
   Direct role
   in negotiations ☐   Specific advice ☐   Gave general
   information ☐
   None ☐

(c) Which, if any, of the following ratified major agreements relating to the new equipment here?
   Branch meetings ☐   Mass meetings ☐   Ballots ☐
   Shop-steward meetings ☐
   Wider union ☐

10. Does your union have a 'new technology' agreement with management?
   Yes ☐   No ☐

If yes:
(a) Does the agreement cover:
   Only your union ☐   Only manual unions ☐   Manual and white-collar unions ☐
(b) How useful is this agreement?
   Very ☐   Fairly ☐   Not very ☐   Not at all useful ☐

11. (a) Do you remember working on the new equipment have:
   Their own separate stewards ☐   Stewards who also cover other workers ☐

(b) Overall, are workers directly affected by the new equipment more or less active in the union than other workers?
   More active ☐   No difference ☐   Less active ☐

(c) How far do workers working with new equipment have problems or interests which mean they see themselves apart from other workers?
   Great deal ☐   Fair amount ☐   Not much ☐   Not at all ☐

(d) In areas where new equipment has been introduced, does your union play a greater or smaller role in day-to-day issues which affect workers than it does elsewhere in this establishment?
   Greater ☐   Same ☐   Smaller ☐
   If greater or smaller: Why is this?
   Fewer/more issues arise ☐
   Members more/less likely to take problems straight to management ☐
   Managers more/less concerned with worker problems ☐
   Other (please specify) ☐

12. As a result of changes associated with new equipment, would you say:
(a) Your members generally tend to be more or less active in the union?
   More ☐   Same ☐   Less ☐
(b) Your union here is more or less united than it was previously?
   More ☐   Same ☐   Less ☐
(c) Relations between manual unions here are better or worse?
   More ☐   Same ☐   Less ☐
(d) Unions here have more or less control over work organization?
   More ☐   Same ☐   Less ☐

(e) Unions here have become more or less concerned about general management policies?

More ☐ Same ☐ Less ☐

(f) The authority of senior stewards is greater or smaller?

Greater ☐ Same ☐ Smaller ☐

(g) The relationship between the workplace and the wider union has become stronger or weaker?

Stronger ☐ Same ☐ Weaker ☐

E. General and Personal

1. What positions do you hold in your union?
   In this establishment/company
   At other levels of the union

2. (a) How long have you worked here?
   (b) How long have you been a steward here?
   (c) Roughly, how many hours a week do you spend on union business in working time?

3. Over the last five years, has management's approach to unions and/or workers changed?

   Yes ☐ No ☐

   If yes: In what ways?

Thank you for your co-operation

Bibliography

Atkinson, A. B., Gomulka, J., Micklewright, J. and Rau, N. (1984) Unemployment benefit, duration and incentives in Britain: how robust is the evidence? *Journal of Public Economics*, 23, 3–26.

Bain, G. S. (ed.) (1983) *Industrial Relations in Britain*. Oxford: Basil Blackwell.

Bain, G. S. and Elsheikh, F. (1976) *Union Growth and the Business Cycle*. Oxford: Basil Blackwell.

Barron, I. and Curnow, R. (1979) *The Future with Microelectronics*. London: Pinter.

Batstone, E. (1984a) *Working Order*. Oxford: Basil Blackwell.

Batstone, E. (1984b) Conflict, community and the recession. Paper given to Sociology Seminar, University of Oxford.

Batstone, E. (1985) International variations in strike activity. *European Sociology Review*, 1, 1–19.

Batstone, E. (1986) 'New forms' of work organization: the British experience. In B. Gustavsen and L. Hethy (eds), *New Forms of Work Organization*.

Batstone, E., Boraston, I. and Frenkel, S. (1977) *Shop Stewards in Action*. Oxford: Basil Blackwell.

Batstone, E., Boraston, I. and Frenkel, S. (1978) *The Social Organization of Strikes*. Oxford: Basil Blackwell.

Batstone, E., Ferner, A. and Terry, M. (1984) *Consent and Efficiency*. Oxford: Basil Blackwell.

Batstone, E., Frenkel, S. and Boraston, I. (1975) *Orientation to work and the negotiation of meaning*. Unpublished paper.

Batstone, E., Gourlay, S., Hevie, H. and Moore, R. (1986) *New Technology and the Process of Labour Regulation*. Oxford: Oxford University Press.

Bell, D. (1974) *The Coming of Post-Industrial Society*. London: Heinemann.

Blackburn, R. (1967) *Union Character and Social Class*. London: Batsford.

Blauner, R. (1964) *Alienation and Freedom*. London: University of Chicago Press.

Braverman, H. (1974) *Labor and Monopoly Capital*. New York: Monthly Review Press.

Brown, W. (ed.) (1981) *The Changing Contours of British Industrial Relations*. Oxford: Basil Blackwell.

Burkitt, B. (1980) *Trade Unions and Wages*. Bradford: Bradford University Press.

Cameron, D. (1984) Social democracy, corporatism, labour quiescence, and the representation of economic interest in advanced capitalist society. In J. Goldthorpe (ed.), *Order and Conflict in Contemporary Capitalism*. Oxford: Clarendon Press.

Central Policy Review Staff (CPRS) (1975) *The Future of the British Car Industry*. London: HMSO.

Child, J., Loveridge, R., Harvey, J. and Spencer, A. (1984) Microelectronics and the quality of employment in services. In P. Marstrand (ed.), *New Technology and the Future of Work and Skills*. London: Pinter.

Clegg, H. A. (1970) *The System of Industrial Relations in Great Britain*. Oxford: Basil Blackwell.

Clegg, H. A. (1976) *Trade Unionism under Collective Bargaining*. Oxford: Basil Blackwell.

Council for Science and Society (1981) *New Technology: Society, Employment and Skill*. London: Council for Science and Society.

Counter Information Services (CIS) (1979) *Report on New Technology*. London: Counter Information Services.

Craig, C., Rubery, J., Tarling, R. and Wilkinson, F. (1982) *Labour Market Structure, Industrial Organization and Low Pay*. Cambridge: Cambridge University Press.

Crompton, R. and Jones, G. (1984) *White-Collar Proletariat*. London: Macmillan.

Crouch, C. (1982) *Trade Unions: the Logic of Collective Action*. London: Fontana.

Dalton, M. (1959) *Men who Manage*. New York: John Wiley.

Daniel, W. W. and Millward, N. (1983) *Workplace Industrial Relations in Britain*. London: Heinemann.

Deaton, D. (1983) Unemployment. In G. S. Bain (ed.), *Industrial Relations in Great Britain*. Oxford: Basil Blackwell.

Deaton, D. (1985) Management style and large-scale survey evidence. *Industrial Relations Journal*, 16, 67–71.

Dohse, K. (1984) Foreign workers and workforce management in West Germany. *Economic and Industrial Democracy*, 5, 495–509.

Dubois, P. (1976) Les formes de luttes dans les usines nouvelles. In Groupe de Sociologie du Travail, *Decentralisation Industrielle et Relations de Travail*. Paris: La Documentation Française.

Dubois, P. and Monjardet, D. (1978) *La Division du travail dans l'industrie: étude de cas Anglais et Français*. Paris: Groupe de Sociologie du Travail.

Edwards, P. (1985) Myth of the macho manager. *Personnel Management*, April, 32–5.

Edwards, R. (1979) *Contested Terrain*. London: Heinemann.

Elden, M. (1977) Political efficacy at work. Paper given to seminar on social change and organizational development, Inter-university Centre, Dubrovnik.

Evans, C. (1979) *The Mighty Micro*. London: Gollancz.

Fothergill, S. and Gudgin, G. (1982) *Unequal Growth*. London: Heinemann.

Fox, A. (1974) *Beyond Contract: Work, Power and Trust Relations*. London: Faber and Faber.

Friedman, A. L. (1977) *Industry and Labour*. London: Macmillan.

Gallie, D. (1978) *In Search of the New Working Class*. Cambridge: Cambridge University Press.

Goldthorpe, J. (1978) The current inflation: towards a sociological account. In F. Hirsch and J. Goldthorpe (eds), *The Political Economy of Inflation*. Oxford: Martin Robertson.

Goldthorpe, J. (ed.) (1984) *Order and Conflict in Contemporary Capitalism*. Oxford: Clarendon Press.

Goldthorpe, J., Lockwood, D., Bechhoffer, F. and Platt, J. (1968) *The Affluent Worker: Industrial Attitudes and Behaviour*. Cambridge: Cambridge University Press.

Gustavsen, B. and Hunnius, G. (1981) *New Patterns of Work Reform*. Oslo: Universitetsforlaget.

Hemingway, J. (1978) *Conflict and Democracy*. Oxford: Clarendon Press.

Hickson, D. J., Hinings, C., Lee, C., Schneck, R. and Pennings, J. (1973) A strategic contingencies theory of intraorganizational power. In G. Salaman and K. Thompson (eds), *People and Organizations*. London: Longman.

Hirschman, A. O. (1970) *Exit, Voice and Loyalty*. Cambridge, Mass.: Harvard University Press.

International Labour Office (ILO) (1984) *Automation, Work Organization and Occupational Stress*. Geneva: International Labour Office.

Jenkins, C. and Sherman, B. (1979) *The Collapse of Work*. London: Methuen.

Kelly, J. (1982) *Scientific Management, Job Redesign and Work Performance*. London: Academic Press.

Kerr, C., Dunlop, J., Harbison, F. and Myers, C. (1960) *Industrialism and Industrial Man*. Cambridge, Mass.: Harvard University Press.

Knights, D., Willmott, H. and Collinson, D. (eds) (1985) *Job Redesign*. Aldershot: Gower.

Korpi, W. (1983) *The Democratic Class Struggle*. London: Routledge and Kegan Paul.

Kumar, K. (1978) *Prophecy and Progress*. Harmondsworth: Penguin.

Latour, B. and Woolgar, S. (1979) *Laboratory Life*. London: Sage.

Lazonick, W. (1979) Industrial relations and technical change. *Cambridge Journal of Economics*, 3, 231–62.

Lehmbruch, G. (1982) Introduction: neo-corporatism in comparative perspective. In G. Lehmbruch and P. Schmitter (eds), *Patterns of Corporatist Policy Making*. London: Sage.

Lerner, S. (1961) *Breakaway Unions and the Small Trade Union*. London: Allen and Unwin.

Levie, H. and Moore, R. (eds) (1984) *The Control of Frontiers*. Oxford: Ruskin College.

Lewin, L. (1980) *Governing Trade Unions in Sweden*. Cambridge, Mass.: Harvard University Press.

Mallet, S. (1975) *The New Working Class*. Nottingham: Spokesman.

Mann, M. (1973) *Consciousness and Action among the Western Working Class*. London: Macmillan.

Marsh, A. (1982) *Employee Relations Policy and Decision Making*. Aldershot: Gower.

Micklewright, J. (1985) Fiction versus fact: unemployment benefits in Britain. *National Westminster Bank Quarterly Review*, May, 52–62.

Minford, P. (1983) *Unemployment: Cause and Cure*. Oxford: Martin Robertson.

Mitchell, J. C. (1983) Case and situation analysis. *Sociological Review*, 31 (n.s.), 187–211.

Muellbauer, J. (forthcoming) Aggregate production functions and productivity measurement: a new look.

Mulkay, M. (1979) *Science and the Sociology of Knowledge*. London: Allen and Unwin.

Narendranathan, W. *et al.* (1985) Unemployment benefits revisited. *Economic Journal*, 95, 307–29.

Noble, D. (1979) Social Choice in Machine Design. In A. Zimbalist (ed.), *Case Studies in the Labour Process*. New York: Monthly Review Press.

Northcott, J. and Rogers, P. (1984) *Microelectronics in British Industry*. London: Policy Studies Institute.

Okun, A. M. (1981) *Prices and Quantities: A Microeconomic Analysis*. Washington: Brookings Institution.

Olson, M. (1983) The political economy of comparative growth rates. In D. C. Mueller (ed.), *The Political Economy of Growth*. New Haven: Yale University Press.

Panitch, L. (1981) Trade unions and the capitalist state. *New Left Review*, 125, 21–43.

Pettigrew, A. M. (1973) *The Politics of Organizational Decision-making*. London: Tavistock.

Pizzorno, A. (1978) Political exchange and collective identity in industrial conflict. In C. Crouch and A. Pizzorno (eds), *The Resurgence of Class Conflict in Western Europe since 1968*, Vol. 2. London: Macmillan.

Rose, M. (1979) *Servants of Post-Industrial Power?* London: Macmillan.

Rose, M. and Jones, B. (1985) Managerial strategy and trade union response in work reorganization schemes at establishment level. In D. Knights *et al.* (eds), *Job Redesign*. Aldershot: Gower.

Rothwell, S. G. (1984) Company employment policies and new technology in manufacturing and service sectors. In M. Warner (ed.), *Microprocessors, Manpower and Society*. Aldershot: Gower.

Rubery, J. (1978) Structured labour markets, worker organization and low pay. *Cambridge Journal of Economics*, 2, 17–36.

Rubery, J., Tarling, R. and Wilkinson, F. (1984) Industrial relations issues in the 1980s: an economic analysis. In M. Poole *et al.*, *Industrial Relations in the Future*. London: Routledge and Kegan Paul.

Sabel, C. (1981) The internal politics of trade unions. In S. Berger (ed.), *Organizing Interests in Western Europe*. Cambridge: Cambridge University Press.

Sandberg, A. (1984) *Framtidsfragor Pa Arbetsplatsen*. Stockholm: Arbetslivscentrum.

Sayles, L. (1959) *The Behaviour of Industrial Work Groups*. New York: Wiley and Sons.

Scarborough, H. (1984) Maintenance workers and new technology. *Industrial Relations Journal*, 15, 9–16.

Schmitter, P. (1979) Still the century of corporatism? In P. Schmitter and G. Lehmbruch (eds), *Trends towards Corporatist Intermediation*. London: Sage.

Schmitter, P. (1982) Reflections on where the theory of neo-corporatism has gone and where the praxis of neo-corporatism may be going. In G. Lehmbruch and P. Schmitter (eds), *Patterns of Corporatist Policy Making*. London: Sage.

Seglow, P., Streeck, W. and Wallace, P. (1982) *Rail Unions in Britain and West Germany*. London: PSI.

Sisson, K. (1984) Changing strategies in industrial relations. *Personnel Management*, May, 24–27.

Sleigh, J., Boatwright, B., Irwin, P. and Stanyon, R. (1979) *The Manpower Implications of Micro-electronic Technology*. London: HMSO.

Sorge, A., Hartmann, G., Warner, M. and Nicholas, I. (1983) *Microelectronics and Manpower in Manufacturing Applications of Computer Numerical Control in Great Britain and West Germany*. Farnborough: Gower.

Terry, M. (1977) The inevitable growth of informality. *British Journal of Industrial Relations*, 15, 75–90.

Thurow, L. (1983) *Dangerous Currents: the State of Economics*. Oxford: Oxford University Press.

Touraine, A. (1974) *The Post-industrial Society*. London: Wildwood House.

Turner, A. and Lawrence P. (1967) *Industrial Jobs and the Worker*. Cambridge, Mass.: Harvard University Press.

Turner, H. A. (1962) *Trade Union Growth, Structure and Policy*. London: Allen and Unwin.

Tylecote, A. B. (1973) Determinants of changes in the wage hierarchy in UK manufacturing industry. Discussion Paper No. 14, University of Stirling.

Undy, R., Ellis, V., McCarthy, W. and Halmos, A. (1981) *Change in Trade Unions*. London: Hutchinson.

White, M. (1981) *Payment Systems in Britain*. Aldershot: Gower.

Wilkinson, B. (1983) *The Shopfloor Politics of New Technology*. London: Heinemann.

Willman, P. and Winch, G. (1985) *Innovation and Management Control*. Cambridge: Cambridge University Press.

Winkler, J. (1974) The ghost at the bargaining table. *British Journal of Industrial Relations*, 11, 191–212.

Index